Julie is an author of nine published books and has worked in the field of psycho-spiritual studies for 30 years. She has lectured internationally in major centres, schools and universities. Identifying the need for an educational programme that encompassed in-depth spiritual self-awareness with intuition, in 1996 Julie founded the School of Insight and Intuition in London, where she was principal for 14 years. During this time she created an accredited Spiritual Healing Practitioner course and a Psycho-spiritual programme. In February 2005, modules of this programme were validated and implemented as part of a BSc degree in Integrated Health at Westminster University in London. In 2005 she received an MPhil degree from Surrey University on the effects of psycho-spiritual development in the lived world of the individual. Julie continues to work as a sensitive and teaches consciousness studies, and psychic and healing development.

For more information see www.juliesoskin.com

By the same author

The Wind of Change
Cosmic Dance
Alignment to Light
Transformation
Insight and Intuition
Are you Psychic?
Insight Through Intuition
Discover your Sixth Sense

THE PSYCHIC'S HANDBOOK

YOUR ESSENTIAL GUIDE TO PSYCHO-SPIRITUAL ENERGIES

JULIE SOSKIN

WATKINS PUBLISHING
LONDON

This edition first published in the UK and USA 2012 by
Watkins Publishing, Sixth Floor, Castle House,
75–76 Wells Street, London W1T 3QH

1 3 5 7 9 10 8 6 4 2

Designed by Jerry Goldie Graphic Design

Printed in China by Imago

British Library Cataloguing-in-Publication Data Available

Library of Congress Cataloging-in-Publication Data Available

ISBN: 978-1-78028-376-0

www.watkinspublishing.co.uk

Distributed in the USA and Canada by Sterling Publishing Co., Inc.
387 Park Avenue South, New York, NY 10016-8810

For information about custom editions, special sales, premium and
corporate purchases, please contact Sterling Special Sales
Department at 800-805-5489 or specialsales@sterlingpub.com

Contents

Acknowledgements

Many grateful thanks go to: Marcus Williamson and my husband Rupert for checking my copy, and their support; to Michael Mann for his encouragement, and all the thousands of people, both clients and students, from whom I have learnt a great deal. Most particularly to all those who endeavour to dissolve their fears, and who try, in whatever way they can, to make the world a better place.

Introduction

What sort of world would it be if we were all balanced human beings? This, of course, is a dream we can only imagine. Nonetheless, it seems to me that we are on the verge of dynamic movement and change and there are the tiny sprouts of enlightenment emerging. They are delicate and need a lot of care. I have long thought that the answer to the world's problems lies not just in politics, religion or science but also within ourselves. Each and every one of us. Of course, exploring and advancing the self has many avenues and I am not so naive as to believe that developing one's intuition and any psychic abilities provides all the answers. However, it can, and does help people blossom, giving them a sense of who and what they truly are, and how to live in this crazy world.

I have written this book from a lifetime of interest and work in the spiritual and intuitive. I started out on my journey with a messianic mission to find the ultimate truth. Slowly over the years I realized that there may not be an absolute truth. Perceptions are born out of our view at any given time and place. In *The Psychic's Handbook* I have relayed information on authorities and models of energies, many of which I have successfully used in psychic, healing and psycho-spiritual education. However, it is good to bear in mind that these systems are interpretations of energy experience. I do not necessarily agree with the interpretations of all the authorities, as any model does not necessarily have to be literally true or real for it to be a useful point of focus. Models may be best used as scaffolding upon which to climb to the next stage. In an unlimited universe there may not be any structures at all, but we mere mortals require some structure to endeavour to understand the sometimes nebulous and subtle energies around us.

Being born and brought up in the UK in the middle part of the 20th century means that my own background and culture is largely Christian. However, in my opinion the best of Christian ethics, morals and principles are present in all faiths. A Buddhist, Muslim, Jew or anyone of another faith, even someone with no faith at all, can just as easily develop their intuition. Over the years I have led groups with people of just about every nationality, faith and culture. The psycho-spiritual process works for anyone who engages their intent to further their progress.

The concept of, 'we are all one' is echoed in many religions, and recently some contemporary science is relaying similar concepts in an 'entangled' universe. This idea presents us with a dichotomy, as on one hand we seem to be moving towards an interconnected world and consequently have to work together. On the other hand, to release worn-out negativities and expand consciousness, it is imperative that individuals concentrate on themselves. Ironically, it is only when the individual's consciousness has risen that their energy becomes clearer and resonates truth. Then, and only then, can they be authentically compassionate and consequently help others. If the genuine intent of the individual is active, it creates a clear resonant energy that goes out into the world.

In the last few years we have seen spiritual healing becoming more and more recognized and it is now officially accepted as a bona fide therapy. This is wonderful news. However, psychics have been labelled as entertainment! In doing this, the powers that be have bundled all psychic work into one box. Once, the seer, priestess and sage were revered by their community; theirs was considered a sacred art, which, like any art, takes training and practice. Psychic practices incorporate a vast array of different levels of work and understanding. In this book I have endeavoured to uncover the rich, rewarding and profound aspects of this wide subject and in some small way have tried to open doors towards good education in the psychic arts. This book gives an overview of psychic perceptions and how to discern the energies. It is written both for the novice and the more advanced student, as well as any who are interested in progressing their lives.

If you have ten fingers and you want to play the piano, with practice and dedication you can learn. You may never become a concert pianist but the music can inspire you nonetheless. It is the same with psychic perception. Anyone, with practice and dedication, can develop this natural ability. Some will become professional, others will simply enjoy the inspiration it brings to them. Being psychic is not only for the few, since we all have this gift if we care to acknowledge and develop it. As well as relaying perceptions of psychic energies in this work, I have incorporated information about the psycho-spiritual process so essential to both our own growth and being a good psychic practitioner.

People fascinate me, whoever they are or wherever they come from; how they come to be what they are and the potentials of what they might become. The effects of this work on the people who develop psychic potential and their spiritual growth is something that has not been delved into rigorously by many. So in this book I draw from my research and experience from thousands of consultations and teaching students over many years. I have related a broad spectrum of associated subjects, which include psychology, psychic and healing development, spirituality and science. *The Psychic's Handbook* gives a practical and down-to-earth explanation of what can often be nebulous experiences. I have also included personal anecdotes and verbatim accounts from students and clients to illustrate and enlighten the reader. These are sometimes humorous, sometimes sad, sometimes philo-sophical, and always true.

Psychic senses can be confusing. Messages coming into the consciousness are often misinterpreted, especially the sources of different levels of psychic perceptions. These energies can take time and experience to discern. How do we know what we are connecting with? Is the information emanating from the subtle energies around the body (auras) or from some discarnate being? Or could they be originating from an alter ego, or the personification of hopes and fears from aspects of our projected selves? Are they from higher sources of truth? If so, what or who are they? Perhaps the medium and psychic just 'smells' out the information from the universal mass of particles to which we all belong? For accurate interpretation of these subtle forces it is essential to know the differences. This book discusses these, often difficult to discern, perceptions.

I hate to see people struggling; I would like it to stop. This is what first brought me into healing and psychic work. However, I have come to realize that struggle is a birthing process that is necessary to push us forward to discover new and better ways of thinking, working and being. Life is a miracle whatever beliefs you may hold. Just to watch a blade of grass growing, an egg hatching, the trees reaching up to the sun and all the myriad experiences that our physical world offers us. We are truly privileged to be here, wherever we came from, wherever we may be going or whatever we may believe.

The jury is still out for me on many of the big questions. What all my senses tell me is that there is some force and energy which, when one engages with it, connects us to the slipstream of universal consciousness. When we are connected to this force it feels right, we instinctively know how to be. My wish is that this book helps you to open your mind, ask questions and seek the truth that is right for you, whatever that may be.

In the current state of the world, I feel the subject of this book is particularly pertinent. Fears abound with financial collapse, global warming and wars. People are therefore being encouraged to look at the bigger picture, to search inside as well as outside themselves. Psychic information can inform us on many aspects of our lives, from personal health to higher consciousness. This can, if properly interpreted, inspire and aid us in both our human and spiritual progress. Intuition and psychic perceptions can play a vital role in how the individual and humanity could move towards a better world.

Well-implemented psychic and intuitive information can inspire, educate and help to move the individual towards wholeness. This is as true for the professional psychic as it is for any other profession. Every person who finds balance and truth in their lives affects those around them, and this helps to move humanity's energy a little further towards what I see as the greatest evolutionary shift for humankind. The world stands on the brink of enormous changes, both material and spiritual. Although this seemingly chaotic state is worrying for many, it may also present us with the opportunity to create a better world and better lives for ourselves. Having accurate psychic perceptions of self and others may assist us in this transformational process. *The Psychic's Handbook* looks at the possibilities that a different level of consciousness could bring to our world.

CHAPTER ONE

Ancient Wisdoms – Future Truths

Psychic does not necessarily mean paranormal although some texts suggest that certain paranormal events may more likely occur here. Rather it refers to psyche as a higher level of development than the rational mind per se.

Ken Wilber

Who can doubt that this is the most amazing, exciting and also challenging time in which to live? A time of mass movement in so many areas of life and living, when humanity is entering a shift so great, we will never be the same again. As the playwright Christopher Fry writes in *A Sleep of Prisoners*:

> Thank God our time is now when wrong
> Comes up to face us everywhere,
> Never to leave us till we take
> The longest stride of soul men ever took.
>
> …

Where are you making for? It takes
So many thousand years to wake.
But will you wake for pity's sake?

We stand on the brink of fantastic information coming to light and although fears persist for some, since the repeal of the witches act in the 1950s it has emancipated so much valuable research into this whole subject. And, in science also, with exciting new discoveries in the area of quantum theory (*see* also Chapter Seven). At last psychics may be able to hold their heads above the parapet. We can build upon the wonderful works of such people as Swedenborg, J B Rhine, Professor Morris who worked for many years in psychical research, and contemporary scientists such as Rupert Sheldrake, Dean Radin of the Institute of Noetic Sciences and many many more. This book does not seek to authenticate psychic phenomena; I leave that to better people than me. It does however endeavour to help in some small way to expand on the rich potentials of true psychic work, that when properly implemented has so much to offer the individual and the world.

It's impossible to say with authority exactly when or where psychic practices started. We know from evidence that ancient peoples used the world around them to auger various portents to assist their lives. By the time of ancient Egypt there was a sophisticated culture full of ritual and worship; a hierarchy of priests and priestesses. In 2000BC the Egyptians devised a method of dream incubation as a technique for evoking oracles (*see* D Radin, *Entangled Minds*). By 650BC in ancient Greece, the seer was an important part of the culture and over the door of the temple at Delphi were written the immortal words – 'know thyself'. As we will see during the course of this book, to know oneself is still crucially important to receive and give profound and correct psychic information.

The word 'psychic' for many conjures up either the loop-earringed fortune-teller or a Hollywood horror film. Both undermine the rich history and etymology of the word. It is interesting to note that much of the current research is done under the heading of psi, pronounced *sigh*, which is the 23rd letter of the Greek alphabet and also the first letter of the Greek word *psyche*.

This term refers to telepathy, precognition and psychokinesis. The roots of 'psyche' – to breathe, life, soul – is allegorically echoed in the Greek myth of Psyche and Eros; Aphrodite, goddess of love, gives the mortal princess Psyche many tests and trials to establish whether she is acceptable for her son Eros. When Psyche finally succeeds, she is given the cup of immortality to drink, following which she sprouts wings. For the ancient Greeks, wings were a symbol of the soul and transformation. Behind this seemingly romantic story lie the principles of psycho-spirituality, as it suggests that through overcoming the trials of life and supreme love, a personal transformation can occur. For this transformation to take place it necessitates a process of 'unfoldment' of self, and various aspects of the individual need to be addressed, which we will look into further in Chapter Two.

The subtitle of this book is 'a guide to psycho-spiritual energies'. What exactly does psycho-spiritual mean? Encompassed in this word are many aspects that in some shape or form relate to the self. In the next section we will look at some of the affiliated meanings that underpin the subject. These include: Psychic, Healing, Intuition, Mysticism, Psychology and Spirituality. Psycho-spirituality suggests that we all possess an inner divine nature which, once acknowledged, accepted and actualized, will lead the individual towards spiritual advancement. This inner essence, or core, is akin to the classical notion of the soul. In mystical tenets and some psychological disciplines the individual is seen to actualize progressively through dissolution of the different 'states', 'layers', 'masks' or 'personas' that cloak this inner being. In mystical literature and theosophical thought, these outer layers are referred to as 'veils of illusions' or 'sheaths'. This is similar to what we now call 'unfoldment'. For this to occur there is need for an awareness and understanding of one's psychological processes through which one can allow the spiritual aspects to emerge. It therefore necessitates the holistic development of the individual. These concepts are present in some modern psychology which is now referred to as, 'third force' psychology: 'Humanistic', and also 'fourth force' psychology: 'Transpersonal'.

Psycho-spirituality has its philosophical roots in the mystical traditions of both the East and West, as well as influences from modern psychology, psychic and healing practices; it has many strands stretching back to ancient times. The ancient canonical Vedic text of the Upanishads, written between 800–200BC, was concerned with the mystical nature of reality and includes concepts of spirituality, which are still in evidence today. Gnostic philosophical ideas appear in the writings of Plato and are present within the New Testament. These concepts came to prevalence in the 1st and 2nd centuries AD when they are thought to have had some influence over the early Christian Church. Gnosis is a Greek word meaning *knowledge* or *insight*. It carries the idea that humans have divinity within. Being aware of this we can connect with our spiritual nature and achieve contact with this highest or inner being.

In the 5th century Dionysius the Areopagite ('Pseudo' – *see* Chapter Four) coined the term 'mystical union' suggesting that we can have a connection with a higher energy or being. The 13th-century theologian Thomas Gallus took up the notion of the 'spark of the soul' and Thomas Aquinas, perhaps one of the best-known Christian mystical scientists, gave us a very modern psychological concept of the integrated man.

Mysticism from various cultures has had an influence on contemporary spiritual practices. These include Buddhism, Hinduism, Sufism and the esoteric Hebrew doctrine known as Qabalah, meaning 'receiving'. This Jewish mystical model found form in Spain and southern France in the 12th and 13th centuries AD, but its roots can be traced back to Gnosticism and the prophetic mysticism of the Old Testament, in which man is able to speak directly to God. These themes sometimes stand apart from religious doctrines, but are arguably at the heart of all of them. However, some mystical ideas were classified as *occult* or hidden, in the West. In many eras the need for keeping practices hidden was a necessity on pain of death.

The notion that one could communicate directly with a divine source was a huge threat to those in power. Occult teachings adhered to the idea that man has endless possibilities through direct contact with God. However, this concept often came into conflict with teachers of organized religions who were fearful of their teachings being usurped. It was primarily to free this knowledge that theosophy, which means 'knowledge of a divine nature', emerged, and it is here that we can pick up our current focus.

The seeds of theosophical ideas can be traced back to sayings and beliefs mentioned in the Talmud, the Jewish literature of the Compendium of Learning which derived from the Gnostics and is also influenced by ancient Eastern teachings. The London Theosophical Society, founded in 1783, is thought to have included William Blake. Towards the end of the 19th century the theosophists began to bring Eastern traditions into the West, believing in the education of perfecting man's hidden power. Of great importance to the movement was H P Blavatsky who lived for many years in the East. Her major work, *The Secret Doctrine* is seen as seminal as it paved the way for others to follow. It was the first time that occult or hidden information of an oral tradition was published in the West. It was Blavatsky who coined the term 'higher self'; she wrote: 'It is the spiritual evolution of the inner immortal man that defines the fundamental tenet in the occult sciences.'

Blavatsky was closely associated with Colonel Olcott, who was the president of the Theosophical Society until his death in 1907. He said:

> Theosophy professes to exclude all dialectical process, and to
> derive its whole knowledge of God from direct intuition and
> contemplation. This Theosophy dates from the highest antiquity
> of which any records are preserved, and every original founder of
> a religion was a seeker after divine wisdom by the theosophical
> process of self-illumination.

Through her personal acquaintance with Blavatsky, Annie Besant, a prominent champion of free thought in England at the turn of the 20th century, became a key advocate of theosophy. She was well known in English society and worked tirelessly to help social reform. In her autobiography she outlines her main reason for promoting this work: 'To found a Universal Brotherhood without distinction of race or creed and to investigate unexplained laws of nature.'

Also of influence to the growth of psycho-spirituality was George Gurdjieff (d.1949), a controversial philosopher, mystic and educationalist whose ideas were widely followed in the 1920s and 1930s and whose influence remains potent to this day. His method was based on the concept of an individual being *conscious* as opposed to being led. Gurdjieff devoted his entire life to the study of Eastern esoteric teaching and passing it on to the Occident. He formed groups called 'Seekers of Truth' for developing self-awareness that were influenced by Sufi teachings and Western psychology, synthesized within an original version of Gnosticism and for alchemy of the inner experience. It was perhaps Gurdjieff who did most to introduce trans-formational techniques and his ideas included T-groups, encounter groups, and transactional analysis. Gurdjieff groups (including the teachings of his student, Peter Ouspensky) still exist in many major cities in America and Europe. Gurdjieff is probably responsible for the notion that radical measures are required to effect a transformation shift.

Since its inception, various groups have branched out from theosophy and it was from its tenet that the German, Rudolf Steiner (1861–1925) developed his Anthroposophy. Steiner was a sensitive intuitive himself, and his edu-cational system was designed for those who 'truly seek to advance human development'. His educational theories challenged the established education system of the time and during his life he set up several Steiner schools, which aimed to educate through connection with the spirit. Steiner schools still exist today.

Without the need for the secrecy of the past, an increasing number of societies, groups and organizations have sprung up since the Second World War, all contributing to the spread of psycho-spiritual activities. Sir George Trevelyan, historian and teacher, often referred to as the 'Father of the New Age', in the 1940s and 1950s made use of ancestral homes as weekend training centres, running workshops in related subjects, and receiving a government grant towards their upkeep. His work inspired many to branch out and create their own organizations.

By the 1970s there was a need to intelligently investigate and expand these ideas in a comfortable place for scientists and medics. The Scientific and Medical Network (SMN) was founded in 1973 by a distinguished group of scientists to broaden the framework of understanding in science, medicine and education, arguing for the intellectual plausibility of a wider and deeper worldview. Geoffrey Leytham, who was a trustee of the Network for many years, explains his understanding of such views:

> I regard the self as being outside time and space ... I regard all individuals as being immersed in the sea of Divine Energy, or Cosmic Consciousness ... A spiritual and paranormal experience such as telepathy would seem to follow quite logically on this assumption of such a universal system of consciousness.

In the past, most of these groups have evolved outside the body of mainstream educational organizations, but some aspects of psycho-spiritual work, often with such titles as Stress Management, Alternative or Complementary Medicine and Personal Growth, arc now present in educational bodies including universities, and by the time I was writing my MPhil thesis in the early 2000s there were copious academic papers written from various disciplines on the subject of self and spiritual development.

The readers of today are more fortunate, the Mind Body Spirit market has exploded and there are now many available. However, the bandwagon of the New Age has produced books, some of which have no real authority, research or validity. I would therefore urge new students of this work, to be inspired to read as much as possible, but not to lose your good sense in the process; in my experience, if something seems too far-fetched and ridiculous, it probably is!

The path to spirituality, and indeed psychic development, is unique; no two people find exactly the same inspirations and words that are right for them. Test it out. Think for yourself. What works for you might not work for others and vice versa. If your energy and intent is true, you will find your way through the quagmire of material. In the end, every road leads home, but some roads take us far off course. Eventually we will find what we need, but only for a time until the next shift, the next part of the path emerges.

There are many ways into the human psyche, but few have ever thought of psychic development as a tool for the innermost workings of their being. Indeed, the whole subject of psychic development as an educational tool is

When I first wanted information on deeper and spiritual subjects (although at the time I knew no title for them) I was 15 years old. An ardent reader at the time, I use to go to the local library every week and get five books out, which was the maximum allowance. I trawled the shelves looking for something, I didn't know what exactly. As I was standing by one of the shelves, a rather nondescript, beige-coloured book literally fell into my hands. It was late and I had to go, so without looking at it, I just took it along with others and left. It was not until later that I even read the title – it was called *The Initiate*, by his pupil. (After his death it was published under his real name Cyril Scott, a 1920s musician). Many years later, coincidently a student of mine and successful musician herself, lived in the same house as Cyril Scott!

As I read this book, with every line, every part of my young being knew there was truth in it. Having found this book my interest was excited, so the next week I went back to look for more. Talking to the librarian, who was also a neighbour, she exclaimed, 'How on earth did you come across this? This book is kept in the vaults.' I told her where it was – she looked amazed. I asked if there were any other books on similar subjects. She now looked completely perplexed. This isn't the sort of book I would expect a girl of your age to want to read!

In fact this book was virtually the only one I could find at the time. The upsurge of the New Age was only in its infancy and I simply had no access to any reading material to assist me. It wasn't until some years later that any relevant books came my way.

largely left unexplored in any rigorous fashion. The media portray it as enter-tainment, and academics and scientists are still, on the whole sceptical. As part of this book I aim to explore the very real possibility that development of the psychic aspects of self can, along with learning from real life experiences, serve in a most profound way. The dichotomy is that psychic development, on its own, can lead the subject down the road of glamour and illusion. At its worst it leads to fortune-telling and the word 'telling' is illuminating; to *tell* someone anything disempowers. To fully educate is to do the opposite; drawing out the individual's innate knowledge thereby giving the power back to them. Applying a form of heightened intuition, together with acknowledg-ing psychological aspects of the self, can enable awareness of both the true feelings of others, and oneself.

In the first development group I attended I had observed that all the people present were not just sharpening their psychic abilities but were also transforming their lives, whether it was through better health, better relation-ships or just greater contentment. This observation fascinated me; what was going on? What was this group doing to create these changes?

As we shall see, the 'self' is the fundamental part of any intuitive or psychic energy and communication. Currently the *Oxford English Dictionary* has a long list of definitions related to the self, which describe the emotional, mental, physical or spiritual aspects. In the last 40 years a vast industry has grown up around self-help groups and therapies and 'self' has become somewhat of a jargon term. In psycho-spiritual studies, the spiritual aspect of self is seen to be the higher aspect of the individual. However, the term 'higher self' can be confusing because this might be seen as the innate, core and soul aspect of self which can also be referred to as the 'inner' self, nature or being. Conversely, the lower layers of self include the more mundane or known aspects i.e. the social, emotional, mental, psychological, ego or per-sonality selves, and in contrast with the higher Self they do not necessarily make contact with the essence, spirit or soul of the person. The Western culture's concept of the self usually refers to the outer layers of personality, which need not include the inner, core or spiritual self. I therefore prefer to use the word 'highest' self. However, psychologists such as Jung and Assagioli and humanistic psychologists such as Rogers and Maslow have sought to incorporate this 'higher' aspect of Self within their work. *(Note: To differentiate between the various aspects of self in this work, reference to the higher Self will use a capital S and the lower self a lower-case s).*

The negative aspects of self, found within the physical, lower mental and emotional energies, are seen to be like veils that might obscure the true inner nature or highest Self. These need to be parted or drawn away as the individual journeys deeper and deeper towards the core of oneself. Spiritual development, therefore, is not so much concerned with accumulating information, as understanding it experientially, i.e. in real life situations and experiences.

Jung defines the 'higher' Self as: The god within. God is an emotive word to many, as it suggests an authoritative being that somehow maps out one's whole life; a man with a long beard; an immovable force. And it can be a negative trigger word for those who have come under the tyranny of enforced concepts with which they feel no connection. For many academics and scientists it triggers something non-scientific and therefore of no value. Indeed 'the G word', as I refer to it, has become contentious. In the subject of Self-awareness, as we look deeper into the spirit or core of ourselves, a sense of something higher than ourselves is often in evidence. Is this some omnipotent energy? Is this a force that flows through the universe? Or is it something none of us really understands or knows? The interpretation of these experiences is up to the individual; beliefs are not set in stone, they can, and do change. Some would argue that they must; after all, we rarely keep the same beliefs we had as a child. Nonetheless, we can only relate to what we feel and think at the time. Within psycho-spiritual development it is left to the individuals to decide for themselves what feels right, and act accordingly.

Although Jung, like his early mentor Freud, largely denied anything connected to religion, nonetheless he wrote extensively regarding the spiritual, seeing it as 'infinite, spaceless, formless, imageless'. In *A Critical Dictionary of Jungian Analysis* by Samuels, Shorter and Plaut, it states that spirit has a purpose; a kind of intuitive force, which connects and influences disparate events. He not only believed in a spirit world full of discarnate beings, he also made use of dreams and highlighted the necessity of man's conscious relationship to spirit.

'Self spirituality' is used as a common phrase, and although many of its concepts can seem similar to psycho-spiritual studies, there is little consensus on how to obtain deep spiritual Self-exploration. For many these ideas will be first acknowledged through the concept of personal growth or development. Numerous organizations implement various kinds of personal development (PD) days for their workforce, and personal development is also incorporated into many college and university degrees. The word 'personal' comes from the Latin *persona*, meaning 'mask'. Personal growth may therefore be seen to deal with the outer or lower influences; the mask or persona self. Personal exploration can lead to varying degrees of awareness, and, although the end result of this personal search might lead towards what the humanistic psychologist Carl Rogers calls 'the fully functioning person', this may not include any deeper spirituality. Confusion arises regarding the understanding of these terms, as it is possible to undertake personal growth without necessarily being spiritually Self-aware. In psycho-spiritual practices there is a belief that a student can break out from the lower personal psychological patterns, wherever they originated, and thereby move towards greater awareness.

During the years of my research the whole subject has expanded and has received much more scholarly attention. 'Spiritual' generally relates to the non-physical. Spirituality can also refer to an awareness of one's inner self and a sense of connection to a higher source; it might be perceived to be common to all religions, but need not be connected to any. Religions are seen as a particular doctrinal framework that guides beliefs and structures on how people live their lives. Spirituality can also pertain to profound inner experiences, which enable the growth of both the positive and creative aspects of self.

In the context used within this work, spirituality is not confined to any particular religion or dogma, but rather it is used according to its *Oxford Dictionary* definition, which refers to the 'essence' or 'core' of an individual. Ontologically, every individual, regardless of their culture, has a core part of Self which is considered the highest aspect of Self, and spirituality is thought to be realized through personal encounters and experiences with the numinous. This concept is integral to psycho-spiritual practices, and in this sense learning is achieved, not just in the head or even the heart, but actualized in the living world of the individual.

So what has intuition got to do with all of this? Again, the word 'intuition', like spirituality, has different meanings. Some assert that intuition is a sophisticated form of reasoning, not some kind of magical sixth sense. Others suggest that intuition is something subjective, non-scientific, and consequently immeasurable. Some schools of thought claim a connection between reasoning and intuition. According to mystical traditions, contact with intuition is often achieved by a state of stillness, or meditation. There are many ideas on what intuition is, including the intellectual mechanics of arriving at ideas without going through any rational, logical or analytical steps. Jung describes it as the psychological function that explores the unknown, senses possibilities and indications, which may not be readily apparent. All these give some sense of availability and accessibility. Not necessarily something learnt, but like sight, smell and taste, readily present. Maybe its immediacy is the reason it goes unnoticed, ignored or taken for granted and therefore becomes hard to analyse.

Intuition can be associated with psychic practices, and has often been denigrated to a fantasy or unreal state. This dismissal obscures deeper possibilities. It is unsurprising that science has been reluctant to investigate what seems to be a nebulous, dubious and unscientific subject. Yet, although intuition is by its nature a psychic experience, using it for personal insight does not make it a fortune-telling device, nor a form of spiritualism, i.e. talking to the dead. For the purpose of psycho-spiritual learning we are endeavouring to reach the highest or deepest level which might be described as the in(ner) tuition, or the inner voice or nature of the soul and spirit. Jung thought that 'psychic reality may be a form of self expression' leading to personification of the self which for Jung was, 'an empirical demonstration of psychic reality'. By this token, acknowledging a psychic reality, at least for the individual who senses it, as part of spiritual Self-development might assist the self-awareness process.

In the past, it was believed that truth was out there waiting to be discovered. However, postmodernism has questioned basic assumptions about knowledge itself and challenges this view. Postmodernism suggests that knowledge paradigms are social constructions. In a world where many realities and religious beliefs intermingle, there are multiple realities, and as such it becomes increasingly difficult to maintain one reality as the only truth. People have often relinquished their responsibility to any number of religious organizations, doctrines, political persuasions, families or sects, and feel secure in doing so as it gives them a sense of permanence. With instant global communication, we now live in a world not just of one culture or religion but also a world of many beliefs. One of the main objections to the postmodern idiom is that it deconstructs and disintegrates any view of consistency, sense and meaning. If this is so, who, or what, can be our authority? This book inquires into this question, asking, can a form of contemporary spiritual Self-awareness, including the individual's own intuition, assist one's innate knowledge and truth?

Many writers and artists down the ages who have had experience of an inner voice have mentioned a form of intuition:

- When your Daemon is in charge do not think consciously.
  Drift, wait and obey – Rudyard Kipling
- Intuition always comes before reflection because it operates more rapidly – Frederico Ruiz
- To some elementary laws there leads no logical path, but only intuition supported by being sympathetically in touch with experience – Albert Einstein
- It is by logic that we prove, it is by intuition we invent, for logic remains barren unless fertilized by intuition – Henri Poincare

Plato said that a poet is able to create only that which the muse dictates. Paul McCartney is reported to have written his perhaps most famous hit, 'Yesterday', after waking in the morning with the whole song in his head. The composer, Federico Ruiz, has said that if he 'thought and reflected too

I n certain cases an intuition has saved lives: My father, who was by nature a very punctual man, told me that in the middle of the Second World War when he worked in the city of London doing vital war work, the buses always ran on time. One day, he left the office at the usual time, and as he was walking down the road, for no logical reason he found himself slowing down. He slowed down so much he knew he would miss the bus and he watched it go past. Less than half a mile down the road the bus was bombed!! He often puzzled on why that day he should for no reason consciously decide he didn't want to catch the bus. That decision saved his life and enabled me to be born!

much, his works would never be completed'. There are numerous references to some inspired force that works through not just creative people, such as writers and artists, but also scientists and inventors.

Evidence of intuition and inspirational connections abound through history, and therefore it begs the question, if its influence can be so productive, why is it not more widely accepted or even used in education?

Psycho-spirituality has evolved and developed for over a hundred years from various different spiritual disciplines, and in the process different faiths, cultures and practices have coalesced into a form of contemporary psycho-spirituality. The associated literature is vast, so in this chapter I have concentrated on the writings and authorities from scholarly inquiry specifically within the growing subject of spirituality.

Contemporary Spirituality

Spirituality is often perceived as a nebulous term, which has many different meanings to different people. Although, to date, a definitive meaning of spirituality is still to be found, effort is being made to establish a definition so we may be able to embrace the subject effectively.

The word 'spirituality' is derived from the Latin word *spiritus* – spirit, breath or life – the essential or core part of the person. Spirit could therefore be thought of as a vital life force, which motivates people and influences all aspects of one's life. However, spirituality is not just thought to be an inner quality. It has also been described as a mode of understanding one's relationship and connection to something outside one's self that provides meaning.

From the many definitions of spirituality it could be deduced that an individual may identify the spiritual sense as something that could be either an external or internal experience. These do not have to be mutually exclusive; usually, the individual is thought to link to a higher power which is generally accessed through the deepest core of self – immanent – but there can also be a connection with a higher power outside the self – transcendent.

Acclaimed biologist Alister Hardy, drawing from the fields of psychology, animal behaviour, psychic research and anthropology, propounds the hypothesis that: 'Spirituality is natural to the human species and has evolved because it has biological survival value.' Hardy seems to suggest that there is a direct, intuitive awareness which is ever-present. This is a contentious issue. Are the building blocks of spirituality within us at birth or do they develop? If the definition of spirituality is that we have a 'core' or essential part of self, it follows that spirituality is present in everyone and like all our faculties it therefore has the potential to be developed. These concepts of evolution are a 'hot potato', which have been explored by hundreds of philosophers, religious leaders, scientists and writers.

There may be various differing opinions of the meaning of spirituality but one of the commonalities in relevant literature is that there is a difference between spirituality and religion. Religion means to *tie together* and is therefore seen as the organization of spirituality and facilitates the making of meaning to our world. Religion usually has a set structure that teaches people about a god, or gods, and the way to live their lives. Therefore it need not be a personal lived experience but a set of values to underpin society, life and living.

Nevertheless, both the religious and spiritual concepts relate to qualities of life that go beyond the ordinary physical and material states; the qualities that suggest there is something more to life than material existence. Indeed many people who consciously follow a spiritual path start with the recognition that, 'there must be more to life than this'.

Religions organize, and provide deep and rich traditions for the practices of being spiritual. They also have social structures and officials in the form of priests and elders to ensure the purity and propriety of practice. Alternatively, contemporary spirituality relates to the experiential journey and relationship with others, powers and forces which seem beyond the scope of everyday life. To be spiritual is to be open to 'there must be more than this' in life, and to encounter and nurture a relationship with it.

Taken from the more orthodox position, developing one's own spiritual truth alone is often used as an argument against spiritual Self-awareness, for where is the comfort of the society, the tribe and practices that have been built up over hundreds and thousands of years? Religions offer support to the community and often hold society together. Having a shared culture allows growth and progress of the peoples involved. Nonetheless, although the structure of religions and religious leaders may give support to their own tribe or sect and propound moral ethics, they have also used their ideals and teaching as an excuse to execute terrible things throughout history. In the *Journal of Psychology and Theology* an interesting point is made by Dallas Willard, when he talks about the behaviour of Christians:

> ... the result is that we have multitudes of professing Christians who may well be ready to die, but obviously are not ready to live and hardly get along with themselves much less with others.

He is talking here specifically about Christians, however the same could be applied to most other religions. Contemporary spirituality, however, demands authenticity, a need to live our beliefs and not be told what they should be. I have heard many people say that if we got rid of religions there would be world peace. I suspect, however, it would make little difference. Religions are tribal. If you took away religions and religious leaders, other leaders and their ideologies would replace them. Perhaps if we stop needing our tribal aspects we will transcend division and wars. Nowadays, with more immediate and efficient communications around the world, being able to watch apparent insanities in the name of a god or religion, should it surprise us that in many cases religions seem to be losing their credibility?

Richard Dawkins no doubt would agree, as he writes copiously and articulately on the evils of religion, particularly in his book *The God Delusion*. He externalizes the whole subject, missing the point of the inner experiences and senses. He makes good rational arguments, he is erudite and intellectual but through lack of understanding he, like many others, puts religions and spiritual endeavours all in the same box. In doing so he waves aside personal experiences by using the mentally ill to further his argument.

At school I was part of the debating society and we were asked to develop not just an argument on one side but also stand and talk with rational arguments for the other. A good rational logical mind can do this with ease. The point is, we can choose what we want to believe and clever people can make clever arguments to support their beliefs.

In the genuine discovery of Self, one needs to take responsibility, think for oneself and, through understanding of mind-sets, true motives and patterns, choose what is right for you. This requires rigorous examination of what is going on inside one's self. People such as Dawkins propound, often through lack of knowledge or care, that religion is similar to any intuitive or spiritual aspect. Psycho-spirituality, as discussed within this book, need not have any connection with organized religions, but does draw from some of its philosophies and practices as tools for investigation of self.

Generally psycho-spiritual practices do not stipulate that the student has to follow any particular belief system. They do, however, encourage the mystical notion of the transcendence of human understanding and the ability of the individual to communicate directly to a higher energy, whatever that is believed to be by the individual. They also usually suggest that spiritual unfoldment is possible for everyone including those that have no religious beliefs at all.

Because of the personal nature of contemporary spirituality, it seems likely that any consensus will continue to be elusive. Nonetheless, increased intelligent debate and discussion on the whole area is encouraging the emergence of spirituality.

Health and Wellbeing

The whole area of spirituality has in recent times branched out to many different areas including health care and research, causing the subject to flourish over the last 20 years. Many articles in referenced health journals have stated there may be some correlation with spiritual practices and better health, discussing the real value in the healing process for spiritual involvement. There has been the suggestion that working with patients must include recognition of the interconnection of the body, mind and spirit, and the need for this integration if true healing is to occur. Other comments refer to the use of spirituality in helping patients to gain a sense of control over their lives. Patients have been reported as saying that they feel enriched and empowered when a spiritual dimension is integrated into all other human dimensions, increasing a sense of wholeness and wellbeing, giving them hope, and a sense of purpose.

Spiritual resources are also seen to be particularly relevant in dealing with situations of severe stress. Previously the medical profession has been suspicious of the spiritual aspects of their patients, however, some researchers have even suggested that spirituality be included as part of doctors' training. The other side of the argument says that certain religious beliefs and activities can adversely affect both mental and physical health and that, far from freeing, it can become restraining. The idea being that:

> … some types of spiritual and religious beliefs can encourage an unquestioning obedience to a single charismatic leader or that it might promote religious or spiritual traditions as a healing practice to the total exclusion of research-based medical care and therefore be likely to adversely affect their health.

> (*See* Larimore, Parker and Crowther)

It could be said that any belief, of a spiritual nature or not, that 'restrains' is likely to be counterproductive to health and spiritual growth. If spirituality is seen to have a positive effect on the physical aspects of a person, might it not follow that it can have a positive effect on other aspects of self?

Spiritual Psychology

It was in the early 1900s that Roberto Assagioli began developing a form of spiritual or 'transpersonal' psychology, which he labelled 'psychosynthesis'. He maintained that we possess a super-consciousness described as the 'psyche', which contains our deepest potential, the source of the unfolding pattern of our unique human path of development. This super-consciousness or deeper aspect of Self continually invites us to levels of healing and wholeness, hence the word *trans* in this context means 'through into another state' and 'beyond or above the personal'. Other major influences on transpersonal psychology include William James and Carl Jung; the consciousness research of Stanislav Grof and the views of Ken Wilber are also pertinent. The transpersonal approach pushes out the boundaries of psychology. It acknowledges the spiritual aspects of life and also the deep need in us for transcendental experiences.

John Rowan suggests that 'transpersonal' is a clearly defined term because it is better stated than spirituality and more widely researched. In The Transpersonal, he cites refereed journals in the subject, where it was defined as:

> The systematic study of non-ordinary states of consciousness
> especially when such states may be considered religious or
> mystical experiences and the models of human personality, belief
> systems and therapeutic practices that are pertinent to such states.

It has been suggested that the psychological and the spiritual are interwoven and often cannot be separated. In this way we need to address the person as a 'psycho-spiritual unit'. The term psycho-spiritual can therefore be used as an alternative to 'transpersonal'. Words often go through phases of acceptability. I use the word psycho-spiritual because it includes both the spiritual and psychological aspects of self, so important to both spiritual growth and psychic development.

The main focus of psycho-spirituality in this book is the development of the Self and, in common with transpersonal psychology, it deals with aspects of the individual beyond the personal state. However, although there are many similarities between transpersonal and psycho-spiritual practices, not every transpersonalist openly embraces the worth of subtle energies, or intuition.

Intuition

The argument against intuition is that it is unpredictable and unreliable, so how can we can deal with the inconsistency that in one type of investigation intuition is considered to be irrational, while in another series of studies intuition guides people to true responses? It is true that intuitive information can be seen as eccentric in nature, as it rarely follows any set model or format. So given the uncertainty of this subject, why choose intuition as a navigator for one's life? Is it a reliable source of truth? It could be argued that there are many better ways to find one's spirituality; following a religious practice, or finding an authentic spiritual teacher, for instance. Another criticism is that intuition is deterministic and therefore does not give the individual room for free will or expression. However, the reverse could just as easily be argued, because as intuition comes directly from the person in the moment, the individual is therefore free to choose his or her own direction.

In *Transpersonal Psychologies,* what could be called a seminal work on transpersonal studies talking about spiritual psychologies, Charles Tart says they:

> conceive of intuition as one or more powerful cognitive faculties that work on principles other than logical rationality, and that work outside of conscious awareness … further intuition is seen as something that can be cultivated and that can give a more profound understanding of many things other than reason.

This idea that intuition can be cultivated is not common and one that has rarely been addressed, but it could be argued that like any quality – mental, physical or intellectual – it must be possible for it to be trained and developed.

In an article by Christian de Quincey, he draws attention to research on indigenous peoples and notes that prior to the influences of the West, people worked with what 'felt' right; once reason was introduced, that same feeling was 'interspersed and masked with the desire to strive to please'. The consequent result was the 'obliteration or suppression of consciousness by reason'. Many of those who follow the New Age and spiritual development are heard to say 'it feels right'. If the feeling is true (and this in itself requires a complete honesty of self) it is not such a bad way to live, however, there are pitfalls with the feelings. Do they come from an innate truth or are they like most things born from fear or desire?

Quoting Stanford anthropologist Richard Sorenson, de Quincey continues to say that indigenous tribal peoples have:

> ... lived their lives based on integrated trust and a sensual
> intuitive rapport between the people. Their communication
> was spontaneous, open and honest. For them truth–talk was
> affect-talk.

This does not mean that reason was not in existence in some form before the arrival of Western man, but if, as this suggests, there is some truth that logic and reason can seek to please and consequently distort one's actions, the person stops being honest to oneself and others. Authentic spiritual Self-awareness requires openness. We need therefore to ask what stands between our truths? The educationalist R S Peters tells us that:

> ... our wishes and fears limit how we see the world ... If this
> becomes too structured in terms of our own personal wishes and
> fears, it can lead to windowless tunnel vision, to a peep-hole on
> the world determined by our own preoccupations.

If fear limits our world, could it cloak our truth, and if so might it affect our communications with the inner being or Self? If we eradicate our fears, negative patterns and assumptions, might it bring us closer to our inner self and enable contact with our inner being? Accessing intuition is thought to provide a readily accessible decision-making tool, which might aid the process of unveiling aspects of self that cloak the core or true Self. It is argued that intuition may not be correct, however, decisions born out of logic can just as easily turn out to be incorrect. Just as there are different types of intelligence, I suggest there are different types of intuition ranging from the animal survival instincts to the highest or deepest level; the in(ner) tuition, or the inner authentic nature and the voice of spirit or core Self. (*See* Chapter Two.)

Professor and psychologist, Abraham Maslow, referring to the inner nature says that it is:

> ... cloaked and *weak*, it persists underground, unconsciously, even though denied and repressed ... It speaks softly but it will be heard, even if in a distorted form ... It has a dynamic force of its own pressing always for open uninhibited expression. This force is one main aspect of the will to health, the urge to identity. It is this that makes psychotherapy, education and self-improvement possible in principle.

So how can we hear this soft inner voice that often is obscured? Can religious notions guide us through? Can logic discern its elusive nature? Intuition may not be all that is needed for this task, but it might give access to this inner sense.

Mystics through the ages concur that depth insight and intuition come in the spiritual unfoldment process and can, with care, be utilized to assist, not hinder, our journey. Carl Rogers says as a:

> ... psychological function, like sensation, feeling and thinking, intuition is, 'a way of knowing'. When you know something intuitively, it has the ring of truth; yet often we do not know,

whom we know, what we know … learning to use intuition is
learning to be your own teacher.

Can this 'way of knowing' or higher intuitive knowledge really be employed
to act as the pilot which drives the person forwards, enabling better understanding of oneself and assisting spiritual transformation? Can it give a
person a better connection and understanding of their inner spiritual nature?
If so, where do we start to find this elusive inner nature? Maslow suggested
that, in the majority of individuals, the inner nature is there unconsciously
and that it can be obtained by a state of stillness. But how does the individual
obtain the required state of stillness to perceive the inner nature? If we take
the mystical approach, making a connection with the inner or higher Self may
require us to uncover or dissolve the veils that obscure contact. To assist this,
transpersonal methods are believed to move and dissolve the outer persona
and lower self to assist the process.

Recently, integrating spirituality and psychotherapy has become a significant area of research. One of the reasons for this combination could be that
the individual's spiritual journey is not always straightforward and affects
students in very many and diverse personal ways. The growing literature
reflects this and suggests some form of therapeutic input in the spiritual
learning process. It has been suggested by Diana Whitmore in *Psychosynthesis
in Education* that they can complement each other:

> This means therefore the therapist has two roles. One is the role
> of psychotherapist the other of a priest, teacher, and spiritual
> guide. In the past we might have gone to one or the other. In
> transpersonal therapy there is a fusion of the two roles.

One could argue that combining the roles of psychotherapist and priest
would present all sorts of problems, not least of all because however good the
training of the therapist, it might not provide them with the spiritual disposition to take on the role of priest or spiritual director.

Whereas for most there is little dispute in the value of therapy, is it really possible that therapists may also 'stand in' for lost religions and faiths? It might be argued that a form of spiritual education that embraces aspects of psychotherapeutic practice is not so surprising in this modern climate, but this fusion of roles might make some uneasy. For instance, does this mean that spiritual teachers need to be psychotherapists as well? Previously, 'being spiritual' has been left to organized religions. The concept of learning to be your own teacher, which stands at the heart of contemporary spirituality, equally does not seem to lend itself to the use of a therapy. However, employing therapeutic methods in psycho-spiritual learning might assist students in understanding themselves. As the New Age writer Caroline Myss says: 'the mystics have come out of the monasteries!' There is some danger here, as many development groups are run by people with little psychological knowledge, or even worse, people who have read something of psychology superficially and therefore become part of the psycho-babble that may have some validity for some people, but will do little to help the person with deep psychological problems and may even do damage. What may be just as bad as the charlatan, is the person of good intentions who is ignorant!

Nevertheless, over the last 50 years with the upsurge of interest in transpersonal psychology and psychotherapy, together with a much greater awareness of other cultural religious practices, the importance of the person is being acknowledged. It is increasingly thought that the more healthy concentration on the self, far from removing the person from a god or spirit, it becomes the very means that allows a first-hand communication with a higher power. The Self therefore takes centre stage in our observation and inquiry. Therefore, knowledge of at least some aspects of psychology may not just be an advantage, it might be a necessity.

Psychotherapy often identifies the need to 'let go', and this concept of release from negative mind-sets and experiences that no longer serve us is familiar to anyone who has trodden on the spiritual or even personal development path. Some suggest that intuition is an aid towards this process as it is seen that intuitive listening is being open enough to let the unexpected come, in a relaxed, detached light. This suggests the need for some form of meditation or quiet contemplation to allow the intuition to be heard.

However, 'letting go' of negativity can be very psychologically messy and uncomfortable, and this being the case, someone untrained in the psychological process may either be unable to assist, or may even exacerbate the problem. This promotes the argument for some psychological knowledge.

Psychological inquiry addresses personal meaning, and spiritual practice looks beyond our ordinary human concerns towards the realization of the ultimate. John Welwood, among many, suggests that psychological work might serve as an ally to spiritual practice by 'helping to shine the light of awareness into all the hidden nooks and crannies of our conditioned personality'.

Welwood is describing some form of loosening effect on the whole psyche, possibly in line with the classic notion of the dissolution of the 'veils of illusion' or in contemporary parlance 'unfoldment' but, as he says, this needs a special kind of therapy. So can psycho-spirituality marry the necessary elements for the task?

In psycho-spiritual development the lower aspects of self dissolve, allowing the higher or inner Self to emerge, giving access to an inner knowing that is not based on learnt knowledge but on an intuitive sense. This is seen to bring a different state of consciousness when an awareness awakened to this world is transformed. With the major changes and difficult situations our planet is experiencing, there is a real argument for a psycho-spiritual integration, one that develops 'a fuller richer human presence that could fulfil the still unrealized potential of life on this earth', according to Welwood.

The combination of the psychological and spiritual is a relatively new concept and there still exists suspicion towards any psychic perceptions. Some religions still see them as evil, ignoring the fact that any communication with God could be considered some form of extrasensory perception. If we are talking about lower forms of psychic work that may inflate the ego and consequently lead people away from their spirituality, I have some sympathy with this notion. Indeed many mystic writers do warn against psychic work, nonetheless, most acknowledge, at the very least, that it is part of the spiritual process that may in time become redundant.

To the extent that any stage of development is not permanent, I would concur. However, this does not take into account the different levels of psychic and intuitive awareness, as there is a big difference between the lower forms of instinctual intuition and the higher form that encompasses a profound sense of the spiritual. Used productively this can be the very quality that ultimately leads the individual towards their spiritual redemption.

It was William James who first provided the enduring conceptualization of identity development naming 'the material, the social and the spiritual as aspects of self'. James described, this as the 'spiritual me': 'The true, the intimate, the ultimate, the permanent me which I seek ... the core and sanctuary of our life.'

The Hebrew word for soul – *nephesh* – is mentioned hundreds of times in the Old Testament, but it has no consensus definition and although one of its meanings is to breathe, it is thought the soul unites with the divine spirit and is therefore seen as an important aspect in maintaining a state of wellbeing. It was Plato who gave us the notion of 'the divinity of the soul, its imprisonment in the body and its need to purge itself of all bodily concerns'. Whether, or indeed how, we have to 'purge' ourselves is debatable, but the notion of ultimate truths is still alive within the psycho-spiritual movement.

With the expansion of democracy, post World War II, and the development of the already established belief in the spiritual and moral goodness, individual salvation was promised through the liberation of self and in this climate Carl Rogers and Abraham Maslow were able to convey the concept of self-actualization as the directional trend evident in all organic and human life. They and others see the innate urge to expand, extend, develop and mature, bringing us towards some spiritual progress.

Of course some are suspicious and criticize any development of self, seeing it as a narcissistic preoccupation, but the concept of 'Self-actualization' can be seen as similar to the mystical idea of a pathway to spiritual illumination. This notion is echoed in Gurdjieff's 'self remembering', Jung's 'individuation of Self', Almaas' 'personal essence' and Maslow's 'self-actualization'. Some find the whole concept an arrogance of humanistic ideals and purport that it is based on an irrational notion of the limitless power of humans to govern the world. Whereas it is certainly true that inherent in humanistic psychology is the notion of human potentials, this in itself does not automatically suggest one would have limitless power, nor that one would want world domination, but rather refers to mastery of Self, which is thought to instigate greater understanding of others and a greater propensity to engage in the good of all mankind.

Michael Daniels and others also delivered an attack on the concept of Self-actualizing, suggesting it might advocate an 'individualistic self-seeking approach to life and a concern with purely personal gratification'. He also says that preoccupation with mystical experience can 'create a non-rational impulsive and romantic bias that actively encourages ... emotional excess and anti-intellectualism'.

Whereas I have some sympathy with what might be seen as the excesses of self-spirituality, I cannot subscribe to the notion that one has to embrace only the non–rational ideas or indeed just the rational ones. People are multifaceted and have many complex aspects of self. Therefore why can't we embrace both? The rational mind is profoundly useful to us and can monitor our excesses and, although the intuition may seem impulsive, it has an immediacy that logic and rationality rarely provide. It may be perceived to be sometimes defective, but then so can the logical mind.

It has been argued that the concept of self-development could support hedonism, and a preoccupation with that self. It might be true that, like almost anything, if taken to extremes it will have extreme consequences, however, it is believed that with a self-development process individuals become more responsible, creative and flexible.

The orthodox faiths are also generally thought to be uncomfortable with what they see as self-serving spirituality, believing that because it is self-based it is therefore at odds with God. Paraphrasing Maslow the word *self* seems to put people off and therefore is often helpless before the powerful linguistic habit of identifying *self* with *selfish*. In some circles, any mention of *self* becomes almost a heresy of the Christian value to love thy neighbour, seemingly forgetting the next part of the phrase is 'as thyself', that is to love equally others and oneself. Also, the Christian emphasis on compassion for the weak often overrides the acknowledgment of the positive aspects within us and breeds hatred for the strong. This fear of godliness and strength stands at the heart of the acknowledgment of the individual's great importance in the spiritual development process. In psycho-spiritual practice, self-respect and self-love are not thought to remove the person from God but rather become the very means by which a first-hand communication with a higher power is reached, and from that, it is believed that emancipation and autonomy can occur.

The New Age

The term New Age was created by the German philosopher, Eugene Schmalenbach in the 1920s. It has been somewhat superseded by the title 'Mind Body Spirit', although both are generally seen to promote the concept of the importance of self as a way to higher knowledge. Autonomy and freedom are the main features, and most authority lies with the individual's experience.

Some have explored the possibilities of the New Age being a cult but research has found that it is not a religious movement and New Agers move through fluid networks rather than settled collectives. Although some New Agers do join cults, it is noted that others also go to church or are interested in Buddhism and other cultures. They are therefore not a unified organization and often meet each other in lectures, workshops, conferences and fairs. Because of their ideal to live for, and in, the present, they are classed as post-modern, but the genesis of this culture can probably be traced back to the turn of the last century with the influence of the Theosophists. The movement began to take shape soon after World War II and accelerated at the end of the 1950s and into the 1960s when the youth culture and the 'anything goes' attitude arrived. The educationalist Sir George Trevelyan who had an influential effect in the UK promoting New Age beliefs from the late 1940s up to his death in 1996, stated:

> ... the New Age concept that if you change man and you change society. Try to change society without the inner change in man and confusion will be the sole result.

(See *Sir George Trevelyan* by Frances Farrer)

More recently the title 'New Age' has become rather passé. The term 'New' is in any case technically incorrect, as much of its influences and practices are revisited old or even ancient disciplines; it describes a broad group of contemporary movements, therapies and quasi-religious groups. Some draw on Eastern or other non-European spiritual traditions and most reject the previous dualistic mind-body distinction.

Whatever title we use, the whole New Age, Mind Body Spirit movement has undoubtedly had a social and cultural effect. To paraphrase John Rowan, in this culture it is common to believe everything, accept anything and not question anything. Unfortunately, in my experience of lecturing and teaching within these movements, there is some truth in this statement. Contemporary spirituality as seen in the New Age and Mind Body Spirit circles is seen to remove people from the authority of religion and the safety of authoritative leadership. When we consider any kind of psychic development, or indeed development of any kind, it intrinsically suggests that one can grow, become better and train oneself. This requires discipline, self-responsibility and some form of evolving of self. Like any training and development we must at some point find some guidance and teaching.

Although one might need an experienced teacher to find a way through what could be perceived as the thick undergrowth of egoist narcissism, equally a dynamic teacher could be thought to be counterproductive. Founder and Director of the Human Potential Research project at Surrey University and a respected expert in the field of facilitation, John Heron has been particularly tough on Eastern teaching which has seen some resurgence in recent times; he suggests that, 'this kind of induced spirituality sets up dependency with chronic spiritual projection and becomes subject to authoritarian direction and indoctrination'.

Heron is particularly critical in *Sacred Science* when talking specifically about Buddhist-type training schools which he says:

> … are expressions of an exclusively male and rigidly authoritarian
> oriental system in which masters have an all-powerful role
> imported to the West. I think it is highly dubious metaphysically.

It is dubious too in the way it is used to legitimate spiritual power over people, by telling them what an impossible, unregenerate mess they are in without direction from those who claim to know the road to liberation. Authoritarian abuse has run amok with the spread of Buddhism in the UK and USA.

Clearly Heron is not enamoured with the revival of some aspects of Buddhism and he is correct in that many of the strict Oriental systems are male-dominated. In terms of spiritual Self development however, even though they may have revived ancient practices, these are generally modified to accommodate Western minds and also, far from being led by, or indeed filled by, 'exclusively males' they have a very high percentage of females. Indeed many recent writers have actively propounded the rebirth of the Goddess suggesting that the feminist movement is a spiritual movement as well as political, because it addresses the liberation of the human spirit by healing the fragmentation of the male and female energies within. Nevertheless, I do agree with Heron regarding some highly publicized and charismatic leaders, whatever their faith or religion. Some people feel the need to follow and will, if not careful, come under the spell of disreputable leaders. I have seen otherwise sensible people lose all intelligence in this way.

The abuse of power in teachers is reprehensible. In orthodox organizations and schools, hopefully this would be weeded out and the teacher would be sacked. However, there is no such body in the psychic, or psycho-spiritual world and it is largely left to the individual to monitor what is right for them.

I once came across such a leader, who claimed to have extraordinary psychic abilities. He ran groups, mainly of women, who swooned over him. I later was told by one of his ex-students that he told the women he possessed a 'golden wand' and they were privileged to receive it!! I will leave further details to your imagination.

So the question emerges – who do we get to help us in this psycho-spiritual process? There is no specific training for this area, and many teachers are self-appointed. This of course does not mean they don't have something to offer, but picking up the previous point of the psychological process involved, and the development of self being so individual, how can one teacher be all things to all people? This being the case it is likely that the individual is at some point in their development forced back within themselves to find what is their truth and how they choose to live their lives. It is now widely known that astrologically we have just entered the new age of Aquarius. The ages last around 2,000 years. The Aquarian age is about the individual, so does this suggest that individuals, at some point, are left to themselves ultimately to find the strength, the knowledge and the divine within?

The argument for emerging modern spiritual practices is that there is value in the multi-variant spontaneous coming together of different faiths, genders and practices which puts power in the hands of the individual to find what suits best. Although it can be an absolute minefield amongst some of these practices that are so diverse and unstructured, and have very little real desire to intelligently examine themselves. Therefore I share some sympathy with the scepticism towards the more dubious Mind Body Spirit practices. Some of the more reputable therapies including health and healing have recently gone a long way to bring themselves in line with professional and rigorous standards. For example, spiritual healing has now been recognized as a bona fide therapy. This has meant that healing organizations have had to get their act together, create a sound structure for learning and examination. Just as you would not go to an amateur to fix your electricity or plumbing, why go to an amateur for healing? Of course, as in all things, standards still vary, but in healing at least there is a common goal to be professional, to attend good training and keep the practice of one's own self-development alive.

Mysticism

Contemporary spirituality has concepts in common with mysticism down the ages. Like spirituality, the meaning of mysticism appears confusing. Indeed the very word 'mystic' has in some circles come to stand for something nebulous, inconsequential and sometimes just nonsensical. It is generally thought to mean a belief in a personal union with God, and being mystical refers to a transcendence of human understanding.

It has been reported that there is an increase of mystical experiences among females, the educated, the affluent and older persons. Further research on the correlation of aspects of the spiritual person suggests that mystical experiences attract extrovert and sociable people, with excitement-seeking, carefree and optimistic personality traits. Historically, however, the mystical type is introverted and reflective. More research needs to be undertaken to examine the use of personality-type mysticism, as my direct experience of students with a mystical bent is that they vary widely in personality traits.

In F C Happold's authoritative work he suggests there are three types of mysticism:

Nature Mysticism is the sense of oneness with nature and the world. It has pantheistic meaning in the sense that all is in God and God is in all; a sense of immanence especially in nature.

Soul Mysticism is the hardest notion for the Western mind as it is the idea that the soul is put into a state of complete isolation from everything that is other than itself, the main objective being the quest for its own self and right knowledge of itself.

God Mysticism is when the 'real' self is thought to be absorbed into the essence of God whereby 'the individual personality and the whole objective world are felt to be entirely obliterated'. In the West it is seen that the soul or spirit is deified so that it becomes God without losing its identity by a process of union and transformation.

There are elements of all three types of mysticism, as described by Happold, present in contemporary spiritual Self-awareness, although the concept of God Mysticism with its processes of union and transformation of Self is most frequently expressed. The one quality that binds all the definitions of mysticism is that it is something experienced by the individual. It is perceived as an inner sense whereby the mystic relies not on deductive reason but on intuition to guide them. As a result of direct intuitive experience one finds not only a coherent pattern which is not contrary to reason, but also a certainty of a sort, which cannot be given by philosophy.

If it is correct that we come to the highest spirit through direct intuitive experiences, might it suggest that the conscious use of intuition may be helpful to spiritual development? The 'internalization of spirit' is seen to be at the heart of psycho-spirituality and although contemporary spirituality shows strong inclinations towards the Eastern mystical traditions, similar notions are to be found within Christianity, for example the Christian mystic St John of the Cross and St Teresa of Avila (*see* Chapter Five).

Mysticism is described as having both an intrinsically personal quality with a belief that one is in communication with a divine being, and also a sense of impersonality with a strong sense of timelessness and oneness. The personal experience has often been related to a religious experience connected to a deity within the individual's faith, so it could just as easily be seen as a unity with Allah or Yahweh or Christ. Research into the mystical shows the described experiences to cross faith and culture.

With mystical experiences there is often a feeling of a profound connection to something beyond the mundane, something powerful and intrinsically divine. Maslow says these peak experiences are:

> ... only good and desirable and are never experienced as evil or undesirable ... the experience is complete and needs nothing else. It is sufficient to itself ... It is reacted to as wonder, amazement, humility and even reverence, exaltation and piety.

The good feeling associated with these experiences, as described by Maslow, differs from some mystical experiences that can be traumatic to the life of the individual, and although may not be thought of as 'evil' they can completely deconstruct the person's life which the phrase 'Dark Night of the Soul' so aptly describes (*see* Chapter Six). Peak experiences seem to have the effect of softly calling the individual's soul, showing another perception and a promise of better things to come. Conversely, some deep mystical experiences can sometimes seem destructive to the present status quo, and although they too may reveal a different way of being they can have the effect of disrupting the person's life.

Assessing what is *real* with someone's transpersonal and mystical experiences is fraught with difficulties. Mediums and psychics have in the past been burnt at the stake, ostracized or kept imprisoned. Ken Wilber in *The Atman Project* relates a similar difficulty when assessing real spiritual awakening. He says that because certain mental illnesses and spiritual emergence are both 'non-rational they appear quite similar or even identical to the untutored eye'. And they can be 'profoundly mistreated and misunderstood'.

By this token it could make someone experiencing psychosis think the voices in their head are really the voice of God, or equally make truly transformative inspiration seem like madness. Wilber states that 'orthodox psychiatry will continue to see saints as insane and sages as psychotic thereby proving itself a proudly tenacious impediment to the growth and evolution of humanity on the whole'.

This alerts us to the difficulty for the untrained to differentiate the real mystical experience from mental illness. These short references open up a much bigger discussion. It seems clear that modern psychiatry, and indeed spiritual facilitation, needs to become more aware and be properly trained to observe the differences if we are to avoid unfortunate consequences. I have seen many good people go astray when confronted by some spiritual experience they cannot rationalize, and otherwise intelligent and hard-working people simply 'losing the plot', believing they are the voice of God or some such entity. This can have disastrous effects on their work, their families and themselves.

William James lists the characteristics of mystical experience as: 'I was in heaven, an inward state of peace and joy and assurance indescribably intense, accompanied with a sense of being bathed in a warm glow of light.' James states that these experiences are not related to the intellect in the usual sense:

O ne professional and educated man told me that many years ago, at the beginning of his spiritual journey, he genuinely thought he was Jesus. Believing this he reasoned he should be able to walk on water. He went down to the river and stood on the bank. He looked at the water and thought – perhaps not!

> Although so similar to states of feeling, mystical states seem
> to those who experience them to be also states of knowledge…
> They are states of insight into depths of truth unplumbed by the
> discursive intellect. They are illuminations, revelations, full of
> significance and importance, all inarticulate though they remain
> and as a rule they carry with them a curious sense of authority.

It might be argued that the best way to deal with these experiences would be in a religious context. However, religious practice might interpret the experience within its own creed, maybe even giving prescriptive answers to something that may be intrinsically personal or born from basic psychology and animal behaviour. And if, as we have seen earlier, they are interpreted by psychiatry, they could equally be misinterpreted. James also suggests that intuition is the key to deep transformative mystical experiences, but different aspects of intuition can also be misdiagnosed. Nonetheless, if it is a possibility that in the right hands intuition can assist some spiritual transformation, maybe the time has arrived to actively train and utilize it.

CHAPTER TWO

Expanding Perceptions

Tell me and I will forget, show me and I may remember. Involve me and I will understand.

Confucius

The exploration of self is a journey. It is an adventure as gripping as any thriller; more exciting, more challenging, and more real, because this is the story of your life, a story in which you are your own hero or heroine. It is said, there is a story in everyone and that is likely to be true, however, stories generally relay the events in one's life. Lurking behind these are layers of self, psychic unseen influences emerging briefly only in dreams, during in-depth psychology or when some drastic life situation enforces this awareness. How many of us are aware, really aware of what or who we are? Aware of our intentions, aware of our true motives, aware of what lurks in our own personal Pandora's box? Dare we open its lid? Dare we peep inside, and if we do, what will we find?

Some years ago whilst I was trying to explain to a woman at a party what Self-development was all about, she exclaimed, 'What would you want to do that for?' Her reaction is not unique, as living life would seem complex enough without delving into the sometimes misty aspects of self. If you want to keep the status quo, then she is right. There often comes a point in life, however, when we question what is the meaning of our existence. It's what I call, 'there must be more to life than this' syndrome. Is life just about a good job, nice home, lovely children? For some that is so, but are these things really satisfying? If you have millions in the bank and all the things money could buy, are you any happier? Judging by recent surveys of countries in the world that are the happiest, the West comes pretty low, and yet we are generally the most prosperous. Indeed the highest on the surveys are countries that are poor, yet most people still chase the dream. In over 30 years of this work I have not seen anyone completing a sound spiritual programme being less happy; indeed, deep awareness of self generally brings greater contentment, whatever the bank balance or the marital status.

In the last chapter we saw evidence that to be in a clear, transparent space allows much greater access to psychic faculties. We are all multifaceted beings, governed by many aspects of life and living; our genetic inheritance, our family and tribal influences, and our own unique experiences. We see the world through our own eyes. We interpret the world though our own thoughts and we make judgements because of it. What is pleasing for one may be awful for another. As we mature in life we develop mind-sets and ways of dealing with situations. These again are different for different people. Our fears and our pleasures are not the same. It is important therefore if you are genuine in your desire to work in the psychic fields that you must take these different aspects into account. The ways in which you react and approach your world will frequently not be the same as others.

To know another person in an empathetic state is a form of mediumship. Few people are really empathetic in the true meaning of the word; to be able to genuinely feel what another feels, without one's own thoughts and nature projecting onto the other. In daily life this is unlikely to be possible all the time, and indeed it is not advised. However, with training it is possible to achieve clarity and empathy, if only for the duration of the psychic link. Only when we know how another feels, thinks and reacts, can we truly give guidance and help. And the guidance that we receive for another may not be the same as the guidance we would give ourselves. If a psychic is cluttered by personal negativities and fixed ideas or is not clear in themselves, they will never be able to give accurate psychic perceptions.

When you are young and keen to drive a car, you have to learn how to use the vehicle first. If you just got in without training, and tried to drive, you would likely hurt or kill yourself or someone else. In much the same way with any psychic work you have to learn your own vehicle, i.e. yourself. Without this knowledge it is misleading, messy and potentially dangerous. You sometimes hear people say they are natural psychics, which may be so, however, it still means you need to learn about yourself, uncovering any negative aspects and mind-sets that prevent you from being in a free clear space.

It is widely acknowledged in counselling and psychology that working closely in any therapeutic practice can bring about 'transference'. This is when the patient, client or student projects onto others their feelings and ideas, which derive from previous figures and experiences in life. The term transference was first used and described by Freud who said that:

> ... a whole series of past psychological experiences that are
> revived, not as belonging to the past, but as applying to the
> person or the physician at the present moment. Some of these
> transferences have a content which differs from that of their
> model in no respect whatever except for the substitution. Others
> are more ingeniously constructed, the content has been subjected
> to a moderating influence ... And they may even become
> conscious, by cleverly taking advantage of some real peculiarity in
> the physician's person or circumstances and attaching themselves
> to that.

Educationalist and facilitator, John Heron says in *The Facilitator's Handbook*:

> When transference occurs, participants unconsciously transfer
> to the group leader, from the hurt child within, hidden and

repressed feelings about a parent or some other important
authority figure from the past.

Rather than ignore or dismiss transference, students can openly acknowledge
it in their classes to aid the self-awareness process, helping them to see what
it is they may be mirroring in others and what they need to observe about
themselves. This mirroring or transference is not just put upon group leaders
or therapists, it can, and does, happen in one's everyday life; it happens with
parent to child, it happens in relationships and it happens with friends.

I have observed that often the transference is projected onto someone who
is deemed safe, albeit unconsciously. In this way we can see how a mother, for
instance, often bears the brunt of the fears of her offspring, as most mothers
are unlikely to abandon their child. It can become a distressing experience
for the recipient, as loved ones off-load their fears and accuse the other of the
same fear. However, it can be transformed if it is acknowledged; it can also be
disastrous in any relationship when it is not. In a psychic reading when the
psychics do not know themselves, they may transfer onto their clients. This
is unhealthy, incorrect and possibly harmful. As we all at some time transfer
our fears and indeed our hopes onto others, it becomes obvious that this must
be understood and realized by any practitioner. Good advice from Heron is

---

I n my early days of teaching I had a lady on my course who, at the
end of the first session, got up and announced to the class she
could not possibly return as I 'reminded her too much of her mother',
upon which she abruptly walked out. I was completely taken aback,
but intuitively realized she was, in some way, mirroring what was
obviously not a good relationship with her mother onto me. I had
already observed that this could happen in a group situation, but at the
time was unaware of the existence of the concept of 'transference' well
known in therapy situations.

---

that 'a knowledge and observation of transference can be put to work and used to motivate learning'. From my own experience with students who have actively acknowledged transference, it is more likely that negative aspects of the transference process will already have been dealt with. It is then very much less likely that the student will project onto the leader, other members of the group, or even those to whom they are giving psychic readings.

One should also not overlook the possible occurrence of some form of counter-transference from the facilitator. To minimize this, the leader of any psychic and psycho-spiritual group must also look at their fears and projections. There is much that one could say about facilitation skills, but perhaps the most important thing for a leader in this field is to have done the work themselves, and use their intuition in any and every unexpected situation that may arise.

In the beginning, learning about your self is a bit like opening Pandora's box; you do not know what you will find. Your biases, your prejudices and your assumptions hinder you from clarity of perceptions. The word 'clairvoyant' means clear sight and that is what we must strive for. Over the hundreds of students of psychic development I have trained through the years, I well understand that when they first arrive in class they are naturally very keen to receive psychic information; beyond doubt, personal spiritual development is the best and ultimately the quickest way to achieve this.

It is true that a psychic can project the future, and if they are dealing with a simple soul, a person who drifts through life, it is likely their predictions will be correct. However, anyone who has owned their own will and even has a little raised consciousness, will have some control over their life; we can change, we can decide, and we can make our own fortunes. A good psychic will give an accurate overview of the situation and project, not predict the future. In this way he or she is giving the client the choice of where to go and how to make their life better. To be a counsellor is to be in a position of power. To be a psychic is also to be in a position of power and, as such, this means taking full responsibility for our readings. It is vital we use this wisely. It is not our job to control another's life and indeed it is counter to the real value of a good psycho-spiritual practitioner.

S ome years ago in one of my groups, there was a lady who told me that some years before, her marriage was stale, she felt it was going nowhere, and wasn't sure what to do about it. She knew nothing about psychic work and had never visited a psychic, but she thought to herself if only she knew, really knew what was going to occur she could deal with it. She found a tarot reader who immediately picked up that she was having marital problems and said, 'You might as well pack your bags now, the marriage is over.' She walked out knowing that this was not what she wanted. She wanted her marriage to work. She set about making it work and 20 years on is still in the marriage and happy. The tarot reader picked up the problem and projected what she thought the outcome would be. But, and this is a really important point, we have free will. Confronted by this information, her mind and heart became focused. She changed the situation.

Through my work in the psycho-spiritual field, I have investigated a spiritual programme which embraces these concepts, alongside the theory that the individual's own intuition can assist spiritual and personal development. This research did not, however, attempt to authenticate psychic phenomena specifically; it deals with our psychic and intuitive perceptions of different aspects of self and our world. Even if you deny the validity of these intuitions, people's experiences, valid or not, create changes for those involved; once a perception of the world is altered, it alters the responses. In the field of self-awareness, this is something we cannot ignore. Alongside the intuition we also cannot forget the more basic animal aspects of ourselves as they can become apparent in personal investigation. The discoveries we make along the way may not always be to do with the mystical, but may also involve basic animal behaviour.

The use of intuition in the psycho-spiritual process is thought to put individuals in command of their own awareness journey, and spiritual Self-

I n the summer of 1975 I found myself in a development group run by a spiritualist medium. We started by 'opening up' – a phrase used in psychic meditation, meaning that we are connecting and opening to some force or energy beyond ourselves. We then spent the evening linking to dead people!!! Since I had not lost anyone close, never knew my grandparents, and wasn't sure if what was going on was real, I sat there uncomfortably thinking, I shan't come here again. Then, at the end of the session we 'closed down'. This is the process of bringing one's energy back to oneself and closing any leaking energy. It's very hard to describe what the experience was for me; the only thing I can say is that, in that moment I felt 'me', for the very first time in my life. This closing-down procedure had somehow brought me into myself. I had never felt so good and strong and I began to realize why the healer who had advised me to join this group had suggested it. The question then remained, what the hell was going on?

Perhaps I should add here that I am a natural-born cynic; on a school report at the age of 11 my teacher wrote she 'had never known someone so cynical so young'. I am naturally curious about what really makes things tick and I was extremely curious about what was going on in these meditations. Why, over the weeks was I observing a change in all the participants? Some older members

development is seen as a pursuit of a higher form of knowledge. This may be much better understood by more subtle means and therefore requires different methods of learning.

It is commonly thought that a psycho-spiritual teacher cannot give the student the information but can 'give birth' to the inner knowledge of the highest Self. This concept is true to the etymological meaning of 'education', suffered physical problems, some serious; all got better. What was going on? A fellow student said to me one day: 'I know I will never be a medium, but I know this is making me a better person.' Yes!!! I could see this in others and I could see it in myself. I had become aware of my actions, my intentions, my feelings and my weaknesses and my strengths, and knowing something internally tends to change the way one lives one's life.

I had never thought to become a medium, but I continued my development at a London psychic school and was utterly fascinated by the process of self-awareness and transformation that occurred. To my surprise I was then asked to become a medium at the same organization. I did this willingly, however, I knew this was not the end of the story. I started teaching, developing a simple self-awareness process alongside psychic development. I had observed that training the intuition could be a major tool in self-development. In 1996 I wanted to concentrate on the spiritual Self-development aspect and opened my own school. Within a year I started a postgraduate research programme at university to examine the process in a more rigorous way. This academic research broadened my knowledge of the psychological process necessary to aid my students on their own psychic and spiritual Self-development.

from the Latin, *educare*: to draw forth, or, lead from a latent condition. This 'drawing forth' suggests that some potential, dormant, hidden or veiled state is already in existence. Psycho-spiritual education therefore is seen as an emancipation of the highest Self. It involves leading a person through the process of finding a deeper relationship with their inner true self and consequently finding greater truths and morality. However, moral judgement is seen as being specific to the individual and does not necessarily need to be grounded in an organized religion.

Finding a good psycho-spiritual teacher is not always easy and it is likely that at some point in your journey you will need one. In past times, this would be left to a priest or guru. Nowadays you can open any Mind Body Spirit magazine, or go onto the Internet and find adverts for masters and teachers. Often these will promise you complete self-realization in as little as two days, usually at some exorbitant cost. Whilst sometimes you can learn from a bad experience with a teacher, it is clearly not the quickest way to progress. Those who want to be led, may be drawn to ill-informed, unscrupulous or downright charlatan teachers who will, at best, not get you very far, and at worst lead you down blind alleys that could take you years to claw your way back from.

A good teacher will inspire and draw out of you the necessary knowledge to assist you to think for yourself. A charismatic teacher can easily give you an experience, can rouse your feelings and make you feel good. If there is no substance in their teaching you will find you have to go back and back, rather like a drug addict getting their fix. If the leader is working with the astral energies (*see* Chapter Four) it is particularly easy to rouse a group of people, who will all walk out saying how marvellous it was but in reality they have not progressed one jot. That doesn't mean of course there are not exceptional teachers in this field. Choose carefully, and never be afraid to walk away, even if everyone else thinks they are wonderful. If your intentions and motives are real, the energy of your true intent will draw you to the right teacher. Finding the inner core true self is seen as an unfolding process, and like a mystery book each new page reveals the sometimes foggy and noisy atmosphere around and within us. As each layer, each veil, is lifted, the individual moves and changes, enabling a greater view.

How many of us say we know ourselves, only for some life situation to show us that we know very little? Why? Have you looked? How do we become the best we can ever be? How can we lose our fear? And how may we be able to think for ourselves? Confucius said: 'What the superior man seeks is in himself, what the small man seeks is in others.' This is as true today as it was when he wrote it thousands of years ago.

Psycho-spirituality encompasses the deeper aspects of self as well as the psychological framework by which we live. The derivation of the word psychology, is worth noting as it means, soul, the word or sign. For many years psychology has concerned itself largely with aspects of the mind and behaviour. This was due, at least in part, to Freud, with his strong antipathy to religion. Freud stated:

> … a person's relationship to god depends on his relationship with his father in the flesh and oscillates and changes along with that relationship, and that at bottom god is nothing other than an exalted father.

This statement is apparently removing God from the transcendent into personal relationships. However, we need to put Freud in the context of the era in which he wrote. This was a time of sexual repression, an era of moving away from organized religions, where science was taking a hold and those who considered themselves to be scientists felt unable to express fully any associated spiritual concepts. Jung also uses the word 'psyche' interchangeably with the German word *Seele*, meaning soul. This suggests then that Jung included the 'soul' in psyche's meaning, as he propounded that it pertained to the 'numinous'; suggesting it has a spiritual quality, and therefore he seems to propose the presence of divinity. Lately there have been many suggestions that Jung did include the transcendent in his work. He also used the word in much broader terms to include all of the psychic processes, conscious as well as unconscious. Neither Freud nor Jung, the fathers of modern psychology, would have used the word 'spiritual' in quite the same context as within these pages, and it is left to us to surmise whether or not they would have agreed with the modern concept. Spiritual development has grown in a modern climate that has allowed us to examine individual values, choices and cultural notions, somewhat freed from the restrictive values of the past.

So where to begin in this process? We are looking to create stillness, emptiness and clarity. We are also looking to shift our perceptions. If you watch a movie that has been made in 3D, then watching in 2D you will not be able to pick up the nuances of the depth of the 3D that is present. And so it is with psychic work; slowly the deeper aspects will come into focus.

From the very beginning of your psycho-spiritual journey you need to practise observation; *detached loving observation of self.* Detached, in a way that you observe yourself as an onlooker; loving, because love stands at the heart of the spiritual practice and observation, with a truth and honesty that hold no bars. In this process it is important not to judge yourself negatively; we all get things wrong at times, we all make mistakes, and we all have been unfair to others and ourselves. It is only the fool who believes he or she is always right. Observe and ask, do I want this? As you go deeper into your journey you will have less and less desire to cause harm. In any case, when we do cause harm it almost certainly will rebound on us. This is the notion of karma – the law of cause and effect.

Contrary to popular belief, the idea of karma is not just an Eastern theory, it was also present in early Christianity. Karma suggests that every action produces its inevitable result. There is a misconception that karma is something from which one has no escape or control; but by consciously acknowledging it, the individual is able to operate more effectively and implement more informed choices.

The belief in karma, or any other concept is not mandatory to psycho-spirituality, however, the student is asked to observe the cause and effect of their own actions, thoughts and emotions. In this observation the student becomes aware of how not just their actions, but also their thoughts and feelings affect their lives. It often requires an unravelling of mind-sets and responses. What is going on? Why do people react to us in a certain way? What happens when we change our thoughts and feelings?

Some students observe a pattern occurring somewhat in line with what Jung called the principle of 'synchronicity' or meaningful coincidence of outer and inner events that are not causally connected. According to the principle of synchronicity, inner unconscious knowledge links a physical event with a psychic condition so that a certain event that appears accidental or coincidental can become meaningful.

The observation of any possible synchronicity is thought to assist the

I had a friend who upon finding herself pregnant in the early 1960s, when it was still not socially acceptable to have a child out of marriage, prayed to her god for guidance. The next day she received a letter from an old friend who told her of her recent abortion. My friend took this as a sign, and also had one, only to regret it bitterly for the rest of her life. Was this really a sign? Was it coincidence? Was it what she wanted at the time, only later to find out that she regretted it?

students' awareness of themselves and their world. One must be careful here, as sometimes the unconscious needs of the individual see things that happen in their lives as an excuse to do what they want.

It would be nigh on impossible to loosen the outer veils that cloak our inner light without looking to the psychological aspects of self. There are many ways to do this. Some believe that just by attunement to higher forces their negativities will dissolve on their own. Sometimes this is true, but most of us have some hidden aspects that, as they start to emerge, will reveal psychological aspects which require help and assistance. This is where some sound work with the modern psychotherapeutic applications can help. For instance, emerging in the field of psychology is a form of spiritual psychology coming under the heading of 'transpersonal'. Transpersonal psychology recognizes the spiritual and transcendent states of consciousness.

Uncovering the lower aspects of self is thought to aid the conscious decision to dissolve outworn negative patterns from wherever they originated, by being able to interpret and communicate with both the everyday world and the realm of subtle forces. In the past, psychological issues were brought to the priest or shaman. However, a good development group or group therapy can allow any issues to be articulated within a collective experience. A gathering of people with a common goal, especially with the aid of meditation, mutual respect and love, allows healing to take place. Working within a good group in psycho-spirituality can effectively become the social fabric with students finding assistance and support. In a group situation, healing occurs when we have the ability to interpret and communicate with both the everyday world and the world of subtle forces. Meditation is a form of attunement both to self and higher energies. Like any practice it takes time to 'listen' to the energetic forces moving in and around the individual and consciously bring them into balance. Healing and self-healing are seen as integral to the psycho-spiritual process as without the release of anything that obstructs the inner connection, clear insight and in(ner) tuition (intuition) cannot effectively take place.

Becoming emancipated and being in a clear space, is similar to Jung's concept of individuation. For him this was nothing less than divesting the self of the false wrappings of the persona, and the suggestive power of primordial images. Individualization necessitates the examination of self, separate from the opinions of a person's tribe or sociological group. There are, however, strong arguments against individualism; doing your own thing, i.e. following the idea of living an authentic self-determined life, might be seen to lead us away from moral, social and religious obligations. Concentrating on oneself can suggest self-indulgence which is a common argument against self-development work, as it is thought that without a strong moral frame of reference the student has nothing to measure or guide them in their spiritual journey. But, does giving a set of morals, however important, possibly hinder the individual in finding authentic spiritual concepts and ethics first-hand? It might be only through deep knowledge of self that one can really know and ultimately be in union and integrated with all that they are. Self-knowledge is thought to bring autonomy. Autonomous people have been shown to have a stronger position in life as they are unencumbered by the need to please others. They are shown to have a natural self-reliance. Being autonomous does not necessarily negatively affect their ability to have close relationships. Autonomous people know who they are, and this, in turn, means they feel less threatened by being different from others.

The educationalist Malcolm Knowles also believed there is a need for individuals to find themselves:

Increasing evidence is appearing in psychological literature that complete self-development is a universal human need, and that at least a feeling of movement in this direction is a condition of mental health.

Psycho-spiritual studies would certainly concur with these basic sentiments and also take them further, believing that self-exploration is an essential part of, not just mental health, but the holistic health and education of the individual.

The First Stages

The student begins training with simple meditations. The practice of meditation is used for many things; relaxation, health, and contentment, and in the context of psycho-spiritual development we use it to become familiar with our selves, in a quieter state of consciousness. Meditation is not, as sometimes perceived, getting 'spaced out' or running away. It requires focus and like any new skill, it takes practice and dedication. It requires honesty of self. That seemingly innocent statement 'honesty of self' is at the route of any real progress. Most people would tell you that they are honest with themselves. They blithely go through life using the models laid down by parents, society, the Church and other authorities without a thought as to whether it is really right for them. To be honest with ourselves we have to go deeper, we have to listen to our innermost desires, thoughts and emotions. In very practical terms it is in the listening to one's breath where many forms of meditation begin. In some cultures the breath is more than just a physical movement, it is also perceived as the life force. To close your eyes and listen within, being conscious of the regular rhythm of one's own breath is, in itself, often enough to bring someone to a meditative state. In meditation the heartbeat slows and the lactic acid concentration in blood decreases where blood lactic acid is related to anxiety. The skin resistance increases and changes in the pattern of brain waves have been noticed, as has an increase in slow alpha waves. These brain wave patterns are not the same as in sleep.

Meditation brings a sharp increase of focus. Many different methods suggest concentrating on a sound like a mantra, or images such as a candle or flower, and any of these can assist. Because this work is about self, the student's own breath is probably the best focus to use. It should be stated here that, particularly in the early stages in meditation, the shift of consciousness might allow the still elated ego to believe in all sorts of ego-boosting notions. In extreme cases this could lead to withdrawal into a fantasy world, a sense of grandiosity, vanity and dependency. This is also true of spiritual development and we will look into these falsities later. For this reason alone it is much safer for the student to have a good teacher, one who can spot any difficulties as they occur and quickly nip them in the bud.

There have been many scientific experiments conducted on meditation since the early 1980s, when Herbert Benson of the Harvard Medical School monitored changes in body heat and oxygen levels during meditation. Experiments have gone on to become highly sophisticated and many are too detailed to relate here. What is very clear is that the brain shows quite distinctive changes whilst in a meditative state. There are now numerous books on meditation, and it is good that the individual finds a technique that works for themself. Psychotherapist and writer, Lawrence LeShan says that meditation assists, 'the attainment of another way of perceiving and relating to reality and a greater efficiency and enthusiasm in everyday life'. Meditation can help in so many ways in one's life and not just for psychic development, although some form of meditation is essential to the process. Meditation, however, does not necessarily have to take up a lot of time, nor does it have to be complex.

Before you even begin to meditate it is important that you engage your will in the process. Ask yourself, what you want from this? Do you want to find the deeper part of yourself? Do you want to delve within? And why do you want to develop your psychic faculties? What is your true motive? These are crucial questions to ask; a teacher or a book can give you wonderful techniques but neither a teacher, book nor any other instruction can engage your will for you, without which nothing will be achieved. There has been a common misconception that in any psychic work you just sit passively and some marvellous things will be revealed. Without your own engagement of will and intent it is like looking for a radio station at night when the airwaves are full. You will obtain fuzzy, inappropriate and sometimes destructive messages.

Meditation is somewhat different from prayer, although the two may overlap. Prayer is usually used to find solutions. Gurdjieff dismissed most prayer as 'useless fantasy'. Nonetheless he advocated a process of what he called 'conscious prayer', but to do this Gurdjieff states you must 'know yourself'. Prayer in its usual mode might be thought of as petitionary; a form of supplication to God or other deities, whereas meditation is seen as attunement or at-one-ment to a higher force. This simply means you consciously and willingly tune your highest Self to the highest energy of good. 'THE HIGHEST GREATEST GOOD.' Whatever your personal beliefs of the highest greatest good are irrelevant – 'energy follows thought'. You engage your will and intent to the best you can. You can't get higher than the highest, you can't get greater than the greatest and you want to link with the best and good. In this way you are not seeking something outside yourself alone, you are seeking to join with, and to become part of the slipstream of universal consciousness.

The terms 'prayer' and 'meditation' can cause confusion. Whether you are a believer in a divine being, or God, or nothing at all, you can meditate even if you cannot pray. Meditation properly refers to internal psychological practices intended to change the quality or state of consciousness of your mind. Prayer, on the other hand, is only effective insofar as there is a supernatural or non-ordinary being that might respond to it. Who or what are people really praying to anyway? If you belief in a god, by whatever name, you will pray to that god, but what is really going on here? Are you perhaps talking to the higher or unconscious aspects of self? Meditation need not have a dogma and is proven to have many benefits in particular stress-related situations. It allows the individual to be in a relaxed, calm state, open to looking inside with less apprehension. It allows the outer 'noise' of the world to subside, which enables contact with the inner or higher Self. It also enables the person to be focused in the present in a state of 'mindfulness', which is the ability to observe one's own moment-to-moment changing experience.

In *Open Mind, Discriminating Mind,* Charles Tart describes altered states as:

> Significantly and discretely different from some baseline to
> which we want to compare it. Since we usually take ordinary
> waking consciousness as our standard of comparison a state like
> nocturnal dreaming or meditation is an altered state.

Many therapists of different persuasions use some form of altered state to assist them in their work and it is used in the psycho-spiritual process also. This is applied because not only do different states provide different information to the experiencing individual, some may in fact provide more information than is available in the usual state. In these higher or most inclusive forms of consciousness the usual normal or lower self is expanded. Therefore, achieving altered states is thought to give students a different view of themselves and others.

Just a few minutes a day in the correct space will begin the process of opening oneself up to the spirit within and the spirit outside; it may be unhelpful in the beginning to try to achieve lengthy meditations. Meditation works not by the length of time it takes, but by the quality of the energy employed. That said, some obtainable discipline in your meditation could assist you. We all lead busy lives, have work, family and responsibilities. Five minutes every day will build up this discipline. Some of my students with young children say it's impossible to sit down with their babies and toddlers around. When necessary, do your meditation in the bathroom! If you allow any outer noise or distraction to impair your attention you will never be able to obtain the focus where and when you want. After all, in the middle of the country there is still the sound of birds! Yes, its nice to have relaxed, pretty and clean surroundings, however, you are moving your energy into a clear space wherever you do it. It is not recommended that in the early days you try to meditate in a crowded place, like public transport, as this might open you up to other people's energy before you have really established where your energy and that of another, starts and finishes. This bleeding of energy is very common in natural psychics and it also occurs with good friends and partners. Part of the necessity to create a meditative state is to harness your own energy field and know what other energies are affecting you. You need to feel completely safe within yourself and the surrounding energy field.

Often in the first stages of spiritual self-development, the student is thrilled, excited and amazed that they have had such subtle and psychic experiences. The teacher is obviously also pleased for them but one must hold this experience in its reality. Some students go overboard at the first stage; if one is growing a fragile plant a weed or two may need to be left in the ground for fear of breaking the newly emerging plant. This is a delicate balance; here the ego is still fragile. If one were to scold someone for getting it wrong, they are almost certainly going to be disheartened at best, and downright aggressive at the worst. The facilitator must not be prescriptive and must at all times take the Socratic stance of asking the right questions to allow the student to see any upset of balance for themselves. In learning to ride a bicycle the person will swing from side to side and sometimes fall; they need to experience this sway to feel the balance, and so it is with psychic awareness, they must feel the equilibrium themselves and then they will gradually balance themselves.

At first the student may feel absolutely nothing and this can be disheartening, especially if they are part of a group where the other members are relaying their excitement in their experiences. I knew of one student so disheartened that she simply copied what the others were saying. Taking her at face value it was a couple of weeks before I really homed in on the fact that she was receiving nothing. We are so conditioned to doing and saying the right thing; it is very hard for the student to admit they are not getting the same as others. There are no prescriptions here; the student needs to learn to be authentic. Often they try too hard. Here we are beginning to deal in subtle energies and subtle energies are *subtle*!! The process needs to be both focused and relaxed and this all takes time. Encouragement is essential but it must be genuine encouragement. Some teachers bolster the ego by telling the student they have great talents, and that they are natural healers. Actually we all are. They may be told they are getting special messages, or that they are powerful. All these things might seem to help, but it's a bit like telling someone they can sing when they are tone deaf. It is disastrous to allow this form of misapprehension, as the student starts believing all sorts of rubbish including that they are the new Messiah! I have personally come across many such people. These are not necessarily people who are loopy or dropouts; they can be intelligent and otherwise highly responsible members of society who just lose the plot.

The Chakras

The focus on breathing into the seven centres of the chakras is often used for meditation and energy work. The chakra system has been well written-up over the last 30 years and there are some excellent books going into depth on this subject, for example *Wheels of Life* by Anodea Judith. Why do we use an Eastern system of energies? And is this system essential? The answer to this question is, no. Nonetheless, it has been shown to work well and its use has proved to be an effective tool in the process of awareness, psychic and healing development; it allows the student to focus on different aspects of self, uncovering and healing any imbalances. Breathing into each chakra centre, spending some time feeling and sensing what is happening, uncovers many of the cloudy aspects that obscure the real self. This ancient system of subtle energies can be reviewed many times throughout development, working in similar ways to a spiral educational process; this is when areas of learning are revisited, each time bringing deeper and more profound learning.

Chakra is a Sanskrit word meaning 'wheel' or 'disc' and relates to seven vortices of energy for the reception, assimilation and transformational processes. In recent times the chakras emerged in the West through the theosophy movement. In the preface to the first edition of his seminal work on chakras, Charles Leadbeater says:

> When a man begins to develop his senses, so that he may see a
> little more than everybody sees, a new and most fascinating world
> opens before him. It is simply an extension of faculties with which
> we are all familiar. And to acquire it is to make oneself sensitive
> to vibrations more rapid than those to which our physical senses
> are normally trained to respond.

Chakras are a system of spiritual evolution both on a personal and global level, and their subtle make-up can only be explored through non-conventional means, including meditation, yoga and self-development. In the Indian tradition the centres are referred to as the lotus flower; analogously, like that flower we are rooted in the mud and darkness of the depths, but ultimately we bloom under the light of the sun. The lotuses are allocated a certain number of petals to each centre describing the rate of vibration or frequency of the energy of that chakra. These also correlate to seven colours, which the chakras throw off depending upon the speed of their revolution. Colour is light vibrating at different frequencies, and the analogous notion is that as the pure white light of spirit comes down into the physical worlds it splits like a prism, reflecting the colours or energies through the human energy fields, breaking into the corresponding colours of the chakras. It is seen that the current of energy creates a pattern like the caduceus, the symbol of healing. This current of energy is called the *kundalini*. The kundalini concept of the unfolding serpent has long been associated with healing and its caduceus logo is still being used as the symbol for medicine.

Caduceus Symbol

The kundalini energy is said to lie dormant in the unconscious of all men and women. It sleeps in the lowest centre at the base of the spine, like a coiled snake waiting to rise. Once this dormant kundalini energy is activated it starts to unwind from the Base chakra centre. It is thought to travel in a figure-of-eight path, rising up through pathways or meridians of energy to which the chakras are connected. This spiral-like unfoldment process is believed to change the energy of the individual, as they go step by step into greater awareness of self, raising their consciousness, and seeing the greater picture for themselves and for the world.

This process creates a series of shifts or initiations, until the kundalini's pathway leads to the top centre where connection is made to the highest spiritual energy. This brings union to the highest source and, in turn, brings a profound change in consciousness, leading to enlightenment. These qualities or centres are not perceived physically, they interrelate to the physical by psychic subtle essences or energetic attraction, which are activated by life force or 'pranic' energy. This 'pranic' (Indian) or 'chi' (Chinese) energy has various different names globally; in the West we simply call it 'subtle energy'. The raising and heightening of this subtle force through the seven chakras therefore could be perceived as a stepping stone towards higher consciousness and spiritual integration. Communicating with each centre, we can be more in touch with hidden aspects of the psyche and begin to unlock the negative aspect of being, which we may not have observed before. We also can see the strength of these aspects and how they, in their natural and balanced states, can positively affect us.

The simple table right looks at the colour, state, intention and psychic connection to each of these seven vital aspects of self. Over the years I have watched the different levels of intuition in operation and linked them to the chakras. (These levels will also be further examined in Chapters Three and Four.)

Base Instinctual senses are those that put us on our guard from danger, most often equated with an animal sense of knowing.

Sacral Tribal senses connect with care for our group, whether that is family, society or the environment; a sense of 'knowing' the tribe or family needs or fears.

Solar Plexus Personal intuitions alert us to people's feelings, thoughts and what they are emitting e.g. their emotions; a sense of sympathy towards others. It can also be a sense of fear or threat.

Heart Loving empathy assists any healing and balancing processes whether for self or others; a sense of being able to help or heal.

The Chakras, Intent and Levels of Intuition

Chakra	Colour	Key Aspects	Method	Statement of Intent	Levels of Intuition
Base or Muladhara	Red	Survival Physical safety	How to survive in the physical world	I learn through what I *have*	Instinctive
Sacral or Svadhisthanna	Orange	Emotions Creativity	How one understands and uses feelings Creative force and drive	I learn through what I *want*	Tribal
Solar Plexus or Manipura	Yellow	Self-worth The lower mind Sympathetic connection with others	How we measure ourselves within the community	I learn through what I *can and can't do*	Personal/auric
Heart or Anahata	Green	Love without judgement Balance	How to understand and forgive	I learn through *love*	Balance Mediumship
Throat or Visuddha	Blue	Spiritual connection Communication	How to communicate without fear	I learn through *commu-nication* and truth	Inspirational Channelling
Brow or Ajna	Indigo	Insight The higher mind	How to perceive higher qualities and potentials	I learn through clear perception and *intuition*	Clairvoyance (clear seeing) Vision
Crown or Sahasrara	Violet	Higher consciousness Depth Inner knowledge	How to surrender	I learn through *knowing*	Alignment/Knowing

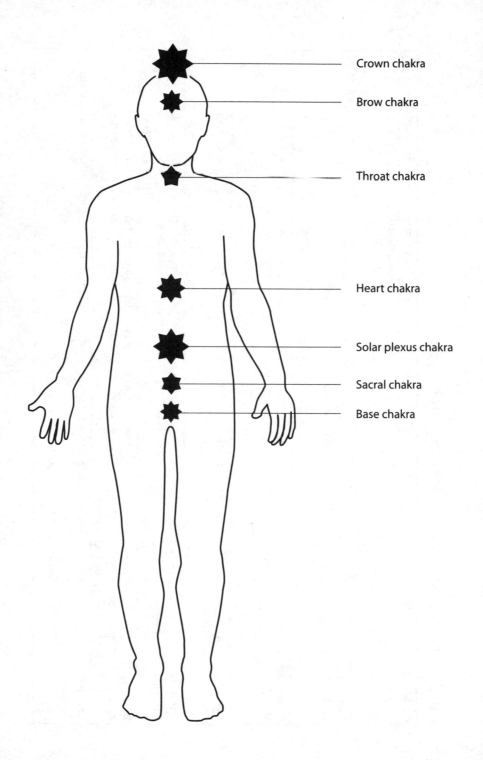

Crown chakra

Brow chakra

Throat chakra

Heart chakra

Solar plexus chakra

Sacral chakra

Base chakra

Throat Inspirational links take us towards attunement to unseen forces, a sense of linking to some spiritual entity, which is likely to be dictated by the beliefs of the individual. For example, a Catholic might feel the presence of Mary or Jesus. A Muslim might feel the presence of Allah. These senses can also feel like an angelic presence and may be acknowledged as some form of information, advice or guidance beyond the mundane.

Brow Vision gives us a sense of the greater picture beyond selfish personal concerns, metaphorically seeing situations beyond the clouds. People such as the Dali Lama and Ghandi exhibit these types of visionary traits.

Crown A pure sense of knowing beyond fear. It is the true altruistic aspects of self and others. Alignment to the highest source of energy.

Processes of Psychic and Psycho-spiritual Learning

Many people have been brought up in a culture of structures, from learning the alphabet, tables and generally putting things in boxes. This is troublesome in a subject where there are no limits and, sometimes nothing to hold onto other than one's own sense. Therefore the use of a system of energy is a very helpful tool in combination with meditation; it gives the student seven notes or states connected with self: physical, creative, self-worth, heart, communication, awareness of things unseen, perception of insight and connection with the highest force in the universe. Note the word highest here. Some people use the phrase 'higher self', but the 'highest Self', whatever that might mean to the student, takes them into the possibilities of something far beyond the little or ego self.

In some schools and disciplines the ego is thought of as something bad, and it is true the ego often gets in the way of this form of work. However, to tell someone to lose their ego is rather like telling someone to stop living in the physical world. It might be that some divine being reaches a state of losing the ego, but if this is true it is certainly an unattainable dream for most. You could argue that this shouldn't stop us trying and I would resonate with this idea, but the dangers of telling someone to get rid of the very thing that gets them up in the morning is counterproductive.

We can only advance by unpeeling, bit by bit, each layer of noise and negativity. Many cultures have noted the highest possibilities and tried to enforce them on ordinary people with disastrous results. The strongest instinct in humans is survival and procreation, so restricting the human sexual urge in priests has caused warped and abusive behaviour. It may be that in the ultimate spiritual state one loses any sexual urge, but if this is so, I suspect it only comes at the very last point of departure into the transcendence. To force a person against his or her most natural desires is not what spirituality is about. Balance is key in all aspects of life and living. Another example of enforcement is to insist on inappropriate fasting. We need food to live. I have personally come across many people who are literally killing themselves because they have been told that one should fast, or eat no meat or live on air! The notion that not eating meat will make you more spiritual is particularly pertinent for most of the population of the West who are blood group O (*see The Eat Right Diet* by Dr Peter D'Adamo). People with this blood type will find it extremely difficult to become vegetarians and in many cases will detrimentally affect their health. Eating meat or otherwise will not advance your spirituality. This mistaken concept arrives because many spiritual schools, particularly in the East, insist on it. The Indian race is made up of over 90 per cent blood group AB, so they are the perfect vegetarians, and they have evolved to be so. Most of the West has not. Some limited fasting can assist during short periods of intense meditation. Check with your doctor if you are in any doubt and I really do not recommend fasting to anyone over the age of 55 years, particularly if you have never done this before. It is important that you do not lose your good sense in any of the processes of spiritual growth. Listen to your own body, heart and mind without judgement; it is really not advisable to let anyone tell you what to do if it in anyway feels wrong. Only the truth of your being knows what is really right for you.

The intellectual mind is a wonderful thing and is extremely useful in the ways of the world. Nevertheless, for some who are particularly academically minded, in the practice of spiritual development it is often a stumbling block in shifting the perspective towards one of sense, feeling and intuition. You might have heard people say, 'get the mind out of the way', which seems somewhat harsh and I am certainly not advocating getting rid of one's reasoning and intellectual ability. However, its use when we are trying to sense and feel energies, especially in the early stages, can get in the way. I would rather describe it as the wrong instrument for awareness of more subtle energies. There is a careful balancing act to be implemented; to abandon one's intelligence is dangerous in the extreme and it can take us to some of the unsavoury states i.e. illusion, fantasy and even mental aberrations.

Meditation takes the student into a silent space, very often for the very first time and, alongside the use of the seven centres of the chakras, will bring focus into different levels of life and living. At first it is important to keep the concentration to the lower centres – the Base – that are the physical aspects of life, which includes survival. In the modern world this also entails work and money. The Sacral energy is the creative and sexual energy. It is important to learn how to use this powerful energy to create rather than destroy. As in all energies, one can use them positively or negatively. For instance negative use in the Sacral may come in an infatuation, fantasy relationships, or to take sexual power and use it to control another person. The Solar Plexus is the third and an important energy as it is where the individual finds their self-worth or lack of it. Many people have been put down in childhood, whether at school being told that they were stupid, or the experience of failing exams, or not reaching the expectations of parents, friends and society. Meditation here is about what is really important to the individual. What matters? Do they feel good about themselves? What effects do they have on others and what effect do others have on them? The experiences of the individual's childhood here is often very relevant to how they see their world and how they respond. Here we examine whether the mind-sets established throughout their lives really serve them. It is their choice and if there is something they want to change, working through it will help them. This is where even a basic knowledge of psychology is of use.

Spiritual and psychic development is fraught with difficulties; illusions of how one should be, or how one ought to think, can be dictated by the notions of others. One needs to look carefully, deeply and honestly (there is that word again) at oneself, what is good and right and, more importantly, have the courage to see it through, even if sometimes that means others will not or cannot see why.

One useful guide is to stop and check yourself every time you say the word 'should' or 'ought'. Who says you should? Who dictates what you ought to do? There are no shoulds or oughts here. Often by picking up on these concepts you can ask yourself where that impression first came from. Maybe it was from a teacher at school, maybe it was from a partner or parent, from some official or religious leader. Or maybe you are even saying these things

---

I often do an exercise with my students to identify their biases and prejudices, and it frequently brings up all sorts of things that have become so deeply rooted, they are not observed. On one occasion I had a student who immediately identified she had a prejudice against 'middle-class, middle-aged men'! As many of our prejudices come from lack of knowledge of the very people we are prejudiced against, I suggested that having identified the person or people concerned that they seek out such a person and engage in some communication with them. On this particular occasion the student was horrified and rejected the idea out of hand. The following week she told us that the very next day she had been stuck in a lift with a middle-aged and middle-class man for over an hour! She did engage with him and found that they had some common ground! Asked whether she would carry this prejudice on through her life, she had to admit that she now could not do so.

I am not suggesting you try to engage with a mass murderer or a terrorist, but many of our assumptions about people are simply

---

to yourself as an excuse to do something you really want to do but can't, for whatever reason, admit it to yourself. Are these things really what you want? To ask yourself what you want is an important question and may, to some, seem rather selfish. To ask this question is vital because only then do you begin to come close to the truth. What you *want* is true. What you *should* do, may not be! And there is no good energy in falsehood.

Practising meditation and chakra work over a period of time, with the help of a good facilitator or therapist, will gradually loosen the outer and superficial areas of your being. It will bring to the surface anything that needs to be looked at and perhaps discarded. There are many good exercises that can assist you, however, without your own good intent and use of will these, in themselves, will do nothing. Meditation, transpersonal exercises and

---

caused by the fact that we do not know them. Experiences can also cause prejudices but again if we look deeper they too can be absurd. I had a friend years ago who was raped by a man of a certain nationality, after which she hated all men from this race. This is simply unintelligent thinking although quite understandable. There are nasty people of all races, classes, political and religious persuasions. There are also good and loving people from the same. I once had a man tell me he hated anyone who voted in the general election for a certain mainstream party. This is also ridiculous thinking and these kinds of thoughts will not in any way serve in one's ordinary existence or in spiritual progress. To practise harmlessness is always a good, however, practising love and light when it is not truly felt, is both dishonest and energetically unsound and no good will come of it.

If you have your energy firmly in your heart, you can speak the truth kindly and generally it will be received kindly, if not always agreed with.

---

positive affirmations will also help, however, if you have not dealt on a deep level with the cause of the negativities you wish to lose, you won't achieve any long-standing results.

You also need to question your thoughts and feelings; do you have any biases, prejudices and assumptions? The reality is that it is extremely likely that we all have some.

Experiences from others who have gone through the process of psychic and spiritual development can be helpful, as many things that emerge for one person will be similar to another. So here I have relayed verbatim quotes from some of the many students who have undergone psycho-spiritual learning that I interviewed at length in the course of my research. To protect the privacy of the interviewees, I have not named or labelled the quotes. Although these experiences are specific to the individual students concerned, I have chosen these in particular, as they speak of aspects of the training that frequently occur with all students.

The first quote is taken from a student who relays their feelings at the very start of the training.

> I thought this isn't going to work, this is fairground stuff, and this is mumbo jumbo magic and very silly. But I'm here and I'll have a go and I was a little scared because I thought, I'm going to fail and I'm not going to be able to do this. I had all these images and so obviously I was linking to something and thought, oh that's a bit strange, I can do this. This taught me to trust more, go with the flow and not immediately to have a rational explanation, a logical explanation. I found it difficult, but deep down I knew there was something in it.

People arrive in one of these types of groups for all sorts of reasons; sometimes it is simply that they came along with a friend, other times it is just curiosity, often it is because they have encountered some psychic experience that they wish to investigate, and most often it is because they have had a sense of something existing beyond the mundane. The same student continues, that she often went home full of questions thinking:

> I do not know what I'm doing here. And yet there was enough
> that I felt oh yes I do know what I am doing here. I think one
> of the things that struck me was I was given permission to talk
> about myself and this was a very different idea for me, because I'd
> had friends who'd been in therapy for years and all the rest of it
> and my judgemental attitude to it was, I'm much too busy looking
> after my family and I thought it was self-indulgent and it was a
> breakthrough that you could actually think about yourself, that it
> was actually a good idea to think about yourself. I learnt to be in
> a different way and now I come at life from a different angle, not
> abandoning logic but using another faculty, intuition alongside
> it. It was good. There were some times when I went home and I
> was so churned up that I would have to deliberately put it aside
> otherwise I wouldn't be able to sleep. I began to ask questions
> about myself and I now admit I needed to look at this and I was
> able to let it go in class. Also acknowledging that other people
> are different from me. If I wrote an academic essay it would have
> been much easier for me. I'd look up my reference and I'd write
> my essay and know I would be on familiar territory. Sometimes I
> was put into unfamiliar territory and some of that was worrying
> for me and some of it was exciting and stimulating. The work with
> the chakras helped me and everything started falling into place. I
> began to make connections with what I was doing in the outside
> world, my work with my own students, and it was helpful.

Finding this process difficult, challenging and sometimes hard, particularly in the early stages, is a recurring theme. However, it is interesting to note that many comments say that deep down they knew it was going to be worthwhile. This has been called, 'a sense of knowing'; this knowing is not an intellectual or rational thought, it is a sense. It is more than a feeling or a thought, it is just a deep inner knowing. As with anything that is worthwhile, it takes some effort and persistence to reach a positive outcome. Psycho-spiritual work is no different. Another student said:

> It was like planting a seed, which with hindsight you can apply. It was setting the scene, and the impact of this stage was that I felt I was going somewhere, but I wasn't sure where that was. The course started to expand my mental capacities, and I was starting to think about things. I wasn't thinking about my own emotions at this time but I was starting to think that my world was not just my work. With hindsight I was looking for something. I won't say something deeper, I don't want to get caught up in that kind of cliché, but I was looking for an experience that was more. I benefited from the focused breath exercises, because a person has an experience within that focused breath which allows them to relax from everything that is going on in their head or around them, and even if they can just go and do that for five minutes a day they are going to have a positive experience, it's a good starting point. I was receiving something that wasn't all coming from my head and I realized that it was important for me to get away from the mental level. When you give someone an experience they don't initially have a language in which to describe it. I think the experiential aspect is quite significant and that this aspect to the work is really important. For most people it is so new on one level that we don't have structures to deal with it. If you were doing it in an academic institution you would be putting it into a mental rational framework and actually a lot of people are beginning to work with something outside that framework.
>
> I began to think about other things in the universe and asking is there a greater role in what I do? I felt like I was opening myself to something completely new for me but it was right. It did have an impact but it had an impact at a pace that I could cope with. I was excited about being able to see the world differently.

When you started talking about the chakras I hadn't a clue what you were talking about and for quite a while I was confused. The confusion was mine and I was too embarrassed to ask. All the way through my life I always found it very difficult to ask for things, but at some point I began to ask. I then realized that this reluctance to ask for things was holding me back. The process goes on for different people at different levels, but the concept of learning to trust yourself, requires you to examine yourself, to understand your own energetic context and be able to distinguish between what's yours and what is not.

Listening to others talk and hearing their experiences is a very powerful tool, which gives you the permission to look at yourself. What was fascinating was that a number of things were being flagged up in other people that were relevant to myself so I was able to watch other people and to reflect on myself, it was actually very powerful for me.

Here the student notes that their perceptions on life began to change. This is likely to be true for anyone who is serious about their progress. This student was beginning to question quite early on, not just what they could do for themselves, but what their role was in the greater scheme of things. This kind of depth is progressive and will take the student into a more altruistic attitude to life and living.

The next student relays a previous experience that brought them to the classes:

I had experienced spiritual flashes and sparks that were a mystery to me but I figured the universe is a mysterious place and one never expects to understand it. Also I had some personal psychic experiences which persuaded me there might be something worth investigating, the strongest of which was when I was visiting my mother our conversation shifted to my aunt, and at one point I stopped and I was aware of my aunt; momentarily I could see her and there was a feeling like a rush of wind around my shoulder, I could feel her, sense her for about 30 seconds, a very very strong feeling and I was completely unaware of what was going on in the surroundings. The following day I got a telephone call to say my aunt had died unexpectedly at that time. I felt this was beyond coincidence as I was not particularly close to this aunt. I believe I had contact with her spirit and this incident encouraged me to investigate and develop my intuitive side and become a competent practitioner as a sensitive healer and medium.

I have heard numerous other examples of such an experience. That is, some extrasensory knowing of the time of a person's death. I have even heard people relate that they have woken up in the night thinking, seeing or feeling the presence of the person who has just died. The next quote is also similar to many other people's experiences:

What was new to me was the learning to breathe into different centres and to visualize light moving. I think that was important in understanding how the mechanism works but there were no real surprises in terms of content because I'd already read quite a bit. I thought the development was incremental and accumulative. However, there was one occasion that upset me in this class when a student told me my energy was concentrated in the higher centres and the mental energy was dominating me. This information shocked me and at first I could not accept it, but in retrospect I concede there may be some truth in it. At the time it made me seriously question whether I could do any more work in this area and I was wondering whether I was cut out for it. Nonetheless, the comment made me look into this aspect then things changed. I tried to open up in a different way. I admit that it's a challenge in a way to marry all these different bits of information that come into you energetically, you have to learn to get used to them.

My life has changed as a consequence of doing the work and it's the accumulation of a set of experiences. I don't think any particular thing triggered a huge change. I found myself slipping between the accepted rational and energetic approaches quite easily as the different senses are used for different tasks.

Another student says:

An inner awareness emerged. It was something that was sort of coming to the fore, that I knew that I had to experience, and then events made it happen because I wasn't voluntarily able to do it. Everything conspired if you like, so it sort of pushed, or I pushed, myself in that direction. I had an awareness of something much deeper being around, and also that there was something that was really missing and something yet to be done that didn't rely on any events or anyone else. I felt a connection to something far greater than myself. I found myself starting to meditate naturally, and I intuitively connected to a higher state through my breath and linking to what I now realized were the chakra points.

I remember quite vividly actually the connection with other people and when we started doing meditation in the group that was immense. Suddenly it felt like electricity and it was such a strong feeling. I mean I didn't stay at that sort of, you know, illuminating state but, initially it was and it felt fantastic, it felt really brilliant. To be part of a group where everyone was meditating and having a sort of energetic connection with each other. It was a really strong feeling. I was able to give precious time to myself, which brought some positive effects, and I especially liked being part of a group. When we started working on the chakra system, that was incredibly powerful.

I felt it was like an unfolding and what I was experiencing was aiding me to unravel things in my life or they unravelled in conjunction with it and that's what I felt all along actually. I went through immense changes and ups and downs and bringing up lots of negativity and all sorts of things happened to me but I was still going through this process which was invaluable. I was allowing myself to have these experiences to become a person who was able to grow.

I also realized the benefit, not just for me, but also for the others in the group. However, I found that exercises when they were focusing on other people were both frightening and illuminating. It was a bit nerve-racking actually when you are focusing on other people. You were on display and being watched by everybody else, and of course I felt judged initially, you know, what people were thinking. I felt on the spot whilst doing the exercises in this class but the benefits were that I became aware that you could focus energy with your mind. This was a new experience and the discipline of having to do it was good. I always had a good feeling about it and looked forward to it every week. I used to feel quite nervous about saying how I felt. Other members of the group gave me permission to speak. It was the first time I was able to reveal personal and very strong things in a group, which was initially scary. I was seeking a validation of both my feelings and actions. I needed the reassurance of the group. I was insecure and very vulnerable at this time. Due to the conditioning of my parents, I was used to keeping my feelings to myself, being part of a group gave me permission to speak for the first time and I found myself able to reveal personal and very strong things in a group. Things were continuing to emerge regarding previous relationships, especially my relationship with my father, which was extremely difficult all through my life. It was a major source of anger and frustration and at this time all sorts of things came up, to a point I realized I needed to do something because there's no point in being able to do things for people if you can't get yourself in order and that was also an incredibly profound realization.

It really had, over a period of time, quite a profound effect on me, you know, focusing on your heart, and understanding that things worked through the expansion of consciousness through your heart and that was an ongoing process. I understood it mentally, but it took a while for it to actually physically manifest itself, it was definitely quite a strong feeling. This feeling has enabled me to move forward and I gained strength. I felt I was connected to both something more powerful than myself and at the same time it felt incredibly strong. The classes were a real focused point and it made me more disciplined at home and I would sit down and have time to myself and try to centre myself, which helped me go through the things I was going through at the time.

Another student relays the realization of energies:

I became aware of other people having energy and me having energy and also what I and others were doing with this. This initially made me feel withdrawn and exposed and it made me feel sometimes uncomfortable. I started getting discerning about the people I mixed with. I felt a bit odd, and I questioned whether I was normal, as I was not fitting in well enough, as everyone else seemed to be. So all my feelings of being different and odd came up to the surface.

I found it very difficult but I never wanted to give it up, it was so compelling. I had to confront things and this felt right and I was spiritually connected and that wasn't a feeling I was getting in any other area of life at the time. I hadn't known such depth before and there was a feeling of knowing it was right. It was tangible and I felt an energy and connected to everybody in the group as an energy it was joyful, an uplifting of one's spirit. I was much more spiritually connected in more areas of my life. It has transformed my life.

71

Working with energies is very much part of the process. Just discovering where your energy is centred and where yours begins and ends is a vital acknowledgement in any form of psychic work. The previous comments from the student who had illumination on a difficult situation in the family indicates something that often arises. Confronting these personal difficulties and allowing them to be healed is a valuable aspect of the work. It allows some of the troubled energy around the student to dissolve, which in turn allows greater clarity, both for the individual and for their psychic work. Many of these comments are positive and all relayed an expansion in some way, but some of the students interviewed said they found the psycho-spiritual process difficult at times.

A further quote:

> It brought immense changes and ups and downs which brought
> up lots of negativity. And if I'm honest, it was a little bit
> uncomfortable. I was challenged by it and was most resistant to
> going into things – a lot came out.

Another student said:

> Everybody benefited individually on a weekly basis no matter
> what level they were. It didn't really matter what stage you were at
> yourself as there was always something you were getting from it.
> [Speaking about a fellow student] they went from saying that the
> issue had been dealt with, to bursting into tears, and then having
> the realization that forgiveness wasn't just about something on a
> mental level, and her physical reactions to the whole experience
> were proof that there was a lot more to think about and work with.
> There was an awful lot coming out and I was watching this woman
> and I couldn't help applying it to some of my own feelings. And
> the synchronicity was that these things seemed to come up every
> week and there seemed to be a process. It gave a lot of people a lot to

walk away with on an experiential and emotional level. The leader of this group very gently but very directly asked her [the student] to look at herself and question whether that was forgiveness, and she and everyone else could see that she had not forgiven her father, so it became a very graphic example of awareness and these things seemed to come up every week.

This comment highlights the effectiveness of observing other people and their reactions and that, *being within a group environment is often an important part of the process, and observation and listening techniques should begin to click in at this stage.*

Observing others and relating it to our own experiences is deemed to be one of the values of group work.

The comment, *I felt very exposed* implies some lack of feeling safe, however, in any awareness work it might be expected that some exposure of self is part of the process of authentic self-awareness. The theory is that if you are exposed you have nowhere to hide and have no alternative but to face up to one's truth, but, facing the truth about oneself is not easy.

They go on to say: *Once I worked through the hurt and looked at myself unconditionally and said OK that is in the past so next time lets do it differently.*

This student had consciously engaged in the transformational process and this shows a positive attitude to exposure. Not all students find this easy or possible. This student had highlighted the benefits of listening to other members of a group and concurs, saying that they, *really liked listening to people, because everyone else's experiences were so interesting and so different.*

Another student says:

I thought it important to make the difference between a mental concept and an energetic reality. We all have areas where this suddenly strikes home. It happened to me a lot and you think oh I know about all this, and on a mental level you do, but all of a sudden the reality happens and you actually have to work with something and its not just enough to look at it and see what is

going on, you actually have to go through the process to change
it and I think this is a key thing when people realize this.

This student particularly remembered, *when people realized how much we are*
influenced by a family member or partner and then there comes a realization
that they can really change things.

Having experiential exercises in classes does not necessarily translate to
experiential learning in the student's lived world. Many students allude to this
and emphasize the requirement to totally engage with the learning and bring
it to actuality in their own lives. This takes time to establish and, *it could be*
days, months or even years before this is realized. It affected my personal life
gradually over a period of time.

There have been frequent comments about the whole process of cutting
negative ties and a realization that there is a need to let go of, dissolve, remove
a layer or 'veil' of unwanted aspects of self to be able to expand spiritual
awareness.

Many students also speak of the importance of being aware of your, *heart*
energy so that there can be a realization that there is a level deeper than the
emotions. Another student said that *as long as a seed has been planted, even if*
you have been a poor student and you didn't catch on at the time, the signposts
are there and then when you think back you know that's what they meant.

Further comments were that there *were a number of things that affected*
me, one was the sense of loneliness but I knew I was going forwards and I
couldn't go back. It revealed that I was very frightened of being alone. I worked
through it over a period of time and I'm not afraid anymore.

The comments about isolation indicate that they might need to reassess
their lives. Some withdrawal from life is written about in spiritual literature
and I have observed it in many students throughout my years of teaching
in this field. It is the point in the process where the individual needs to
withdraw to gain greater understanding of self and their connection with
a higher source. This does not mean that they literally hide in a cave like a
hermit; it is more an inner withdrawal. This can be acknowledged as a type
of bereavement process that occurs throughout any change or death, not

just in a physical sense but a death of any aspects of life. Whether this is perceived as positive or negative depends largely on one's own perspective. Contemplation and isolation from the material world is common in religious orders and spiritual practice and its value is known. In the material world it can be construed as 'unhealthy' and 'strange'. However, it is, for some, a necessary part of the psycho-spiritual process.

The need to be aware of heart energy means the ability to love and be true to oneself. This notion of unconditional love is commonplace in spirituality; not the usual emotional form of love but love beyond emotion and without judgement. The danger of this concept is that by believing in being nice and good, it may detract the individual from looking at the very personal issues they need to consider. If not addressed properly it could bring about a denial of the more negative aspects of self.

Another student said:

> you suddenly become aware of the responsibility that is yours and yours only; it is up to you to implement the work. You can devise a course with tools and techniques but when that person actually understands, it is in their own process. It was hard. You can't take them deep or not, you can offer it but those who have a deep experience are ready and they will have it and those who are not ready they may take it onboard and deal with it later on or they may never. Some people are ripe and some are not, but equally if people have these big issues that are brewing then the sooner they deal with them the better because they would be pretty serious blocks to any kind of self-awareness if they've got some shadow side hanging over them.

The issue of taking responsibility and therefore directing one's learning is an important aspect. In psycho-spiritual practices it is believed that nothing can be implemented in the life of the individual if they do not take the necessary responsibility for themselves. To continually apportion blame on others is not spiritual behaviour and has no basis in reality.

The issue of the very real need for support through this process emerged:

> I think it is remiss in any organization that brings out emotions or personal things that did not have support. You need to define what you meant by counselling and whether to give it carte blanche to everyone as I think this might be open to abuse because plenty of people just want to talk about themselves. By virtue of having a group there is always some form of counselling going on, and it's very healing, and I thought it was good to have one-to-ones, as when stuff comes up you need personal counselling. I did have counselling and it was incredibly helpful. Some people do need to talk and sometimes it might be missed when someone is struggling.
>
> A lot of the struggle is what gives you the strength to work through it and it pushes you onto the next stage of learning. It occurs by working through them personally and in this way you find the answers. For me it was acted out everyday; I used life as an experiential reflection for things that were coming up. It gave me a lot of strength and I felt my real life was walking side by side with this work. However, when I went through a period of feeling empty, I needed some help with someone who understood the work. I couldn't just talk to a friend. I needed to have someone to talk to and was glad that I forged relationships with other students. It was conducive to go to the pub and talk!

Having support in the psycho-spiritual process is essential, however the whole subject of therapy and counselling is open to debate. Hopefully, with a good, sound facilitator in a development group you will receive what you need, although there may be times when you do need one-to-one mentoring with someone who is professional. There are now so many different types of therapy and counselling. Some are excellent, although others will not help at all and may even hinder the process. What we are dealing with here are your own energies, and discussing problems over and over again can draw the very energy

T here was an occasion some years ago when I had inadvertently been quite mean in my words to someone. I realized this and spent the whole day feeling sorry for myself and wondering what I could do to repair the situation. Later in the day I took myself into meditation and immediately I heard the words. 'We do not want your sorrow we want your strength.' We are all at times unkind to others. Constant observation will ameliorate this over time; what is done is done. Learn from it and walk on.

you want to release back to you again and again. The chapter on astral energies is particularly appropriate to appreciating this little-understood aspect.

The comments about students just wanting to talk about themselves sound derogatory, but how else can the facilitator help unpick what is occurring if they do not talk about personal issues, even if this leads some students to be self-indulgent in the process? When there is an increasing connection to a higher source it is usual to find that any self-indulgence diminishes.

Other general comments include that they: *were more open to new thoughts; dealt with emotional issues; let go of fear*; and *had more confidence.* However, any movement, either positive or negative, within the lived world of the individual may be disruptive, so some kind of regular counselling or *off-loading process* was felt essential. This needs to be measured by another student's comment that *there is a need for struggle at some stage, and any method that holds the student too tight might disallow the self-directed process required.*

Working with your intuition can sometimes push you against the tide of authority, current thinking and family desires. How many times have you said, 'I knew I have to do this', or 'I knew I must not do this'? This feeling coming from something other than the rational. The final quote in this chapter illustrates the dilemmas that can be incurred through following your truth and your intuition.

I have been a very, they say, a very courageous woman, in all sorts of things, I was renowned for my courage in doing so. OK, now having challenged a very difficult situation, I then sometimes internally would wobble because I didn't have that internal frame of reference that says OK. So my soul felt split because I challenged it and because I went with that strong intuition, others would say 'I couldn't have done what you did', 'Are you sure that was the right thing to do?' and that's what wobbled me, instead of going back to the very thing that gave me the courage to challenge it in the first place, I would've listened to 'Joe Bloggs' so my internal frame of reference having done it, wasn't strong enough.

And my internal frame of reference or intuition would say, 'This is not right, challenge it', but there are consequences to doing this that were very disturbing and therefore I didn't stay with my initial intuition, but then I did and I saw everything through, and sometimes it caused my soul to be troubled. For example, I was responsible for sending someone to prison and there was a consequence to my actions. So my intuition said this is a corrupt person and I will do something about it. He did go to prison, but my troubled soul came because there were children and a wife.

'Causing her soul to be troubled' indicated she was not sitting comfortably with the deeper areas of intuition. This student also seems to exert personal will to see this intuition through. Intuition does not always follow any reason and might be seen to go against rationale, common sense or even the apparent right thing to do. Intuition may give us another instrument by which to live our life, but, this can open us up to more possibilities and, arguably, having choices can be a double-edged sword, which might at times lead to confusion.

Deep psycho-spiritual work is about really knowing oneself honestly; all the contrived excuses we invent, knowing deep down what is really right despite any possible consequences and following it through, even when the odds are stacked against us. Most importantly we must lose our fear, knowing that on the most important level, in the depth of our being, we are safe.

CHAPTER THREE

Energy Fields, Thought-Forms and Auras

When you stop admiring yourself and let the eyes of the heart open your vision to vast worlds, then all you do will become admirable.

Rumi

It is scientifically acknowledged that energy fields surround all living organisms. Every living thing on our planet radiates energy that can be perceived both psychically and scientifically. This corresponds to writings in ancient spiritual texts, including the Upanishads. Connecting to these energy fields can provide a psychic with a vast amount of information relating to a person, including the physical, emotional, mental, and astral desires and fears. This information is extremely valuable. It not only presents us with a snapshot of the person's life, it can relay back to the person what they are emitting to the world, because, as strange as it may seem, not everyone realizes what energies they emanate at any given time. So it is also a form of awareness. However, if the psychic is inexperienced or untrained, this information can be relayed back incorrectly. So in this chapter we take an in-depth look at what is happening in the auric layers and how they can be accurately interpreted.

The energy field or 'aura' emanates from the individual as layers, pushing outwards and around the body of the person. These layers are often perceived as colours, especially by healers. These layers can be correlated to the chakra system. The first layer is the physical – the 'Base' energy – and this is felt very close to the body. The next layer is the emotional body or 'Sacral', which is slightly further out from the body. The lower mental, the 'Solar Plexus' layer, pushes out even further, and so on. Although you can give a general indication of where you will find each layer, each person is different. For example, someone who had just run a marathon will have an immense amount of red physical energy in their first layer and this could push out several feet from the body, whereas normally the levels would only register a few inches.

As well as use for psychic readings, psychically scanning the aura is also extremely helpful in energy and spiritual healing. Indeed most healers will carry out an auric scan before they implement any healing, as this enables them to know where to concentrate their energies. A psychic will sense these energies slightly differently from a healer; the psychic will receive information and images, relaying these back to the querent, whereas the healer will sense the feeling of the energies and work according to the information they receive. For example, a healer will walk around the body and, most often through the hands, will have a sense of warm, cold, spiky, dark or light, or dozens of other senses. Translating these feelings is common sense; if the healer feels a grey or dark area this needs to be transformed, and so he or she will draw down light to dispel the darkness wherever it is. Alternatively, if the healer feels a scratchy or spiky patch, he or she will smooth it out. A hot patch will need cooling, a cold one heating etc.

Both healers and psychics may perceive colours from a person's energy field. There is no particular big deal about this as most people pick up things from the auras automatically without even knowing about it. We even have many sayings, which indicate that people pick up these colours naturally. For instance we say, 'got the blues', 'in the pink', 'browned off' etc. Also, we use other ways to describe the behaviour or the sense of a person: 'she's scratchy today', 'he's in a dark mood', 'he's yellow', meaning he is a coward etc. What are we saying when we use such phrases? What are we picking up? Colours most often relate to the auric emanations that we receive through our minds as colours. Our minds need something that has some structure. Energies rarely can be seen with the human eye, so we perceive them often as colours or images. The majority of psychics and healers do not 'see' with their human eyes the colours or shapes or other images, they see it in their mind's eye. So, taking as an example the saying to be 'browned off'. We know that means the person is troubled, fed up and not functioning well, but why? Brown is not a chakra colour; it is a colour associated with material things; money, possessions and business. Many people that use this phrase do not know this, but they do know the sense of the person they are describing.

Generally speaking, all bright clear colours are positive, and colours that are sullied or have some muddiness or darkness about them are not, and that is exactly how we can translate them. A clear brown may be a positive sign of balance in the material world of the person, whereas a muddied brown will be the opposite. So it is likely to be that the 'browned-off' person's aura is emanating a muddy colour. Reading the aura is natural. We all do it somehow. What a psychic or healer must do is refine that natural sense. They must understand what they are receiving and get some greater depth as to its meaning.

When you have done a sufficient amount of work in untying negative aspects of self, as discussed in the previous chapters, you can begin to connect with others more clearly. This does not mean you have to be a saint to do this work! It does, however, mean that while you are making the link, at least you know you are in the clearest energetic space possible.

Opening Exercise

A brief word here on posture and body language may be helpful. When opening and implementing this work it is essential that you are comfortable. Quite simply you can implement this work in any position, and I have found that sitting with a straight back helps the flow of energy. When I trained I had a hard disciplinarian teacher, one who probably would not be acceptable nowadays; nobody would dare to disobey her! However, over the years of working in this field I have often been extremely grateful for her methods and the discipline she instilled in us. Try to keep your hands still, because apart from the annoyance that waving your hands around would bring to your sitter, actions like touching your nose in body language can mean you are lying, or uncomfortable and uncertain with what you are saying. People pick up on these kinds of movements. Many psychics find it preferable to keep their eyes shut to concentrate their connections; this again is personal choice.

A positive discipline to clear your own energy before any reading is firstly and most importantly to consciously engage your whole will and intent in the process: *Energy Follows Thought*. Relax. You can implement your own meditation practice that works for you first. A good way of bringing yourself into the right energy is to visualize light or crystal-clear water coming right through your body from the top of your head to the tip of your toes. Then become aware of your breath and breathing. Breathing is something you do every minute of every day without thought. Your breath is your life force, both in a very physical sense and also connecting you to the breath of life in a spiritual sense. Listen to your breath. Do not force or hold your breath, just be aware of the natural rhythm of your own natural breathing. As you do this it will automatically and gently take you into the deeper part of yourself; the part of yourself that is the hub of your wheel so to speak; the part of yourself at the core of your being; the part of yourself that is always still, always light, always strong.

When you feel you are in touch with this energy and with the aid of the rhythm of your breath, consciously breathe this calm energy out and around you, like waves of gentle light. Like ripples on a pond, until that energy is around you and with you and through you, gently allowing it to emanate through the layers of your energy fields, until it expands to the outer levels of your aura. You will be able to tell where that is for you. Usually it is slightly more than an arm's length from your body. To hold that clear energy in place, visualize a golden band at the edge of the aura keeping the energy safely within your own space as this will help to hold that tranquil force. Take a few moments to acknowledge, feel, know and enjoy this energy. It is yours, and no one can take it away, unless you allow it.

When you feel comfortable with this, send your thoughts and energy with firm intent, to the *Highest Greatest Good*; the highest spiritual and benevolent force in the universe. It does not matter what personal beliefs you hold, make sure you affirm that it is the highest greatest good. Direct your energy as high as you can and then higher, and then even higher still; there are no limits other than those you put upon yourself. Then visualize this connection as light coming down, connecting and flowing through your Crown centre; then fill your centres and your whole being with this connection. After implementing this, focus your breath back into each chakra, starting with the Base.

The classical image of a chakra is a lotus flower. Some people therefore like to visualize a flower opening in each centre, and the higher the chakra the more petals open. You can equally use any image that impresses upon you the idea of opening; an opening door or window for instance. Some people like to visualize a spinning wheel where the higher the chakra the faster the wheel spins. What matters is the energy and focus you give to it, and so whatever suits you will work. This simple exercise will become second nature in time. At first it is advisable not to hurry the process. Your own good sense and intuition will inform you whether you have implemented it effectively.

- Beginning with the Base, visualize drawing up the red energy from the fiery inner earth, as if you have your own personal taproot into the deep core of the earth.
- When you feel this is open, breathe into the orange Sacral centre; this is the energy of creation, both on a physical level of procreation and also for the rocket-like energy that sets things in motion.

- Next, the yellow sunlight of the Solar Plexus energy. This is the sympathetic connection both with yourself and others.
- The green of the Heart Centre follows. The Heart Centre is a neutral force; it is the centrifugal force, and the energy of balance and harmony. Here we begin to reach the love beyond emotions; unconditional love of self and others.
- The following blue Throat centre is communication.
- Next the indigo Brow centre is the doorway to the third eye; sight beyond sight.
- Finally, the violet Crown. When you reach the Crown centre, spend a few moments to acknowledge yourself as a spiritual being and acknowledge your connection to the source of 'all that is'.

Next bring your thoughts and energy back to your Heart. Take a few moments to breathe again in this centre, knowing you are connected to the balance of your being, both as a physical and a spiritual being.

After reaching an open and free space, take your energy and thought to the person with whom you wish to link. A very important point to take on board here is that it is wrong, in so many ways, to link to a person without their permission. It's a bit like opening someone's post without permission; no one has the right to do this. It is energetically unsound and no good will come of it. Sometimes a very open psychic person may pick up something without even consciously knowing they are doing it. If this should happen, visualize anything you receive, in light, and let it go. Once you have established your own energy field, through practice, this bleeding of energy will diminish. We live in the material world; if we were always open to every energy around us we would simply go mad. I ask you, would you leave your front door open for any Tom, Dick or Harry or a Mary or Sue to come in? So why would you do the same energetically?

Once you have obtained permission from your sitter, and feel you are in a clear space, send your thoughts like an arrow towards the person, whom we call the 'querent' or 'sitter'. (They do not necessarily have to be physically present for this to be effective). Remember that your thoughts are energies too. The most immediate energy you will connect to is the aura, the energy field emanating from the sitter. You will then be able to perceive the physical, emotional and lower mental or thought energy of your sitter, as we all have these energies working with us all the time. You may perceive these as thoughts, words or pictures in your mind or maybe even just an intuitive sense. Some people are more visual than others so, if you don't receive pictures do not be concerned, just be very aware of all your senses. Making the link with your energy and thought is an action or a male energy. Once the link has been made, wait, listen and be receptive; this is a female energy. It has often been thought that psychic work is mainly feminine. This is inaccurate as without the intention and action of energetic focus you will analogously be like a jelly, and any perception you receive will be hazy and unintelligible. We need both the male and female energies in harmony for any authentic psychic perceptions, as we require balance in all ways.

M any years ago an extremely distraught lady came to me. Another psychic had told her that both her daughters were going to die! Apart from the extremely unethical aspect of telling someone this, it was completely incorrect. Upon working with this lady it transpired she was lonely and her worst fear was the loss of her daughters. The psychic had picked up this fear and relayed it back to her as a fact. This is a common occurrence in an untrained psychic. For example, you could be giving a reading to someone who had just gone for a job interview. If this person thought the interview went well and were expecting to be given the job, an untrained psychic would relay that they would get the job. If the person thought the interview went badly and they expect not to get the job, the untrained psychic would then say they did not get it. Neither of these may be the true outcome as they are born from the expectations of the sitter.

Often a student will say they didn't know if it was their own energy or thoughts they were feeling. This is a good question to ask; doubt is healthy. Whilst in the process of any psychic work, on any level, it is important to let the rational mind rest; if we constantly question everything we receive, one part of our mind and brain fights with the other and assumptions are made that are invariably wrong. It is not, however, a bad thing to get things wrong, particularly in the early stages, as through the continuous attunement to energy we begin to see when we are on key or not. Be wrong at the top of your voice and then comprehend the feeling you had when you were wrong, next time you will recognize the difference. It is similar in energy terms when learning to balance yourself to ride a bicycle; you need to feel and sense the imbalance to gain balance. This means letting go of all preconceived ideas, assumptions and biases. Slowly but surely you will sense when you are on key, you will know by that feeling. Try not to analyse it whilst you are receiving it. Afterwards you can analyse it all you like, but the process of analysis will shift you away from your link. If the preparation has been good and your energy is clear, any impressions you receive once the link has been made, however silly and irrelevant they may seem, will be from the subject. Do not try and embellish what you receive and put your own interpretations on them; 99 times out of 100 if you relay just what you receive it will be correct.

Physical Aura

To begin with it might be easier if you consciously connect to one auric level at a time. The densest, and often in some the loudest energy, is the physical or Base level. Connecting with this you will sense the physical state of the person. Sometimes this can be a little alarming as the other person may have a completely different make-up to yourself, and you may therefore interpret this to mean that there is something wrong. Remember we are all made a little differently. What might seem strange to you might be a perfect balance for another.

There are many different aspects of the physical life and living that we pick up here. You may receive information about the health of the person, but equally you may sense what they have been physically doing during the last 24–48 hours; energies stay in the aura for around two days as long as no other emotional or mental energy is given to them. Be very careful in your interpretation of any health issues. Unless you are a medically trained professional, you must not diagnose them. This in itself can cause dilemmas; if you do pick up something you feel is amiss, gently suggest the person sees a doctor. You can home into areas of the body and implement a psychic scan from head to toe, if this feels appropriate or if you have been asked to do so.

On all levels of connection and in the lower centres in particular, you may pick up fears and desires. Do not fall into the trap of reading these as actual happenings.

People's desires, hopes, beliefs and fears are held very strongly in the aura. It is up to the clarity, experience and good practice of the psychic to discern the difference. The aforementioned woman had been told her worst fears of the loss of her daughters. The interpretation caused a vast amount of unnecessary anxiety and pain, and it was in any case incorrect. It is bad practice, bad psychism, and is certainly not going to help; it may even cause harm to the very person you are trying to help if you misinterpret their fears and desires as an actual prediction. With any good consultation the person should leave you with a sense of healing and upliftment. Of course you will encounter people who have terrible problems and I'm not suggesting in any way that you lie or say something just to make them feel good if it is untrue. However, if you are working with clarity you will receive from your heart the right words, that give the truth in a way which can be accepted and be able to give guidance, assisting that person in their trials. This advice may vary differently from the guidance you would give yourself. Judging another by one's own responses is not good psychism. Again, find true empathy and feel their feelings. This will enable you to be both more sympathetic to their needs and give the correct advice for them.

We are looking for balance in all things; in yourself and in your querent. Many mediums and psychics will speak of the necessity of working from the heart. The reason for this is clear. The Heart is the centre and balance of your energies. It is depicted as a green energy and green is the colour we see all around us when our planet is healthy and balanced. Just as the world is constantly trying to balance nature, so your heart is constantly trying to balance you. When working with the aura, or indeed any other link, make sure your own energy is placed very strongly into your Heart centre. Please note that the Heart energy is not the same energy as the sort of sentimental imagery and thoughts of a valentine card. It is love, but not emotional love. The Heart energy is unconditional and nonjudgemental and is beyond one's normal emotions. It is balance. It is harmony. It is your strength and your healing. When in doubt go to the Heart. When in fear go to the Heart. When in restless imbalance go to the Heart. Make your Heart centre your safe and home base. The constant balancing of your energy will profoundly help your psychic link and also assist you personally. When you successfully make a connection with the Heart energy for the first time, you will clearly know the difference between this form of unconditional love and the emotional type you are used to. It is quite different. It is free. It is calm. It is quietly strong, and it has a resonance of deep peace.

I have often suggested to students that they think of someone they dislike; perhaps a politician, work colleague or someone from their past. Having identified this person I then ask them if they could give a healing or psychic reading to that person, free of their negative feelings? Only by being in a true note of unconditionality can we do this, and this is what we are aiming for.

The Base or physical level is survival. In the modern world this includes work, money, possessions and all the hopes and fears connected to these essential aspects of life and living. Let us not forget we are both spiritual and physical beings. We are animals in our human state and, as such, we all possess animal instincts. The Base level is the level of the instinctual and we forget this at our peril. No level is better or worse than any other. We need to be physical to have the most amazing and privileged experiences in life and living. Our physical world is a miracle of existence and our bodies are an amazing wonder, allowing us to feel, touch, love and reach beyond. Whatever your beliefs about life, and whatever you believe made us come into existence, it cannot be in any doubt that we are truly privileged to have the experience of life, even when our lives are troubled and we are in pain.

Many who are on the spiritual path ignore the fact that our responses are often born out of our hard-wired animal behaviour. This is not bad or wrong, as we all want to protect our world and we all want the best for our families and ourselves. This is no different from any other animal on this planet. We will fight for our survival just as any other animal does; although our methods may be different, the energy and response is the same. Many difficulties people find in their lives are from these natural instincts. Consequently many problems on the Base energy will need to be addressed on that level alone. Whereas spiritual contact and aspirations can, and do, assist us, sometimes the answer is more obvious and closer to hand than we would allow ourselves to believe.

You have probably heard of the 'flight or fight' response. In some shape or form we all respond in this way. The means with which we protect our tribe and ourselves may be complex. They may be wrapped up in altruistic concepts, but the need for survival and protection is still at the heart of a great deal of what we do. To ignore this basic aspect of ourselves is a form of denial. The animal part of us is not inferior, it is a strong part of who we are. In the search for spiritual heights, our basic animal instincts are often forgotten, unacknowledged and ignored. There is nothing wrong in being in a human/animal form. It is part of the whole wonder of this planet Earth. And although our ultimate aim is to raise our energies beyond the Base levels, we will, whilst on this planet, never lose them. Love yourself and others as you are, and embrace the wondrous human family to which we all belong.

The founder of humanistic psychology, Abraham Maslow (1908–70) wrote about the now famous principle of the 'Hierarchy of Needs', in his book *Motivation and Personality*. This principle is depicted as a pyramid. The lowest levels are our most basic needs: survival, food, warmth etc. The theory being that once a person's most basic needs are met, they progress up the pyramid. The next need is to become increasingly social and psychological. And when these needs are met, again they progress to the next level, which is the need for love friendship and intimacy. Higher up is the need for personal esteem and also the feeling of accomplishment. Lastly, Maslow stresses the importance of self-actualization, which is a process of growing and developing as a person, to ultimately attain our individual potential. If we also consider the spiritual aspects of humankind, the ultimate peak of the pyramid must also be what mystics call 'enlightenment'. In many ways this concept is similar to the chakra system. Our basic energies are focused with the Base level energies and as we progress, our own energies and responses lift up to the more spiritual and altruistic. The highest chakra energy also takes us to enlightenment.

I mention Maslow's concept here because it is important to recognize that if someone is in dire need in the lower states, for instance if they have lost their job, have no money and cannot afford to feed their family, this basic energy will take them over. Survival is hard-wired in us; it is the most basic need of us all. If someone is in this unenviable position, when their whole energy and fear is focused on their physical survival, they are unlikely to hear any higher forms of guidance. As a sensitive it is important to meet your querent on their own level. Having established their difficulties, hopes and fears with detached empathy, you can then consciously take your thoughts and focus to the Heart energy, find healing sources and open your channels to practical guidance that will be heard.

We are all responsible for our physical lives. The angels or deities won't put your needs in your lap. What the higher sources can do is direct the person to the appropriate place, thought or situation, which will assist the problem. They do not walk for us. However, in a good reading, even with people in dire need, when you bring in a healing force, the querent will leave in a more open and less fearful space, allowing them to release their stress and therefore see positive solutions to their particular need at the time.

In the early days of any psychic practice, it will be better to concentrate on one energy at a time. As you become more proficient you will be able to direct and link with different energies when appropriate. If you are not musically trained you may listen to an orchestra play and not hear the individual instruments; in time, as your ear gets more attuned, your training will allow you to be able to pick up what every instrument is doing. Psychic practice is also an attunement. It is an attunement to energy. At first the whole sound of the energies blend together. In time, and with practice, you can and must know with which level you are working. When you identify each energy, purpose and frequency, eventually you will be able to improvise and move between the levels more freely. In psychic energies you are training your own instrument, much like a singer would train their voice. How does a musically trained person know instantly the note that is being played? They have trained their ears, and so must the psychic train their senses, which is achieved through practice and constant attunement.

One of the first things you may pick up is the sense of a colour around the person. This is rarely, in the early days anyway, a physical sight, it is an inner sense or sight. If you develop your psychic faculties for healing this sense will, in time, become very evident and it is very useful in the interpretation of someone's health and wellbeing. As a psychic practitioner this sense is also useful, however, there is no point saying to your querent 'I see the colour red' or blue, or whatever it is. They are unlikely to have the same interpretation as you. It's up to you to sense this and relay what it means.

The Base energy is seen as red. As with any colour it is the strength and clarity of the colour that is important. If, for instance, you pick up a strong clear red colour, this is likely to mean that the person is strong and healthy

---

S ome years ago whilst leading a class I looked over to a girl and psychically saw red flashes coming from her arms. It was quite dramatic, so I said to her, 'You feel like you want to hit someone.' 'No,' was her reply, 'I have hit someone today'!!! Her anger was still very present in her energy field. Of course there could have been other interpretations to seeing these red flashes. For instance, it could have been that she had been to the gym and done some extreme exercises with her arms. But psychically I knew it was not this. Trust your senses, your most immediate interpretation is pretty well always the right one.

---

physically, and they are in a good state. On the other hand, if the red is muddy or in anyway not a clear primary colour there is something amiss. If you link with someone who has just had surgery, you would be likely to see red flashes coming off their body, particularly where the surgery has been performed. This is the body's own wonderful ability to heal and its need for more Base or physical energy to bring about balance. If you link with someone who has just done some strong exercise, equally there is likely to be a great deal of red energy coming off them; they have been using their physical energy and that is what you will pick up. This red energy in its negative form also has the resonance of anger.

It is important for you and your querent that you are very clear about what you see. Psychics often get images coming into their consciousness when they link with someone. Yes it is right that you relay the images, but it is also very important you interpret them and relay the interpretation back correctly. For instance, let us say you saw a cat. That symbol is coming to you through your mind. The energies are giving you something that you can take and use in the guidance and connection. So what does a cat mean to you? Your mind is looking for substance and most often the images you receive are telling you, through your own mind, what is needed. Of course sometimes an image of a cat maybe just that; the querent has a love of cats or has a cat that is loved, for instance. Alternatively, they may have an allergy or be afraid of cats. There are, with images, so many possible interpretations. You need to pin down the right one. Being vague and nebulous with your sitter is no help to you or them, and it won't win you any favours or bring new clients. You must be clear, precise and know.

It is useful to cut the word 'something' from your vocabulary. Many inexperienced psychics say the word 'something' all the time. What is something? Something could be anything! You, as the proficient psychic, need to know. If you receive things that you do not immediately understand, breathe into your Heart, reach up to a higher level and open freely your mind. It will come. Remember you are in control of the session, and you are in control of the information. Many untrained psychics say that their words come from another source and therefore they are not responsible for them. It may well be true they come from another source, however, this can never abdicate the responsibility of the words that come out of the psychic's mouth.

Being in the position of giving someone very personal information about their life is putting yourself in a position of power. Any abuse of this power is inexcusable. There are many people who will hang on every word you say. There are even sitters who would implement whatever you say that they should do. Many people are so vulnerable and are unable to think for themselves that they feel they need someone to tell them what to do. Telling someone what to do is not going to help them. Having empathy and a clear overview will enable you to bring in good healthy options, putting the power back into their hands. What they do with the information and guidance you give them is up to them; they may take it on board, they may not. It is not your job and will bring untold difficulties if you get involved with what they do within their personal and private lives.

In many therapeutic practices the therapist is not allowed to communicate with the patients outside the therapy room. So, if they see them at the supermarket they are not supposed to acknowledge them or even say hello. This may seem extreme, but it is a safeguard in keeping their practice very separate from the individual's lives. It is completely up to you how you may

---

V ery early in my work as a psychic, I had a woman who kept phoning me at all hours of the day, to ask me what to do and even what to say. In the end I had to say that her life was hers and it was counterproductive for me to effectively run her whole life. This woman needed some professional help. As psychics, we are not always able to address very serious problems, whether they are health issues, extreme emotional or mental problems. It is not a sign of weakness to know we cannot help sometimes. We cannot be all things to all people and we must not try to sort out what could be a problem that needs very specific and other professional help.

---

deal with such situations. Keeping an emotional distance from your clients is preferable; with a vulnerable person they may want more and more from you.

A short note here on the use of sound in your work. Sound vibrates energy, and with focus on that frequency one can draw one's energy into alignment; rather like having a personal tuning fork. Chanting is present in many cultures and can have the most uplifting and healing effect. There are many good books on the subject of the use of sound. Here I just suggest a very simple exercise, which is particularly good for any ill health and for healing.

Lie on your back and take yourself into a relaxed state. As you breathe through the chakras one by one, feel the sense and the vibration and sound the note you hear when you make this connection. If you are worried about what this may sound like to others, do it when you are alone. If you are not used to singing just hum the note that comes to you intuitively. Feel the strength of the vibration in the centre you are working with. Go through each chakra sounding the appropriate note for that centre. When you have finished go back to the Heart centre and hum into the Heart. I suggest you make these sounds at least three times. This is a wonderful way to balance energy and often allows some intuitive guidance on what our bodies need for good health. The excellent thing about working with sound is that it quietens the mind, and in turn this allows higher intuitive information to reach us. The monks, nuns and sacred musicians over the centuries have used sound to inspire, uplift and help us reach higher energies.

Emotional Aura

Having scanned and relayed whatever you receive on the physical level, the next auric level to connect with is the emotional. As before, remember that energy follows thought; so bringing your own energy fully into your Heart centre, send out again the energetic arrow of thought to your querent's emotional state and relax. Be open to whatever sense, image or thought you receive.

With the previous level of the material and physical state of the person you may sometimes get a physical feeling in your body, with the emotions you may receive an emotional sense. Remember these senses are the querent's own and not yours. Accept and acknowledge the feelings and consciously let them go. To hold on to another person's energy is unwise and in extreme cases could be harmful, as holding on to someone else's energy does nothing to help them and will detrimentally affect you. A visualization you can use here is to see a particular problem that has been revealed to you in a circle of light, and then imagine that this bubble is so light in weight that it floats away into the source of light love and goodness.

What you receive on this level is many and varied. You will almost certainly pick up the particular emotions your sitter is feeling at the time. Since we all have a melange of emotions going on, these often need careful sorting. The two strongest energies we have as human beings are survival and procreation. These are hard-wired in our genes and because of this you are bound to receive information regarding these two important factors. The natural colour of this level of energy is orange. If you psychically receive information as colours, acknowledge how clear the colour is, so as to sense balance of the individual.

As well as the emotional energy, on this second auric level we are touching the creativity of the person. This is the drive, the energy that allows us to move forward in our lives. When focused upon, it can be a wonderful creative force, but when this energy overpowers in a negative way it can be devastating to the individual and the people around them. Most people will use this primal energy in a positive fashion; becoming a parent is, of course, the

---

When I was leading a class, many years ago, I saw out of the corner of my eye orange flashes coming sharply off one of my students. I said nothing at the time; it is none of my business what someone does in the most intimate aspects of their lives. A couple of weeks later this student came and told me he had been diagnosed with HIV.

---

most obvious. Some people may have transferred their creative force into something innovative and artistic. There are all sorts of ways this manifests. A good businessperson is most likely to be using this creative energy, also a writer, a musician, a dancer, an accountant or a scientist. This is the energy that instigates, ignites and pushes us forwards to do something creative, whether that is creating a child, a book, a scientific theory or anything else.

Here you may be touching on things that might be very personal and intrinsically important to the querent's life, their personal relationships for instance, which may include feelings of love, resentments and jealousies. The second energy is tribal, so you might often pick up emotional situations around the family, where they live or even in their offices and workplaces; anything that constitutes their particular social group. These situations, especially if they are connected to loved ones and families, can often be stressful and it is important therefore that you approach these with care and love.

It is here that you will pick up deep feelings, whether that would be about their partner, a work situation or a neighbour. Again, these need careful handling, and we cannot advise someone based on our own feelings. For instance, you may pick up that the person is being bullied in their job, and you might think, well, they should just leave. People get into all sorts of difficulties because of their own attraction of energy and if it is something they have brought to them by their own energy it is unlikely to improve by changing jobs, houses or partners.

You will come across many who have a recurring theme in their lives. Why is this? Why does someone attract a specific negative situation that plays over and over? Clearly this is something the person needs to address in themself. It will almost certainly have stemmed from a negative experience in their earlier life. Many such people think that they can run away from this; if only they could move house, move job, change partner, it will all go away. When we change location, partner or our job we take our energy with us and therefore, before too long, a similar situation will manifest. This feeling of life being against them is one of the martyr, the victim, and the hard done by. With help, this same energy can be turned around, put to positive use and aid the individual to move forward, free from previous negative ties.

You have to use your very good psychic senses to find out whether this person has the necessary strength of character to make changes. It is a sad reality, that for whatever reason, some people are unable to do this. However, giving them something to focus on will assist their own changes. Ask them to see the particular situation/person that is causing grief. Ask them then to visualize it in a circle of light, just as described earlier. Then they can visualize themselves separately in another circle of light, *without emotion*. Once emotional energy is present it is advisable to stop the exercise immediately. If the situation is so ingrained in their life it might be easier for them to visualize the situation/person in a two-dimensional state, rather like seeing a picture on a card. When this is in place, ask them to draw a figure of eight around their circle and the situation/person with which they are troubled. Having done this, ask them, in any way that they want, to visualize cutting the figure of eight in two, so that now the situation/person is separate from their own bubble. Then see the bubble that has the image of the situation/person with which they are having difficulty, become weightless and float away into light. This exercise is cutting the ties of negativity and is similar to the now famous exercises given in the book of the same name, *Cutting the Ties that Bind* by Phyllis Krystal. As long as the visualization does not pull the person back to feel emotional about it, it will work. It has worked for literally

---

I had a student, years ago, who was extremely troubled by her neighbour who was a concert pianist. This might sound lovely, but the trouble was there was nowhere in my student's house where she could escape the sound of the neighbour practising. However lovely the music, it's not yours and you are no longer in your control of your home. She said she was beginning to feel violent towards her neighbour and was extremely stressed. She had no peace. I suggested she did this exercise. She did, and within a very short space of time the neighbour just stopped playing, she knows not why.

---

thousands of people. The intent must be there and the necessary desire to finally escape from the torture of the recurring heartache.

I could relate hundreds of similar stories of the outcomes of this exercise. The most important thing I have found is to implement it without emotion; this is hard when the feelings are so stirred. But try and if you don't succeed, try again. Even if you manage it, for only a few seconds, you break the emotional link, it will have an effect and it will work. We know within ourselves when this has been achieved and, if it is, one need only implement this once. The other most important element of this exercise is not to have any notion of the outcome. For instance, you must not want the offenders to leave, die or any such thing; it must be unconditional. The outcomes of this exercise are often surprising and it rarely pans out as one might imagine. However, if implemented correctly, resolution will occur. You can use this exercise on yourself for any given matter, including those situations that have long gone but still affect you in some way. You can even implement it by visualizing someone who has passed away if their influence is still having a negative impact on your life. This exercise is particularly good with the emotional level of energy. There is nothing so debilitating as negative emotions, particularly for psychic work.

Connecting with this second auric level is also linking into the desires of the person. These can be many and varied. Remember, on the auric levels you will only pick up that which is still present or still affects the person. So, you could pick up a transient emotion, for instance some annoyance the person has had recently at work, but not one that will stay important in that person's life. Alternatively, you may pick up some deep-seated resentment that is rooted from their past, which is still being felt by the person: Most things you receive in the aura are those that have happened within the last 48 hours, up to a week. This is why psychics are able to describe very accurately what the person did in the very recent past. Images sometimes come through that could be quite banal.

Just because you become adept at picking up auric information does not mean you have all the answers. It really is not difficult to link into these kinds of things. Amazing though you think they are, they do very little to progress

I once saw quite clearly the man I was giving a reading to with another man, a friend, putting a white scarf around his neck. This man was amazed, as he had been given the scarf not 24 hours before in exactly the way I had described. He took this as some kind of mystical sign, which it wasn't.

your querent's life. One could say it's proof of a psychic link, and it is, but it is not a mystical or transformative experience and not too much importance should be placed upon these kinds of psychic information.

We receive these types of impression all the time, but few people put much emphasis on them. For instance, when we meet someone for the first time we get a sense, almost immediately, whether we can trust this person, or whether we like them and whether we warm to them. First impressions, as they say, are often the best. When we go into a building for the first time, we immediately feel whether this is a safe place, a happy place or even a bad place. Without conscious thought these impressions are a form of psychic link. Pretty well everyone, even hardened cynics, will receive these impressions; they are so normal to us that we hardly acknowledge them. Training to enhance your psychic perceptions is just acknowledging these sorts of natural impressions, focusing on them and expanding the information around them. So if you get an impression of someone or some place, make that conscious connection with whatever it is, and you will receive why you get the impressions. You can then discover why the place you have just walked into is happy or sad, and why you feel uneasy meeting someone for the first time etc. However, and this is really important, some of the impressions we receive originate from our own fears. Maybe for instance the bad feeling you have towards a place is due to a memory of a similar place where you had a bad experience. This is why it is so necessary to clear as much of your own negativity as possible so your psychic vision is unobstructed by your own fears, desires and needs.

It is for a very good reason that most religions talk, in some fashion, about unconditional love. Whether it is the 'middle way' of the Buddhists, the 'sacred heart' of Christianity or 'unconditional love' in the Eastern traditions. Many religions say we can only reach a state of spiritual transformation by going through the Heart. The Heart centre is unconditional love and only by reaching this higher form of love of self and others can we be a clear instrument. In human existence, being in this state is unlikely to be possible all the time. Nevertheless, little by little, we can clear away the debris that we all accumulate, and we will then receive glimpses, and these glimpses will increase as time goes on. Once you really are locked into the sense of loving, you will want to keep it as much as possible. The hardest time in one's life to connect with this nonjudgemental energy is when a situation or person affects us individually, particularly on an emotional level. This affords us an opportunity to completely release old negativities in our actual existence, for it is only when we have such an experience that we can genuinely know whether it's possible to leave aside our fears and work with harmony and love. This loving state is not just an idea, a thought, or a good vision, it has to be actually real; we have to experience it in our lived world. It is easier, of course, when giving a reading to a stranger, as they have nothing to do with our personal world. They are no threat to us on a personal level. The real transformation is when you achieve the same loving connection in your own world and with those who have in some way wronged you.

Being in a clear space is especially important when psychically connecting with the emotions. Negative emotions in one's energy field are like dark, misty clouds. You can perceive this around the aura of a person suffering with these troubles. We talk about a dark cloud around a person, we sense the greyness, and, particularly if you are a natural sensitive, you will not want to be in close physical proximity to such a person. They feel uncomfortable to be near. This is because they themselves are uncomfortable. It is so important not to be drawn into this energy. Some people experience very grave difficulties in their lives, and if we, as psychics, get pulled into this negativity, even absorbing some, it will do no good at all. A natural psychic's energy can be very porous, like blotting paper. Unfortunately, I have seen many untrained psychics get immersed in other people's negative energies, they then get drained, and in extreme cases can have a complete breakdown. Just as cleanliness in the physical worlds help stave off disease and illness, so cleanliness in an energetic sense will keep us safe. We need to be open, but open in a positive energy. If we have dealt with our own negativities our auras are clear and present no danger. Negative energies can only attach themselves to negative energies. Like attracts like. Unconditional love is a pure energy, therefore nothing can stick to it, nothing can harm it as negativities have nothing to hold onto and cannot grow in this clear energy.

It is no good blaming someone or something else for your feelings. Finding one's own equilibrium in one's own energy means taking responsibility. Ultimately no one makes us do or be anything. We respond to things

---

When I first joined a well-established development group in a major psychic centre in London, I was already well on my way in my psychic training. I'm ashamed to say I was showing off on the first evening when I was asked to link with a fellow student. I knew by then I was good at it, and wanted everyone to know it. I relayed very personal information and finished by saying 'and you really wish you were a man'. I will never forget the look on this student's face; it fell, she looked ashen, and was visibly upset. I knew I had overstepped the mark and got a ticking-off from my teacher. I thought she was going to expel me from the group. Fortunately she didn't, but later explained the necessity of being kind and gentle. My teacher told me the information I had given was correct. The student never returned to the group! With experience we get to sense just how much a person can assimilate at one time. Working with the Heart will allow you to instinctively know and be able to speak the truth, kindly and with healing energies. We are not there to judge someone, or to tell them what to do. We are in service to humanity and must never forget this.

---

because of our own experiences, but even the direst experiences we may have encountered do not have to stay with us. It's hard to let go of a hurt or pain, especially if it is something you have felt for a long time. It's difficult, but is essential, both for your wellbeing in life and to be a clear instrument in any form of psychic work. It is for this reason that most therapists, as part of their training, have to work on themselves first. It is the same for psychics.

In this important area of the emotions, it also includes very personal relationships, including sexual ones. These are sensitive areas and must be treated accordingly.

Lower Mental Aura

The next auric level is what is described as the 'lower mental' and comprises the person's sense of self-worth; how and what they think. The sense of this is something, at one time or other, we have all come across, for instance, when we are in a room with a really pushy person. We rarely like it and we will physically move away from them. This is the Solar Plexus energy. It is an energy that links to what we do and don't want on the material planes. It is also the level that can most easily transfer energy from one person to another.

There are many needy people in this world and some are very good at draining others. They are unlikely to realize they are doing it, but they pull on our energy and this can be quite exhausting. We have probably all had the experience of a friend or acquaintance who is going through a hard time, and wanting to be sympathetic to their needs we will listen to them go over and over their problems. If you have a personal involvement with this person this can be particularly draining if it goes on too long. Bizarrely, I have found telephone conversations are the worst; long ramblings of the person's woes over lengthy periods of time will make them feel better, but are likely to make you feel drained. These kinds of exchanges of energy do not have any long-term advantage. The person may feel better for an hour or two but it won't last, and you will get off the phone feeling exhausted! The needy, having felt the benefit of drawing on your energy, will want more. They will phone again and again to receive some more energy. This is not proper healing energy and is an energetic form of vampirism.

There is a very simple way of stopping this energy leak; simply cover your arms over your Solar Plexus area. The folding of arms is a well-known observation in body language and it says to us the person is not interested in us or is on their guard. In energetic terms you are blocking the leakage and protecting yourself. It works, even when on the phone. If you know beforehand that you will be in a difficult encounter you can visualize yourself in a bubble of light and hold that light around your auric energy field, as described at the beginning of the chapter. The usual distance of the lower aura energy is within an arm's length, so if you visualize yourself in your own energy within arm's length and visualize drawing a golden band around you, it will help to keep your energy to yourself. This practice works well in all sorts of situations that you feel may be difficult or even dangerous.

You may find that a particular colour works well for you and there is no real hard and fast rule for the colour that you use, as long as it is strong and positive. I have found that gold is a good basic colour to use, and if you feel unsafe in a car or other vehicle, silver seems to work very well. On the other hand, I do not advise you to use silver around yourself for preventing energy leakage or as a protection, as it has a very devic, fairy-like quality (*see* Chapter Four). It works well with machinery but not suitable for humans living in the material world. With practice you will have established your own very strong energy field and feel safe and confident in any situation. However, when one's emotions are unbalanced, particularly when caused by difficulties in a close personal relationship, this protection can go astray. So, take just a few moments to visualize dropping any unwanted energy by seeing your flow of energy go right back into the earth. Afterwards, breathe back into your Heart centre, taking a moment to reinforce the feeling of balance in your own energy. It is also important to do this after linking with someone to avoid interference between one sitter's energy and the next, as well as your own energy.

Our thoughts are energy too. Certainly the way we think, and more importantly the intention behind it, changes the way we approach and deal with life. Thoughts and beliefs are very important factors in the state of any person and can indicate just how they are going to proceed at any given time. To psychically link with your sitter's lower mental or thought level, as before, implement your will and send the arrow of energy to the mind energy of your querent. 'Energy follows thought', is particularly relevant on this level as you will be able to pick up the thoughts of the person. In one sense you are reading their mind and, as such, again you must treat this with the utmost integrity and care.

You will find that people have the most transient and sometimes, depending on the person you are reading, very confusing thoughts. When I have implemented this exercise in class, all sorts of thoughts come to the fore; a television programme they have watched within a couple of days, for instance; whether they are going to miss their bus or train, or what they are going to buy in the supermarket. This kind of information has little significance.

Linking on this level you can get a very clear idea of the type of mind of your querent. Some people are very muddled and have very confused thinking that can be the very cause of their difficulties. Being a good psychic

---

O n one occasion a student working with another in a psychic exercise described very clearly a bandage being carefully put around the leg of a person. It was clear to see that she did not have a bandage on so, when asked, the student looked somewhat sheepish as she said she had been watching a hospital soap opera the day before and was struck by the care the television nurse gave to bandaging her patient's leg! It is worth noting that such information rests in the energy fields for a couple of days before dispersing. A week later the student would not have picked up this information. A classic mistake when reading the aura is to give these types of messages much more relevance than they deserve.

---

is often brought about by simple observation of people. It would be almost impossible to do a good job as a psychic if you did not like people. Every single person has their own unique story. Every single person has different experiences and how they use these in their lives is fascinating. You learn so much about people when doing this work, it broadens your mind, it allows you to accept people as they are, and love them anyway. Not just what they do, where they live etc., but also how they approach everything. And how we think, to a very large extent dictates how we govern our lives.

For some years now there have been many books on positive thought, including affirmations to assist the desired changes of thoughts. An affirmation is a short positive statement that reinforces positive thoughts, such as, 'it's getting better and better every day'. Perhaps the leading author on this subject is Louise Hay. In her books you will find positive affirmations on many aspects of your life, health and living. She gives the metaphysical reasons for the complaint and a simple phrase or sentence to repeat. For example, let us take a very common ailment, the backache. In the lower back the metaphysical cause of the pain is a feeling of being unsupported. The backbone, after all, is physically our support for the body. The affirmation here is: 'I trust the process of life. All I need is always taken care of. I am safe.' This simple phrase is putting positive thought out as energy. It can be very powerful and it certainly can help. Sometimes in a reading, if relevant, you as the psychic may receive intuitively such a phrase that will assist your sitter in changing old negative ideas of self. You can also tune in for an appropriate sentence that will assist you, especially for the clearing of bias, prejudices and assumptions spoken about in the previous chapter.

It makes perfect sense that our beliefs and thoughts profoundly affect how we connect with the world, and therefore affect what happens to us because of them. These beliefs may have come from early childhood, although in adulthood these beliefs may no longer serve us or simply may be just wrong. Prejudices perpetuate in families, tribes and society. Hatred and fear of a particular race for instance, born out of a historic situation that may have happened hundreds of years before; the Serbs and the Croats for instance, the Jews and the Arabs. But equally it might be a fear of birds, dogs or any other thing born out of one instance back in time, and reinforced through the family links. Unpicking, releasing and letting go of these kinds of negative thoughts are vital to good health and spiritual progression. It is worth remembering that beliefs are not set in stone. When a belief has become completely ingrained in a person, the belief is automatic, and the person does not even realize they are being governed by it. There is little chance of this changing until either life confronts us with a situation, or we examine all the predisposition of our thoughts. Beliefs can, and sometime must, change. We can choose what we believe and as adults we must examine what is truly right for us.

Some positive affirmations can therefore be of great benefit. Like any other energy, an affirmation only works if the person saying it actually engages their will in the process. They must want the changes. Saying words, without this engagement of resolve, will do nothing; you might as well be reciting a nursery rhyme! Affirmations at certain times in our lives can be a positive step in changing long worn-out patterns, however they are not a panacea of all ills; in themselves they will not give you enlightenment, but they may help you to start the process of clearance of self and damaging mind patterns. Putting out the positive thoughts is an important first step, although complete changes only ever come about when the fear or negative impressions are altered and played out in actual living.

Being aware of your thoughts at any given time is essential when you are working with energies. The saying, 'be careful what you ask for', can just as easily be applied to, 'be careful what you think'! The clearer the energy fields around and with you become, the less resistance these energies have and the more power your thoughts and words emit. The laws of cause and effect are working with your thoughts as well. Most thoughts are transient and therefore have little energy. Alongside any thoughts, if you also give them some emotion coupled with will, the energy increases significantly. 'Like attracts like', is true in all areas of life. Good thoughts generally bring good things back. Bad thoughts generally bring negativity. Don't take my word for this, or indeed anything; watch and observe yourselves, think for yourselves and begin to create your own positive future. The future begins now, in this minute. So whatever bad or negative things may have happened in the past, you can start to shift the negativity today.

The laws of cause and effect play out all the time; mostly things come back to you over time and not just from the person or situation that you sent

---

This was illustrated to me very powerfully some years ago. I was working in London, where parking was always difficult. On a particular day I spent nearly 40 minutes trying to find a space. I was late for my appointment and getting very frustrated. Finally I saw a space; I pulled my car in front of it to back into the space and as I did so another car dashed in. I was so cross and angry I sent out a very negative and violent thought. Immediately I did this I knew it was wrong and tried energetically to retrieve the anger. I was rushed and exasperated and that energy went with it. The next day I had to go again to the same area. This time I saw a space right in the road where my appointment was. I drove into it and seconds later I had a large expensive car hooting wildly at me. I opened my window to a very angry man who accused me of taking his space. It was a small road and I was absolutely sure he had not been waiting otherwise I would have seen him. I tried to explain this but his anger just grew and grew. He was literally jumping up and down, gesticulating and swearing at me and finally he told me he was going to smash into my car. It was an extremely unpleasant and threatening experience. Luckily there were many people around and he knew he would not get away with it. After he had gone, I remembered the previous day and laughed. I knew my anger from the previous day had come back to me! Of course there will be plenty of people who would say it was only coincidence. However, the way this incident occurred, it was so exactly the energy I gave out the previous day – was it coincidence?

---

the energy to in the first place. You may have heard, or even said yourself: 'Why was that person so nasty to me? I have never done anything to them.' Probably you haven't, however, you may have thought something negative or projected this particular negativity to someone else at some time. The effect of your actions and thoughts do not always come back via the same situation or person. When you work with energies you have to be very vigilant in knowing exactly where your energy is. The clearer your energy is, the quicker it returns.

Everything has energy and this includes emotions, thoughts and actions. Everything has an action and a reaction; if you drop a cup, it will fall. This is the law of gravity and so it is with energies. It is not, as some would tell you, a punishment, or a judgement of some god. It is a law just as surely as the law of gravity. I suspect somewhere along the line, this natural law was deliberately interpreted to manipulate and take power over people. There is no punishment, there is only nature. Guilt is an emotion that can be just as corrosive. We all do wrong sometimes. It is good and right to acknowledge this. Learn from it, be aware of it, put it in light and let it go. Move on, knowing that next time you will do better, and be better from this knowledge.

As in the previous auric links, remember that what you psychically receive is just what that person is emanating at that particular time.

Some thoughts are stronger than others. When a training psychic first practises making a link, the impressions will almost certainly feel stronger than they really are. It is your good sense and judgement that will allow you to

---

When I drive on a long journey, I like to sing. On one occasion, driving down the motorway to take a class in SW London, I sang to John Denver's 'Eagle and the Hawk'. I liked it so much I sung it over and over imagining the flight of the birds of prey. That same evening one of my students linked into me. She said she saw two large birds, one an eagle and the other she thought was a hawk!

---

discern what is of real importance and what is not. Being a clear instrument yourself will enable you to distinguish between your thoughts and others.

Astral Aura

The previous three auric energies are relatively easy to understand; we all experience our bodies, our emotions and our thoughts. With the following layer it is more complex. The astral aura, not to be confused with the astral plane, (*see* next chapter) is the emanation of energy from the person that holds thought-forms, desires, addictions and obsessions. Some of these you might pick up from the previous layers, but here they are ingrained in the aura and, as such, are much harder to release. The sense of this energy is porous; it holds substance and, with enough energy from the person, will literally create a life of its own.

These energies are built up through time; a normal thought that you pick up in the lower mental layer will stay present for 24–48 hours. If you feed a thought with enough emotion or mental activity, that energy will begin to register in the astral part of the aura. Someone with a largely emotional make-up will create a desire-based elemental. A more mentally orientated person will create a thought-based elemental. The latter are generally stronger. If either of these are joined with the energy of will, it literally creates a being; an entity within the auric field of the person. The individual then becomes possessed by the energy they have created. A psychic can see these thought-forms or elementals, and the way that these are perceived will vary with different psychics, as each will interpret them in their own way. For instance, one psychic may see a negative thought-form as a snake whilst another may see it as a wolf, or any other thing that represents to the psychic the energy it is emanating.

Over the years I, and many other psychics and healers, have come across people who believe they are possessed. Let me state here quite clearly, that real possession from a dark discarnate being is extremely rare. In the life of a healer or psychic you are unlikely to ever come across it. What you will encounter is a form of possession, not from an outside source, but one built up from the individual's own fears. These fears build and perpetuate themselves, taking root in the astral layer. This is also where you will discover addictions and obsessions where the astral layer will appear dark, have a clawing energy and will be very unpleasant. In these circumstances there will be heaviness; an oppression around the querent. These obsessive qualities can be extremely difficult to dispel and it is certainly recommended that the individual receive good loving healing and therapy to assist the dispersal of this pervasive force. Once a thought-form has been created in this area they are very difficult to release, as this energy can stay in the astral aura for a long time, affecting the individual so profoundly that their whole lives revolve around it. So, for instance, even if the alcoholic has given up drink, the energy or entity they have created will still be around in the astral aura for up to seven years. Healing radically speeds this up and can help to dissolve it completely.

These energies do not necessarily have to stem from a negative source; it is the obsession that forms them. It could as easily start with a very normal or natural desire.

The energies that psychics pick up on this level are important, as they are most often the cause of the querent's difficulties and they may have experienced many years of suffering because of them. Sometimes these are so very ingrained in the whole energy field of the sitter and manifest so strongly in the life of the individual, the person will need some other form of therapy to assist them to unpeel and dissolve them. We cannot imagine that we can be all things to all people; it would take a lifetime and beyond to have the professional knowledge of a medical doctor, a psychotherapist, a psychologist, a dentist, a surgeon and on and on. Our practices are holistic but they do not cover every eventuality. The benefit of psycho-spiritual work is that it can assist in any difficulties, however, sometimes other forms of healing must take place alongside them. In the case of an astral entity, we have to tread very carefully indeed. To obtain these forms of entities the person has held them and given them immense energy over a long period. They are used to this energy, even if it is detrimental and affecting everything they do. Sometimes to even relay the problem will be met with a defensive or even aggressive response. It is important to bring to bear all the loving force that one can,

A lady came to me, desperate to conceive a child. She was turning 40 and had already tried IVF. When I linked with her I saw a very strong image of her holding a baby in her arms. I relayed this image. The next time she came, a few months later, I received the same strong image, again I relayed this to her. The third time she came I still received this image and, as she had not conceived, I questioned it in my own mind. I then tried to project the image of her with a child older than the image I had received. I could not. I asked her if, when she thought of having a child, she ever imagined it growing up. No, was her reply. I then realized that, so strong was her desire to have a baby, she had created a very strong thought-form in her outer aura. In effect she had created an entity of the child she was so desperate to conceive. A desire to have a child is one of the strongest I have come across.

This kind of thought-form is extremely strong and can block out other links. It feels so very real, so tangible, and is often unlike any other impression we normally receive from the aura. Therefore it is extremely difficult, even for the most experienced and competent psychic to determine. The image I received was correct, however, the interpretation was not. The thought-form was so strong that it presented itself to me as a fact. To my knowledge this lady never conceived. The two strongest desires embedded in our psyche are the desire to survive and the desire to procreate. These are natural to all living beings and women who, for whatever reason, find they cannot reproduce can become so obsessed that it takes over their entire life, blocking out everything else. Of course there are many other situations that create this obsessive energy. It can become a real problem affecting both the person's normal everyday living and can create an energy that will, if not checked, dominate or even ruin their life.

to gently inform them of the elemental form and suggest they would be best served by letting it go.

When energy like this is so ingrained a cutting-the-ties exercise on its own will probably not dissolve it completely, although it can be of some help. Some forms of transpersonal work can assist here. There is, for instance, a well-known exercise whereby the client is asked to imagine an empty chair and then see and feel the presence of the person with whom they have suffered sitting in it. The client is then encouraged to talk to the person, drawing out angers, resentments and pains, hopefully to bring some kind of resolution. It is possible for the intuitive psychic to implement this, but, and it is a big but, only try these forms of healing if you are 100 per cent sure you are competent and fearless to do it. If you are not, you could make matters worse. These elemental energies are a possessive force and they do not relinquish their power over the person very easily. In one sense they have created a life, a being, an entity in their own right. In extreme cases these entities will begin to bleed into the astral planes to haunt and possess the person. (*See* also the next chapter).

Drugs and alcohol literally loosen the barriers between the layers of energy fields allowing the auric layers to bleed. This in turn puts them in touch with astral energies, which is one way in which people have psychedelic experiences. There is a good reason why these layers are intact for normal living. It is likely that someone who abuses alcohol or drugs is doing it as a form of escape from a fear or difficulty in their lives. Equally it could arise from the artificial feeling of bliss that some drugs give. Like attracts like, and fear attracts fear, so no good is likely to come of it. Being open in a fear state will attract fear-based energies and, in turn, give life to them in their astral aura. Many patients I have seen as a healer, who feel they are possessed, have at some time in their lives abused drugs.

Some cultures use drugs as a tool for out-of-body experiences, allowing practitioners to meditate for long periods of time, or gain access to higher sources of energy. This practice can only be done safely by a teacher who truly knows what they are doing and should never be implemented with anyone who has fear. As we all possess some form of fear it is a very risky way of

S ome years ago I was called to give healing in hospital to a man
who was very close to death. He had been living and suffering
with cancer for a very long time. When I walked into his room I was
immediately aware that he had a dreadful dark energy over his head.
I held his hand; I knew I had to talk to him about dying to release
him from the fear. He told me he was terrified of dying because in his
younger years he had abused drugs and had had the most terrifying
experience of connecting with a devil-like entity that had subsequently
haunted him. The entity he described was an astral thought-form. He
had no particular religion but was terrified that when he died he would
be forever haunted by this ghastly entity. He said he had done some
bad things in his life and thought this entity was going to come to get
him when he passed, as a punishment. I reassured him, explaining
quite simply what had happened to him, that the entity had no control
over him in a state of love. The bad things he had done were not
heinous crimes and no more or less than most people experience. It
was the entity that made him think this way. I surrounded him with
love and told him he was loved unconditionally and he could let go
and move on into spirit in peace. He died less than 12 hours later.

having psychic or spiritual experiences. It became somewhat fashionable in
the 1970s to believe that drug taking was going to allow the individual to
become enlightened. Whereas it might give you a very different experience
or perspective on life, it is extremely unlikely to give you enlightenment.
Enlightenment can only be achieved in a conscious state of life-long work
on the self. (*See* Chapter Six)

Fear attracts fear, and that fear can, in certain circumstances, become so
strong it hooks into the astral aura and gives birth to fear-based energy. It is
wrong to assume that *all* the energies in this layer are negative. Just as a fear

energy creates a fear-based being, so a loving energy can create a love-based being. This love-based energy could sometimes become the guide of the individual (*see* next chapter). Imagine all your strongest feelings gathering up like a cloud and forming into a shape. Imagine that you communicate with this shape, each time reinforcing the energy of it. It grows and becomes a dynamic force with the aspects of your feelings, whether negative or positive, graphically forming into a life of its own. If this energy is fear, it will play out your worst fears. If it is love, it will play those out too. Love is good, but a love-based elemental, which is almost certainly an emotional love, could equally hold the person back from taking responsibility for their life and living. Take heart, as the amount of energy – whether it be thought, emotions or any other – needed to create these elementals is usually born from years of focused will, and most people go through their whole lives unencumbered by them. Obsessions on any level are not healthy; when you consider what is happening in your energy field with an obsession you can see just how destructive they might be.

To briefly recap – the aura or energy field comprises energies that the person is emanating at the time of the link with the psychic. They are what they think, feel and how they are physically. Auric energies also connect to the desires, fears and obsessions of the individual.

Closing-Down Exercise

When you have finished your connection with your sitter, consciously bring down healing energy to surround them and then consciously disconnect from their energy. It is very important that you also cleanse and close from this connection afterwards; absolutely no good will come from holding on to the other person's energy. So there must be a firm definite disconnection. A quick and easy visualization to use, is to see them in a bubble of light, separate from yourself, and see any residual energy drop into the earth.

After an exercise, whether it be a psychic connection to another, or your own meditation, it is always good to do a brief cleansing of your own energies to make sure you are back in your own positive energy. So once again engage your will and reach up in your mind to the highest greatest good; the source of the universe, and visualize bringing this in as light coming down into the Crown centre. The Crown and the Base centre are always open. The Crown energy links us to the divine, and the Base energy links us into the physical world. Visualize sweeping the light into the Crown and down to the Brow centre, cleansing, clearing and gently closing that centre. The visualization that you personally prefer is fine; it could be the flower petals folding in, the window or door closing, or a curtain being pulled. Energy follows thought. The visualization is only the focus for your energy. After closing the Brow take the light to the Throat centre and again visualize the light cleansing, clearing and closing that centre. From there, do the same into the Heart, then the Solar Plexus and then the Sacral, maintaining the bright clear light as you do so. When you come to the Base centre visualize a taproot-like energy, like a root going right into the very core of the earth. Then draw that energy back up to your Base centre. This final grounding is most important. Affirm that you feel, know and love yourself as a physical being, loving all that you are, and consciously affirm that you will bring joy and love into your life.

In reality your centres will normally be open all the time. Even after implementing the closing procedure, the moment you think, feel and respond to anything, they will open again. The point of closing is not to keep them closed; who would like to be energetically in a steel box? It is to cleanse and clear any residue energy picked up from your link with a sitter. You can use this opening and closing in other aspects of your life and living when necessary. Some people also like to throw a circle of golden or white light around themselves after any psychic work.

In my opinion there has been a lot of nonsense spoken and written about the closing and opening procedure, and elaborate forms of protection that simply are not necessary. If so much energy is given to protecting yourself it can turn into a fear if, for whatever reason, you are unable to do it. My advice is to keep it simple. You are quite safe in your own energy if you engage your will in the process and your intent is only for the highest greatest good. Clearing the centres periodically, whether you are actively working as a psychic or healer or not, is a good practice and will assist you in your own

I once had a client come to me with the most dreadful headaches she just could not get rid of. It transpired that she had been told by the development leader of the group she was in, that she must close her Crown centre! She had constantly tried to do this as the group leader said it was dangerous if she didn't. It was no wonder she had headaches! The Crown (and the Base) will always be open whilst alive. I instigated some healing, opened and cleansed her Crown and her headaches immediately disappeared.

life. Ultimately your greatest protection is an open, loving, pure heart.

The notion that you must always have your centres closed is simply not possible. You want and need to respond to others, you want to feel love and be loved. If you were to be closed energetically you might as well analogously be locked up in a tower. Over the years I have had sitters asking why they do not receive love in their lives. Mostly the cause is that through some previous hurt or fear they have unconsciously closed down their loving energies. This may be all right for short periods, when someone has experienced some shock or deep hurt, but this closure must only be used as a band-aid and the band-aid must come off as soon as possible. Certainly closing your heart will stop you being hurt, but equally it will stop you being loved and stop you loving, and a life without love is very grim indeed.

Like any practice, psychic work is a discipline. With dedication and good motives in place, it really is not difficult. Becoming competent in the psychic arts is just the same as being competent in any other skill. Being a good psychic does not necessarily make you more godly or special. Every soul is a special soul. Take pride in your work, but don't allow this pride to overcome you. It is a privilege to understand and know another human being in this way. If you work well, the benefit to your sitter and yourself will be profound.

CHAPTER FOUR

The Astral Worlds

Millions of creatures walk the earth unseen,
both when we sleep and when we awake.

John Milton

The derivation of the word 'astral' is from the Greek *astron* and relates to a star. The Greeks used it to describe the heavens and the home of their gods. Astral worlds, or planes, are terms used by mediums to describe an existence parallel to our own. Astral planes are notoriously nebulous even for those who continuously work with them. The best way to describe the astral world is that it is a vibration slightly beyond the material worlds through which we can perceive and communicate with an array of different non-physical beings and energies. Like our world, these range from the very dark to the most beautiful and radiant. Every living thing in our world is thought to have an astral counterpart or energy. Even homes and offices will have some astral energy caused by the people who inhabit them, or forceful situations that have occurred there consequently creating a strong energetic resonance.

We all have access to the astral when we are in our sleep. In the sleep state our astral bodies, which are a counterpart to our physical bodies, slide a few centimetres out from the body. For whatever reason, some people have a greater disposition for their astral body to become more active. This has been called 'astral travelling'. In the 1970s it became fashionable to train oneself to astral-travel, and subsequently many books have been published on this subject.

There have been cases where someone on the operating table has been aware of being outside their body and has observed their still physical body, and the motions and words of the doctors and nurses. This type of astral travelling usually occurs without any previous experience, and consequently it can be quite disturbing for the recipient. Those who have astral-travelled have related that when looking at life forms in this state they see an ethereal substance around the body. Inanimate objects are also seen to have a hue of energy around them, born from the thoughts and desires of the owner of these objects. It is possible to train oneself to astral-travel, and interesting though it might be, in my opinion I can see little long-term benefit from this practice for the psycho-spiritual process. I would not advise you to try it unless you absolutely know what you are doing. Apart from anything else, the amateur inquisitive astral traveller may come across some strange entities and unsavoury beings here, usually from what is called the 'lower astral' as described later in the chapter.

There are three main types of dream. The first is like filing information on your computer into some kind of sense and order. This is where the now unconscious mind is assimilating all that has happened during that day. The second, and most often experienced, is the psychological type whereby we dream in symbols. These are the types of dream that can be of use in therapy. Here the mind is accessing the unconscious to inform us of something that we cannot quite reach in our waking lives; things that distress, things that need to come to the surface but we are not quite ready to accept. These types of dreams are most useful in the self-awareness process, and some therapists work with their patients' dreams to unlock deeper awareness. During the psycho-spiritual process it is not unusual for the student to have more frequent dreams and these can be very relevant. A dream therapist once told me that any living thing in your dream, including animals and insects, are a representation of an aspect of yourself. So, for instance, if you dream of someone who you have not seen or thought about for a long time, the question to ask is what sort of person were they? The characteristic of the person is saying something about you. In these cases it might therefore be good to look at what was going on for you at this time of your life, as it is likely to be something very relevant to what you are trying to work out now. This type of dream will only stay in the consciousness for a short time and unless we talk about it or write it down they are often forgotten very quickly after waking.

The third type of dream, and most relevant to the astral, is one where we are not sure whether the dream was actually real or not, on waking. These are the dreams that stay with us throughout the day. They are the dreams where we meet, sense and even smell the person we dream about. These are the dreams that we describe as being 'so real'. The psychological dreams are experienced more as symbolic cardboard cut-outs and stay in our consciousness for a very short time. In contrast, astral dreams are rarely forgotten. The deep experience we have with meeting someone in the astral, leads many to think that we actually have made contact with the person whether they are still alive or dead. It is believed that the astral body of the sleeper and the astral body of the person have actually communicated through the astral energies.

In the previous chapter we looked at thought-forms. In the astral you will find thought-forms also. These have been created by the minds of humans and through continuous desire and energy are registered, not just within the astral aura of the individual, but are now residing on the astral plane. The energy and purpose of these thought-forms are produced by their creators. As we have seen, these can be created unconsciously by a person who has manifested a strong desire or thought force. This usually occurs when the creator has a strong mental image of what they desire, as in the case cited in the previous chapter of the woman who so longed for a baby. This ability has been used purposely by both black and white magicians who have learned to acquire this talent. Strong desires for either good or evil will manifest form and create a semblance of vitality in these artificial entities. These entities go only where they have been directed to go. They can be dissolved and rendered useless by correctly directed positive thought. Some of these thought-forms are deliberately conceived by someone sending out strong mental pictures and in this case it is conscious.

When I visited Jerusalem some years ago, I was aware of an abundance of thought-forms delivered by different cultures over the centuries. One religious place in particular was crammed full of these thought-forms, many of which were born from the pleadings of those in fear. Such was the shock of this energy and the fear-based claw-like astral force, it took me several days to clear. It's worth remembering that not all churches and places of worship have a positive energy.

The appearance of many of the entities we call ghosts can be thought-forms. This category of ghost is often the type who walks through houses and castles over a long period. Some of the supernatural saints and other divine beings of all faiths have been created in a similar way. These can be kept alive through generations of prayer and devotion. These energies are often sensed around statues or particular places in religious buildings. Those who accept the beliefs of these particular powers and are in harmony with the vibration can be affected by them, whether it is for good or ill. In some cases, when a place of worship has been neglected and there is no longer the reinforcement of this energy, it creates a void and a place that has been created in worship and love can now become one of negativity and fear. This is the reason why empty churches will be cleared of the energies by a ritual of deconsecrating by priests who are competent in this task. If it is not implemented, unknowingly this is how generations of fear and hate can perpetuate. The astral energy holds these unfortunate entities and, by the reinforcement down the generations, it can cause the perpetuation of negative energies that may lead to violence and wars. Only by deliberate and desirous positive power of true goodwill and love, will these malevolent energies stop the perpetuation of the destructive forces that we have seen throughout history.

In many cultures we give names to energies through the names of a saint or a deity. The Catholic religion has saints ascribed to various things, for instance, St Christopher for travel, St Anthony for finding things, and St Jude for hopeless cases. The Hindus have thousands of gods ascribed to all areas of life and living. The Greeks also had gods of wars, love, stars etc. If we take the notion of energy following thought, when we pray, are we creating a greater and greater thought-form and personality? Are we possibly even giving birth to these beings through our own focused energies?

To the surveyor on the astral plane everything is as real as the material world. The solidity of all things is relative, as every atom is constantly in motion and there is nothing actually solid in the material world. The vibration on the astral is higher than the physical world, however, as we shall see later in the book, it is far from being the ultimate energy in the universe.

So we can begin to see that the astral plane of existence is fraught with difficulties, and many genuine and competent mediums have fallen foul of the influences and illusions that they can bring. It is for this reason we must first look at some of the dangers they incur. As you progress in your psychic development, layer by layer, veil by veil, the picture changes. Each step along the way holds pitfalls and glamours, which are essential to acknowledge. These are often insidious and cloak themselves in the name of good intentions. In all areas of psychic work we have to be diligent in our own motives. Perhaps here in the astral planes this fact is of the greatest importance.

In the last chapter we looked at the astral aura; the emanation that holds deep desires and fears. It also holds what has been called 'glamour'. This has many implications, one of which means it is subject to the mass energies of the world. This is the same energy that allows otherwise peaceful people to become caught up in violence in crowds and also allows mass fear. This is the energy that allowed thousands of people to be influenced by the compelling energy of Hitler, or the mass hysteria induced by charismatic preachers. The astral energy might also grab you as part of collective grief or exultation. Many unscrupulous people have used this energy to influence the masses to their way of thinking, towards violence or to extricate money for a disreputable cause.

Often, such is the ego of the psychic or medium, they do not always realize they are subject to the destructive energy of glamour. One of the many ways this can manifest is that well-meaning psychics believe they are up against the 'black forces'. They think that their demonstration of commitment has been so good that the black forces will be sufficiently interested in them and will try to hinder their good work. Nothing could be further from the truth. It has its roots in pride and self-satisfaction. It is illusion, and illusion can be rife in this level of work. If we have a pure intent and an open loving heart – loving in the sense of unconditional loving – no black or evil force will be able to attach itself to you. Fear attracts fear, and love attracts love. Only in fear do these rare occurrences of the darker forces take hold.

Such are the pitfalls in working with astral energies, many schools will warn against them. It is true that in the astral the work has its challenges, however, among other things, the astral energy is a frequency through which the vast majority of the world can communicate with higher forces and as well rounded psychics we must, at the very least, come to understand these energies. It is certainly true that ultimately we must rise beyond these levels but, for now, we still have to use them to the best of our abilities to assist the growth of both our querents and humanity.

The books of Alice Bailey describe at length the dangers associated with the astral energies, and I use some of her headings of 'Glamour' to illustrate the difficulties we are up against.

The Glamour of Destiny

This is the illusionary notion that we are special, and have a special task to fulfil in our spiritual lives. The reality is that every single being is special, and has latent abilities within them. When we work with spiritual energies, our best talents and abilities will be utilized, whatever they may be. Beware of anyone, either living or in spirit, who tells you that *you*, and only *you* can save the world, and that you have been chosen above others to do this task. This is a hook to your ego and it will almost certainly be untrue.

The Glamour of Aspiration

The total dedication and absorption in the notion of following the light that allows the individual to literally become blinded by the light! In this state the truth is not seen, and if it is, it is ignored. This is the energy of the 'love and lighters'! That is, those who refuse to see what is real because it might not be all peace and good. In this state somewhere along the line, life will present them with some great difficulty and when it does they often go into a downward spiral of depression, feeling they have failed.

The Glamour of Self-Assurance

This is the overly enthusiastic student who believes that he or she is always right. It is the stuff of fundamentalism and bigotry. We all make mistakes. Acknowledging them and learning from them is an essential part of the path. Only a fool believes they are always right.

The Glamour of Duty

This is the overemphasis on the sense of responsibility. Whereas it is true that we must take responsibility for our own energies, this does not mean we take responsibilities for others. This is the energy of the martyr. It is the energy we have been subject to in the Piscean age, which is now receding. (*See* Chapter Seven).

The Glamour of the Mind

This is the notion that through connecting to spiritual forces you have the capacity to deal with every problem; we cannot be all things to all people. Spiritual forces can, and do, assist us, but our human existence is ours, and ours alone and we must take the responsibility to do what we feel is right.

The Glamour of Devotion

This is the glamour of a dying age. It is the energy of withdrawing from human life, as in retreating to monasteries and ashrams. It has little part to play in our modern era. Everyone has access to truth, we do not necessarily need to go into retreat from the world to find it.

The Glamour of Desire

Here one can cloud and cloak one's real needs and wants. What do you want?

This honest question is the one that will bring you closest to the truth; not what you 'should' or 'ought' to do, but what you really, really want. Identify this, and align your needs and wants to the higher forces.

The Glamour of Personal Ambition

This is self-explanatory; allowing one's own ambition to get in the way of what is really needed. Ambition is good and a useful energy when aligned to the highest greatest good.

The Glamour of Self-Pity

Because the very nature of psycho-spiritual development is observation of self, many students become prone to the negative aspect of what they discover. This is a powerful and deluding force, which exaggerates every condition and isolates people within the centre of their own lives and the dramas of their own thoughts.

Many of these aforementioned glamours are likely to occur at some time on your path. See them for what they are and hold your Heart clear and open. It is then that you can walk with greater knowledge and clearer resonance.

Some years ago I had spoken in a hurtful way to someone. Realizing that this was wrong and that I had certainly failed to 'be spiritual' on this occasion, I pondered much on it and was consequently extremely miserable. After moping around all day, I decided to seek illumination on the matter and took myself into a meditation, expecting to receive some stern words regarding what I considered disgraceful behaviour on my part. To my astonishment the message that came through loud and clear was 'we do not want your sorrow we want your strength'! In other words, do not waste time on what you have done badly, learn from it and move on.

When dealing with the astral energies we really are dealing with unseen forces which are, as such, extremely difficult to understand and to relay succinctly. Many writers in the Mind Body Spirit genre, at best glide over these nebulous energies or do not mention them at all. There is also a difference of opinion between the few authors who do write on this subject, as to the level on which the astral is based. So let us explore this elusive area and, as always, I urge you to think for yourself. Use your deepest and truest intuition and make your own final judgement.

Although man stands on the brink of enormous change in all areas of living, including the psychic ones, for the vast majority of people it is still the astral planes that transmit ideas, visions and inspiration from energies beyond the normal conditions. The easiest way to understand this is to acknowledge that each layer and level has its own vibration, and just as a single point of space may contain vibrations of heat, visible light, X-rays and other aspects of the electromagnetic spectrum, each will vibrate at its own rate and not interfere with the other. Each beam of light contains many different colours, again, each with its own rate of vibration. Tuning into psychic energies is similar to tuning a radio along a dial. The astral tuning can, at first anyway, be a bit like trying to tune your radio at night, with so many stations they bleed into each other and are sometimes difficult to hear.

For whatever reason, some people have a greater connection to the astral and will perceive beings from this plane of existence more easily. Those who have an easier connection to this plane are not necessarily more spiritually advanced souls. As with all psychic senses, a connection is made by a shift of the sensory mechanism on the part of the psychic, and an act of will to engage with this frequency. There are many different vibrations on this plane, and they often fill the medium with excitement and expectation. We must keep a sense of proportion in all of this; as a medium once said, 'just because you link with someone in spirit [i.e. astral] it does not mean they have a greater IQ than you do!'.

Earth Spirits

If you quietly walk through a forest or in the countryside you may sense an unseen presence. This presence is likely to be an 'earth energy' or 'earth spirit'. Under various titles, these elusive beings are present in many cultures including the Valkyrie of Norse mythology and the leprechauns in Ireland. In Gaelic they are called *Sidhe*, which means people of the hill. The Lenape native American Indians call them *Nan-a-push*, which means the little people of the forest. In one of the most extensively researched books on the subject, *The Book of Imaginary Beings*, by Jorge Luis Borges, he describes many of these types of being including a rather obscure spirit called Lamias, that, according to the Greeks and Romans, lived in Africa. Apparently Lamias made whistling sounds and resided mostly in the deserts. Upon reading about these beings, shortly before his death the poet Keats was inspired to compose his poem 'Lamia'.

There are also names for the different spirits connected to the different elements: salamanders are the fire spirits, sylphs are of the air, nymphs are found in water and the gnomes are part of the earth. Other names for this kind of energy include fauns, brownies, trolls, pixies, mermaids, elves, satyrs and fairies to name just a few. These creatures have been sung and written about over centuries, including Shakespeare's *A Midsummer Night's Dream* and Wagner's Ring Cycle. People have reported sightings throughout history, and, if the earth spirits are indeed figments of overactive imaginations as has been suggested, has not humanity taken great pains to invent such a multiplicity of names for these, so-called nonexistent beings?

So what are these elusive beings? It is thought that every blade of grass, every flower, every tree and every living thing has a spirit and that these energies form part of the usually hidden world that co-exists with our physical one. In the past, it was believed that the purpose of fairies was to absorb the life force emitted by the sun, and to distribute it to the solid physical worlds. In so doing they become the essential connection between the sun's energy and the soil's minerals. Different types of earth spirit are thought to have different roles. Some work above the ground and some below. Some work for the expansion of cell growth and some with the mineral, vegetable and animal worlds. The substance of the earth spirits is essentially etheric; the finest aspect of physical material. Their state of being is so sensitive and fluid that it is believed to be changed by thought and feeling. The forms of these beings are many and varied; they may be perceived as light beings and are usually seen as small in size. Fairies are thought to be able to change their shape at will, and with this chameleon-like talent they are mischievous and playful. They have a fluidity of energy and emanation and we therefore very often perceive them with wings and flowing limbs.

The word 'gnome' is interesting for it is associated both with the Greek expression for sound judgement (Gnomon; indicator, 'one who discerns', or 'that which reveals'). And the Latin expression for earth dweller is *gēnomos*. It also means a misshapen sprite that was supposed to inhabit the interior of the earth, and the guardian of mines and quarries. It is believed that in some way these earth spirits assist the process of the living world. The gnomes are said to be very aloof as the gnomic energy is so dissimilar from our own that it is almost impossible for most people to perceive them. They are thought to be very distrustful of humans, which is not that surprising when you consider that it is their job to guard the earth for which many people have scant regard. Most people report that if they inadvertently wander into an area where gnomes reside, they experience an uneasy sense and feel a need to get away as soon as possible; they literally feel they are being ejected from the gnome's territory.

These ethereal energies are very subtle and illusive. There is a danger in making too close a connection with the earth energy, devic worlds, as after experiencing their particular energy, people may find it difficult to return to the normal human state. The fairy's evolution is thought to be parallel to our own, but rarely to interrelate. I have met in my life a handful of people who I have felt to be of a devic or fairy-like nature. For these people life is very hard. Their appearance is often elemental. They usually have pale skin and they often incur some kind of eating disorder. Strangely, they rarely live in the country but favour cities. This may be because they can be more anonymous and need constant human energy around them to maintain their human existence. They prefer their own company with few, if any, friends and are self-reliant. In some cases, if they have the inclination, this type of energy in a person will allow them to become exceptional healers.

In olden times people blamed many and varied things on the fairy folk, such as mysterious deaths of animals and illnesses. Cramps and bruising were particularly ascribed to the fairies who were supposed to pinch people in their annoyance. They were also blamed for plant blights and even for hair being tangled. They were often accused over things that went missing. In the past a great deal of superstition revolved around the notion of fairy folk, and elaborate protection methods were employed against their intervention. These included turning clothes inside out, the use of bells, bread, salt and daisy chains as well as prayer and the cross. Enchanting and delightful these connections may be, however, it is important to remain balanced and grounded at all times.

In the previous chapter we looked at thought-forms and elementals. The earth spirits' energy can overlap thought-forms, and there are innumerable descriptions of fairy folk that seem to be similar in quality to elementals. We know that psychically we can create a being from thought energy, and fairies have been said to change their shape by accessing the thoughts of human beings. Where one starts and the other ends is a good question to ask. Could it be that the energy emanated by the earthy spirits gives off a resonance, and because we as humans can only identify things with form, we personify them and give them shape? Children have often been told that every time you say a fairy doesn't exist, you kill one. Energy follows thought, and if indeed these are manifestations of these thoughts, maybe it is so?

Angels

Just as the earth energies are seen to be the etheric energy that protects living things in nature, likewise angels are seen to protect and guide us. Angels form a part of many belief systems and appear in the literature of many cultures. We communicate with them through the astral frequencies. They have been described as spiritual tailors, continuously repairing our etheric bodies and,

I n a lecture I gave some years ago in Cyprus, I made the point that angels are something most religions have in common. It was a surprise to me therefore that a member of the audience, got up and shouted to me. 'How dare you say angels are anything other than Christian?' Upon which she walked out! I felt saddened by the fact that I was trying to illustrate something that different religions have in common – clearly this particular lady did not want to know!

as such, they are often depicted as being very close to us and work within our aura. One of their jobs is to guard us while we are asleep, ensuring that we are not bothered by lower astral beings.

Down though the ages, angels have been acknowledged, not only by Christians, but by many other cultures; the angel Gabriel is said to have dictated the Koran to the prophet Mohammed, and it was an angel that stopped Abraham from sacrificing his son – a significant moment in Jewish history. Christians know well the story of the annunciation to Mary concerning her forthcoming child. An angel appeared to Joseph Smith in 1823, an event that led to the writings that became the Book of Mormon and to the founding, in 1830, of The Church of Jesus Christ of Latter-day Saints.

Some of the oldest known artefacts are of winged angel-like beings. They were used as images in ancient Egypt; in the Greek pantheon, the wings of Hermes and the winged Eros represented the spirit that carried messages between the gods of Olympus and the lesser gods of Earth. The angels were seen as emissaries of the gods in Greek mythology and the god Apollo was perceived by the Greeks and the Romans as an angelic being of whom it was said nothing false or impure might be brought near him, for he was a cleaning and enlightening power.

Judging by the many books about angels that have been published in recent times, it seems that somehow the angels are currently in our psyches. Many mystics and poets have also written about them down the ages. In the

Old Testament is the story of Jacob's ladder where the angels travel up and down to levels of heaven determined by their own type.

Perhaps the most cited reference to angels is attributed to Dionysius the Areopagite in the *Celestial Hierarchy*. The writings attributed to Dionysius the Areopagite spread over a few centuries and therefore often come under the heading 'Pseudo-Dionysius'. We may never be completely certain who wrote the *Celestial Hierarchy*, but what is clear is that it has had an enormous influence on subsequent Christian theologians. In *Celestial Hierarchy* it speaks of the nine orders of heavenly Angels: Seraphim, Cherubim, Thrones, Dominions, Virtues, Powers, Principalities, Archangels and Angels. In this model the highest angels carry out planetary and cosmic missions, while the lower orders help manage the affairs of the earth. The Cherubim and the Thrones are said to have the most wisdom and are the closest to the Divine Source.

In the first hierarchy, the Seraphim are described as the flames of love. Their task is to transmute the darkness, which they do as a song of creation and celebration. Theirs is a vibration of love and creativity. These beings are thought to be in direct communion with God and, as such, are beings of pure light and thought. The name 'Seraph' means healer, doctor, surgeon and higher being. The serpent image of this angelic order symbolizes rejuvenation and its logo, the caduceus, is still used today as the symbol of the medical profession (*see* Chapter Two). This image originally appeared as a wand in the hand of the universal god Hermes, who was believed to be one of the Seraphim.

The Cherubim emanate and manifest the flow of light force. This Hebrew word means both 'one who intercedes' and 'knowledge'. The concept of our own friendly cherubs originated here, however, these high powers are not truly represented by the sweet images with which we are so familiar; theirs is the energy of divine knowledge and wisdom.

The Thrones administer higher justice, holding the balance of all universal laws. Dante described this highest order as the 'place of pure love, pure mind, pure will and purest spirit'. In Jewish lore they are described as the 'Great Wheel' or the 'many-eyed ones'. Interestingly, from their description they might have been confused with modern ideas and visions regarding extraterrestrials, and some ET sightings have given rise to theories that they are indeed angels.

The second hierarchy consists of the Dominions who govern us, the Virtues who devise strategy, and the Powers who carry out the divine plans and protect against evil influences. It is also said of the Virtues that they preside over the movement of all the celestial bodies, including the galaxies, the suns, the stars and all the planets, and that their high powers help to hold the threads of the cosmos together. They strive to balance the polarities of matter and spirit. The Powers seem to act as holders of the energy between the different layers of the cosmos, keeping each energy in its rightful place. Dionysius the Areopagite says that it was the 'powers who resisted the efforts of demons to take over the world'.

The lowest angelic hierarchy consists of the Principalities, the Archangels and the Angels. These watch over all the nations, the world leaders and the great global movements, and they also are said to have the rather perilous task of being the protectors of religions.

Whatever the hierarchical level, the angels are constantly working with us to heal and help us on our spiritual path (*see* also Chapter Five). Those with whom we have most contact, other than our own personal guardian angels, are the archangels. Most of the angels' names end in 'el' and the derivation of the singular 'el' is interesting; it is an ancient word with a long and complex etymological history, which has a common origin with many other ancient words in other languages. Among the many meanings are brightness, radiant, and shining ones.

In the 13th century Thomas Aquinas devoted an entire treatise to angels in his *Summa Theologica*, and said:

> Every angel is of a different species and each species is higher
> or lower than the other. Angels do not reason as men do from
> premise to conclusion, but from the knowledge of a known
> principle and this straightway perceives all its consequent
> conclusion with no discursive process at all.

Their knowledge therefore is intuitive and immediate.

It is said that nature abhors a void and it seems Aquinas was in agreement; he believed that the existence of angels was perfectly logical; the perfect universe must have a precise and orderly arrangement of all things that were created, and an orderly universe cannot have any voids, therefore for him it was a logical necessity for the universe to include angels. This echoes some modern scientific thoughts, suggesting the existence of an entangled energy connecting everything in the cosmos.

We cannot describe angels without at least mentioning what are considered to be the dark angels. The dark angels in Christian terms began at the Fall; the beginning of time. Lucifer was the name given to the infamous fallen angel, however the name Lucifer, far from meaning dark, means a 'light being' or 'bringer of light'. So how has this contradiction occurred? Apparently God asked his higher angels who would be willing to help humanity by offering constant challenges and temptations. Lucifer volunteered, but, because of the nature of his work, that is revealing light through darkness, he received bad press and latterly become known as the devil, instead of his true nature, which is the great awakener. In one tradition Lucifer was described as the guardian of the planet Venus; the planet of love! Over a period of time,

---

Curious about angels and their place in the universe, some years ago I spent an entire term with my students connecting to the nine levels of angels. Much to our surprise the energy we received from most of them was not the gentle love and light that we have come to associate with these beings. I had a sense at the end of this project that in some way the energy we call 'angels' was in someway holding together matter and anti-matter; physical and spiritual forces, like a never-ending stream of gossamer strands. I cannot of course, rationalize this. Maybe one day scientists will discover the holding force of the universe and explain to us what it was we perceived during these sessions.

---

the name Satan gradually came into use, taken from a Hebrew word which meant adversary. From the 3rd century onwards Satan gradually became synonymous with the concept of the devil, and developed as a separate entity in apocryphal literature.

Descriptions of the Fall tell us that the angels were the first beings to become separated from the Source. God breathed both angels and humans out into the cosmos to gain experience. The angels then abandoned free will as they desired to be completely part of the will of God. So they were directed not to take on physical form but to work alongside mortals. However, some of the angels decided that they did want free will, and through that freedom they chose to leave the divine unity. Gradually they drifted away from the Source. Those which fell away took on human bodies, and those which drifted the furthest away became demons. The derivation of the word 'demon' is illuminating. In Latin *deus* means god and the Greek *daemon* means 'genius, a god-like form, an intermediate between god and man'. The so-called devil, in my opinion, is a travesty that is most likely born out of fear. The creation of the devil as an entity may have originated principally out of an ecclesiastical desire to control the populace through fear.

Dark angels are representative of chaos, and it is through experiencing chaos that we gain knowledge of ourselves. How else can we reach an understanding of good and balance without experiencing the opposite? So in this way the dark angels, far from being against us, are the very energy that enlightens and transforms. The English mystic Edward Carpenter in his poem 'The Secret of Time and Satan' gives us the best and most apt description of the true meaning of Satan or the devil. Extracts as follows:

> I saw Satan appear before me magnificent, fully formed, feet first with shining limbs. He glanced down from among the bushes, 'come out' he said with a taunt. 'Art thou afraid of me' and I answered him not but sprang upon him and smote him. And he smote me a thousand times and lashed and scorched and slew me as with hands of flame and I was glad, for my body lay there dead and I sprang upon him again with another body and with

another and another and again another. And the bodies, which I took on, yielded before him but I flung them aside and the pains which I endured on one body were the powers which I wielded in the next. And I grew in strength till at last I stood equal in might exultant in pride and joy and then he ceased and said, 'I love thee'. And lo his form changed and he leaned backwards and drew me upon him. And he bore me up into the air, and floated me over the topmost trees and oceans and around the curve of the earth under the moon till we stood again in Paradise.

'The pains which I endured in one body were the powers which I wielded in the next', fittingly describes the illumination we receive from the difficulties we incur. As William Blake so aptly put it, 'Evil is only the deprivation of good, and when the soul emerges from this illusion of evil, Lucifer resumes his original status as one of God's great Archangels'. For most people, angels are the embodiment of divine or unconditional love. We connect with this energy through the Heart and they are the epitome of good in the astral worlds. If we are to work within the astral we can do no better than call upon this radiant, nonjudgemental and pure energy to assist our task.

Lower Astral

When the veils between the layers of energies start dissolving, many students have had the experience of the rather disturbing lower astral energies. On numerous occasions I have had students tell me they see faces, particularly when they are trying to go to sleep. These faces are not ones that they recognize; they stare closely as if they were in an invisible zoo looking out from their invisible cages. These have been called 'lost souls'. They can cause no harm other than the reaction of fear that they might induce. Of the many souls that have left this earth, some, for whatever reason, are unable to move swiftly on to the higher reaches of the spirit worlds. These then wander around and any person whose energy is beginning to open to the astral world is likely to come upon them. In Christian terms these are the souls asleep until the trumpets of judgement will awaken them. As the student begins to work more clearly in his or her own Heart and light, these experiences will very quickly dissolve.

Among the energies in the lower astral are some who also want to cause mischief to those they can communicate with on the earth plane. These souls masquerade as divine beings. They can only attach themselves through one's ego and incompetence. They will tell you all sorts of far-fetched things. Usually they give themselves important names: Egyptian gods, famous people in history, or some name that has particular importance to the recipient. Maintain your common sense at all times. Remember, the higher the energy, the less likely it even has a name. A good and important rule to remember is that no benevolent being will ever tell you what to do.

Here on the lower astral you may encounter the atmosphere of seedy places and people who have succumbed to acts of debauchery. All sorts of unsavoury places and people such as drunks, drug abusers and those who

I once worked with a lovely genuine medium. However, she started going through a very turbulent time in her emotional life and, to my surprise, suddenly told me that she was channelling the Dalai Lama. Upon hearing what he was supposed to be saying it was obvious that this was certainly not the Dalai Lama or any person like him. She unfortunately very soon afterwards had a complete nervous breakdown and had to give up her mediumship work. This energy was undoubtedly from the lower astral. So good are these energies at causing their mischief and masquerading as something they are not, that even experienced mediums may from time to time fall foul of them, either due to some unresolved fear or, like the aforementioned lady, when they are going through some negative fear-based emotional and personal experience.

have lost, for whatever reason, their dignity and their true sense of self. Occasionally these astral energies may try to influence a living person, usually one who is similarly overcome with drugs, liquor, fear or malevolent thoughts or actions. Unfortunately when they do, they strive to draw the person into further degradation and debauchery. Beings resident on the lower astral will eventually become bored or sickened by their state. It is believed that the disgust and revulsion for such things will then lead them to a desire to move forward into a more pleasant area of the astral. Alternatively, the experience sets up a desire for reincarnation whereby they may find themselves again in a similar negative energy. Just as it is possible and desirable to shake off one's darker traits here on the material plane, so it is in the astral. In nearly all cases 'living out' results in 'out living' and even the lowest energies are likely to raise their vibration over time.

Mediumship and the Afterlife

The most common communication with the astral is through a medium who contacts the dead. It is believed that when someone dies, their astral body continues and is registered on the astral plane, where the medium is able to link with them by shifting their consciousness. When psychics connect with this particular frequency they literally become mediums of communication between the two worlds.

Mediumship can be a joyous art in that it connects people with their loved ones and gives great comfort. For self and spiritual development it also offers an opportunity for some release from hurt, fear or pain. Arguably, the most valuable part of this work is when some issue caused by a departed parent, lover or friend can, through this contact, be expunged and therefore free the client from what may be a lifetime of misunderstanding and hurt. Sometimes the medium can use the link to allow both the person in spirit and the sitter to communicate so that some unresolved negative influence can be dissolved and profound healings can take place. We, as psychics and mediums, can only present an opportunity. We cannot make and should not wish to make the sitter do anything that they would not want.

This was made abundantly clear when many years ago I had an elderly lady come to me and immediately I made the link I felt a very strong connection to her mother. When I relayed this she shouted, 'send her away'. At the same time her mother in spirit was frantically telling me that she had had to put her up for adoption at the age of two because she could not, in days before social security, look after her properly. It was a very difficult decision for her, and had caused her great distress. Unfortunately the sitter would not allow me to relay this. She continued to shout at me to send her mother away and said if I continued with the link, she would walk out! She asked how could any mother do such a thing, and said that her mother ruined her life by giving her away. Because the sitter would not listen I could not explain the circumstances of her mother's decision. The bitterness of this lady was palpable. She was elderly, probably in her late 70s; I wondered if, in this lifetime, she would be able let go of the pain that she had carried all her life. I felt desperately sad that a real opportunity was lost. However, this was her choice.

The process of separation of the spirit when it breaks free from the physical body at the time of death has been described as the breaking of the silver cord, that is, of the etheric string that binds us to the physical body. There is a reference to this in the Bible (Ecclesiastes XII. 6) where death is spoken of as the time when 'the silver cord be loosened'. Much has been said about what happens next. It seems that the soul is greeted by either a light being, or a loved one already in the spirit world. This could be a husband or wife, mother or father, or someone whom the individual has loved and trusted.

We tend to believe that sudden death is preferable and is the best way to leave the physical body. A conclusion, no doubt, born out of compassion and of not wanting our loved ones to suffer any unnecessary pain. From a physical perspective this may well be true, however, from the spiritual point of view it may be quite the opposite. There are many documented cases of spirits turning up at their homes, not knowing they are dead, particularly in the case of a sudden accident. And according to many accounts from mediums, sudden death can make the transition very traumatic. Therefore it is likely that the better way for the transition from the physical planes to the astral ones, are when death comes gradually, as in old age when perhaps the person is spending more and more time asleep. In sleep they are in an astral state that leads them closer and closer to breaking free from the physical world.

What happens next depends greatly on the level of consciousness of the person who has recently departed. It works as a type of magnetic force and this attraction of energy means that each soul will be drawn to the energy and experience most conducive to them. It is my understanding that no two people have exactly the same experience, although generally they will be shown to a place wherein they come to terms with, and then exorcize, all the struggles of their life, and where they will become acclimatized to their new state. It is thought that the stages of the afterlife somewhat mirror our own, with seven levels, and whatever vibration you emanate will draw you naturally to the similar level in the astral.

The 1930s medium Geraldine Cummins gave titles to these levels. She was an author, playwright and medium who wrote 22 books, 15 of which were transmitted or dictated in the form of automatic or inspirational writing. *The Road to Immortality*, in which the seven levels of the afterlife are described, purports to be coming by means of mediumship from the departed FWH Myers, a scholar who founded the Society for Psychical Research in 1882. The seven layers contain details of how the soul may progress through to higher spiritual levels or planes. They may also be read as levels of spiritual progression on the earth plane that have a correlation with other models. (*See* Chapter Five.) Using the titles of Cummins, here we look at these levels:

Matter

Upon passing into spirit the soul acknowledges the actions, feelings, thoughts and situation of their physical lives:

M any years ago I went to a talk by a wonderful medium, now passed, who referred at length to the level that Cummins calls Matter. She gave a comprehensive description of what it was like. She explained that very soon after passing, we all experience our lives again, rather like a sensorama film. The difference being that in this instance, not only do we experience our lives, but also the effect we had on others. We will feel and think what the other person felt and thought, in connection to our behaviour towards them. Through this process we are able to fully understand just what effect we had on everyone in our lives, acknowledging what harm or good we did. This seemed rather startling, however, she went on to say that most of us, far from finding mainly bad things, the recently passed are most often surprised by just how much happiness and good they have done in their lives: things we don't even think about, what we did for our family, smiles we gave to neighbours and friends. The generosity of spirit we have shown in our lives without even thinking much about it. She said that most souls are basically good, and therefore the good we have done far outweighs the bad.

Judgement

After the previous experience the soul can be purified. Choice is made here, not by our desires or selfish hopes or fears, but by the quality of our vibrations. It is thought that at this point we can quickly return to life through reincarnation, or spend some time in the many layers of the astral worlds. Many mediums will tell you that people who have taken their own lives, will quickly return to the earth plane to continue what they had not finished in their cut-short lives.

Summerland

This is the layer through which most mediums communicate. It is here that the soul can literally create its own reality from desires. You often hear mediums describe the place where the loved one is residing as a garden or some other beautiful place surrounded by love. This is the reality of the departed; perhaps in their life, they loved their garden, so in the astral world they have chosen to recreate it. Here the soul's surroundings are only limited by its own mental and spiritual development. During the sojourn in Summerland the soul comes to recognize itself in a much more objective fashion, at the same time realizing how it could live more fully if it used its untapped potential. Timing in the afterlife is often perceived very differently from our own time. However, it is not thought to be healthy for any soul to reside in Summerland for any great length of time. It might be that the soul literally waits for another loved one to pass, before they themselves move on.

On this level the impression the medium has is of a real living being. The sense is that the person in spirit is just as real as we are. They may see the person vividly, however, not always how they were at the time of death; often the departed reveal themselves at an age when they felt at their best. It is for this reason that discovering the age of the person in spirit is

---

I once came across a soul in spirit who had been a miser in his life. In spirit he had a huge amount of money that he spent years and years counting! This puts aside the notion that you can't take it with you! Actually, here you can create anything that you want. Another experience I had was coming across a World War II pilot, who had put himself in a mess room exactly like the one where he had spent so many hours and days before he had died. He had surrounded himself with other young pilots who had also died. This was a place where, in his short life, he had some respite from the anxiety of the war, so this place was recreated in the astral.

---

problematic. If the medium links to the departed before they arrive in Summerland, the most likely impression they will have is of exactly what experience the departed had prior to death. Here in Summerland, the soul will already have left behind the possible traumas of their own death and put themself in a place of peace. As time passes there is a natural process of disintegration and all that has gone before fades. The soul has less and less desire to be connected to the earth plane. Having whatever you want eventually loses its attraction and increasingly the spiritual aspect grows.

Colour and Light

At this point the soul has lost its interest in having everything it wants and is bored with what has now become illusion land. It then makes a conscious decision to move onwards. No longer subject to illusory ideals it is now sensing the wonder of the Source, the light, universal consciousness or whatever descriptive word you wish to use for the highest possible energy in the universe. The deceased is shedding their outer image, and consequently mediumship on this level has no form with which to link. Communication is therefore only on a mental level. This energy is equivalent to the unconditional Heart level, described earlier. It is the alignment to light, thus creating a prism-like energy echoing all colours of the spectrum.

Flame

Here, most, if not all, old worn-out ideas from the earthly life are resolved and discarded, and worldly ambitions are left behind. There is a burning up and burning out of the old mental energies. If the soul reaches this level, the vibration is such that negativities and old patterns can be purified much more quickly and more easily than a lifetime of therapy in the material world. This stage is a full dissolution of the individual state, and group consciousness occurs through the purification flame of Source. Gradually through an attraction of energies, other souls are brought together and they then stay until there is a critical mass of group soul energy, enabling them to move forward. Mediumship on this level is communication with a group soul; the teachers, angels and hierarchy of divine beings whose sole purpose is to advance consciousness.

W hen I was working as a medium, I had a client who wanted me to contact a friend of hers who had passed the year before. I opened up the channels and immediately felt enveloped in the most wonderful white light. There were no words and no thoughts, just absolute joy. I felt this somehow to be the energy of this lady's friend and I knew that she had completely let go of any image or personality. I relayed this to my client. She said that she was a bit disappointed not to be able to talk with her but could completely understand my description, as her friend had been the most saintly woman, who had lived her life in complete love. I felt I had linked to a very high level of 'white light'. If everyone could experience this energy it would certainly take away any fear of dying.

White Light
This is a stage of pure reason. All emotions and desires as known by humanity have gone, replaced by the aligned true desires and pure thoughts. Beings here are capable of living as white light without any form. Mediumship with this level would be conceptual and inspirational only.

Timelessness
Oneness with all that is. From this we emanated and to this we will all eventually return. This is pure thought, pure light and absolute truth to which we all aspire.

My understanding of these levels is not that we all go through them one by one, but automatically we are drawn, by the attraction of our energy, to the level at which our consciousness is attuned. It might be, for instance, that the aforementioned lady never went through the lower levels but having cleared negativities and fear during her human life, and no longer subject to material desires, she moved directly to the fifth or sixth level. By the time we have become encased in the sixth level of white light, any human desire would be eliminated and the need or want to reincarnate would disappear. Most mystics, occultists and spiritual teachers agree that the highest level is beyond description, where we become at complete oneness with the divine Source, at which point all personal hopes and fears completely dissolve away. We are encased in all that is, with no earthly needs or desires. The self is completely obliterated and we are just light.

Trance

Trance has many purposes and states. It can be self-induced or may even occur involuntarily. For instance, one can automatically go into a form of trance whilst sounding a mantra or chant. Dancing to a rhythmic drumbeat or music may also induce a state of trance. Its meaning is from the Latin *transire* to 'pass over' or 'to cross', and simply put, it is when someone is in an altered state of consciousness. Therapists, including hypnotherapists, psychiatrists, psychotherapists, psychologists and NPL practitioners, among others, sometimes use a form of trance. It is used as a relaxation or inspirational energy to aid a healing process and can also be utilized for planting suggestions into the minds of people in trance. This can be for good or ill.

In meditation it could be considered that one is in a form of trance, however, it can also occur when doing the most mundane and repetitive things. If one is driving for instance, on a familiar and well-used route, the driver may go into an autopilot state. It can also be observed in athletes and dancers, when fully centred in their action they are operating in a trance-like state.

There are many accounts of mystics, seers and religious figures going into trance to obtain information. The classic one is the seer at Delphi in ancient Greece, who was trained in the art of inducing trance for divinatory purposes. In mediumship we talk about a state of trance when an entity in the spirit or astral world takes control of the medium. In early spiritualism, around the beginning of the 20th century, it was a common occurrence for the medium to give up full control to a spiritual entity. This necessitated a complete devotion and a lifestyle similar to that of a nun, for as the entity takes over the body, the physical aspects of the entranced medium are affected. For early spiritualists it was thought to be a way of convincing the public that a higher being was bringing forth greater forms of knowledge that could not otherwise be obtained.

Full trance is a very particular form of mediumship and, in my opinion, should only be considered on the rarest of occasions. It might sometimes bring through higher teachings, however, these can be obtained in other safer ways (*see* Chapter Five). It is particularly problematic to know for certain from whom one is receiving contact, and that the entity is what they purport to be. It is certainly not for the inexperienced medium for many reasons, the main one being that it is very easy for a lower astral energy, masquerading as someone else, to speak through an untrained medium. This can bring a variety of problems including sometimes physical or mental illness.

Long-practising shamans have an advantage here, for they have built up over many generations a powerful link with their ancestors, whom they know and trust. Various tribal peoples around the world use some form of shamanism. 'Shaman' was a word that was originally applied to the semi-religious practices of certain Siberian tribes, and later used for tribal cultures across the globe. Shamans in trance are thought to leave their bodies, and it was noted by missionaries at the turn of the 20th century that they seemed to rely on a technique of ecstasy involving a close relationship with the spirits. It is not hard to imagine the reaction of the missionaries to these activities! They were of course convinced that trance was the work of the devil and set out in earnest to eradicate the practice, and to convert the people to what they considered more godly pursuits. As education was brought into these new lands and the peoples gradually became more Westernized, their use of trance as a way of life somewhat decreased. It is interesting and perhaps amusing to note that from the turn of the 20th century, as tribal peoples became more Westernized, spiritualism, which is similar in principle, was becoming popular in the West. Thus, as the white man laboured self-righteously to expunge a form of spiritualism from foreign lands, it was already taking root at home!

Shamanism in all its forms has subsequently enjoyed a revival and is popular in Britain and in the USA, where they have the rich background of the Native American energy upon which to draw. In this culture they consider their dreams to be of no psychological significance, rather they regard them as journeys into distant worlds, or visions to warn and help their tribe. It is therefore not surprising that many mediums have attracted personal spirit guides who are thought to be of Native American origin.

Full trance requires a synchronizing of energies between the astral entity and the medium. This means that there will be some depletion of the medium's physical energy and so they need to be of a physically robust nature because he or she is literally taking on the vibrations of a different entity, which will disturb the bodily frequencies. The old-school trance mediums were very tough indeed, with many of them living to great age. Many people simply do not have the correct constitution and therefore are not equipped for this task. Those without the necessary physical as well as emotional and mental temperament can become ill, and even if you are strong and able to take on this rarefied type of work it can take as long as seven years for the body to adapt.

An old argument in favour of trance work was that in this state, less of the medium's ego personality was present, and therefore more spiritual information would be received. However, even in full trance there is always something of the medium present and there are other ways of dropping the personality without completely giving away control. There are indeed so many illusions, dangers and glamour involved in this form of work, that unless you are 100 per cent confident and have a fully experienced teacher, it is better to steer clear altogether. The medicine wheels of the shamans are set up to make communication with a specific spirit, as a kind of ceremonial service to spirits through ritual and symbols. In this way they contact the appropriate energy, making any mismatch less likely.

There is a great mystique around the idea of an entity or spirit speaking through a medium, and many people seem to throw caution to the wind with the expectation and excitement of it. For the inexperienced it can seem very glamorous to have a being from another world communicating through you. It should nonetheless be borne in mind that having a conversation with a party who happens to be in the astral or spirit world does not automatically mean they have a better or more knowledgeable view of the truth. Shamans draw upon the knowledge of their ancestors, which is commendable, but do their ancestors have all the answers either? They can only speak, as any of us do, from their own perspective, which may be wholly irrelevant for us in the modern world. We must always come back to the essential awareness that no one has the right to rule us, and it is foolish to surrender our control to any being, living, dead or however high they may be. The fact is that no genuine advanced being would ask this of you anyway.

Unfortunately, one of the most reckless things that I have come across is when a person (even someone in a development circle) is asked to open up in a trance state and wait for any entity to speak through them. This is rather like picking a telephone number at random and expecting the person at the other end to be a higher being with all the answers. This sort of pot-luck activity is highly dangerous and is certainly not to be recommended. Some people think it fun to try a random connection, but since very few people are without negativity, and like attracts like, this can in some cases attract a dubious entity. The effect of this sort of unsuitable communication is also highly disruptive, both to the physical body and to the nervous system. A bad link formed in a trance condition can take days, weeks or even years to sever.

Trance mediumship did have a rightful place, particularly in the first half of the 20th century. However, in my opinion, if you will forgive the pun, it is a dying art. As we move on into strange and exciting changes on all levels in our world there are other more expansive challenges and opportunities for the medium. If you are determined to open up into a trance state, whether it is for mediumistic purposes or for health concerns, make sure that you know where your therapist and your energies are connecting to first. Carelessness in this work will effectively create an unstable spiritual time bomb destined for unpredictable but inevitable detonation. Any form of psychic work, particularly mediumship, requires years of training and dedication if one is to remain stable in all situations.

A medium who wishes to work in trance needs a good wholesome and grounded teacher. Never be afraid to walk away from a teacher you find to be insufficient. A good teacher for one person may not be the right one for you. Also, be somewhat wary of any teacher who demands a following, as they are more than likely to be deficient at best and dangerous at worst. And, like any other walk of life, there are unfortunately some complete charlatans. Implement your good sense at all times. It's not so much that there are many charlatans in this field, although unfortunately there are some. The danger largely lies in the fact that even people who put themselves up as teachers, may be well-meaning but may themselves lack the sufficient experience and knowledge required. At all times, implement your highest will. Asking for only that which is the *highest greatest good* is a valuable mantra and focus for all psychic work, and is particularly necessary in the astral worlds.

If you are still set on this form of psychic communication you can assist the connection by visualizing a symbol, or a name, as a kind of password in the astral. Create the thought around what you desire and perpetuate the energy constantly. Even when you are working 100 per cent for the purpose of the higher good, when you finish with your symbol, whether through loss of interest or when you no longer use it, this energetic gateway will remain open. Without focus running through it, a vacuum will have been created. This vacuum will be filled, and it can just as easily be replaced with a disruptive negative force. So if you choose to work in this way make sure you put in some form of energetic safety clause, and agree with an angelic energy or guide that when you have finished with the connection it will dissolve in light (*see* also next chapter).

Occasionally, through weakness of character, a person will invite a dark entity to them, believing that this will give them power, to make them rich overnight or to confer upon them some unearned status. Nothing comes from nothing, and everything that happens to you is a result of the energy you emit. If there is no generating energy then there will be no manifestation of wealth or power. If some power is initially received, this will be transient and cause suffering. People who appear to get rich overnight have, in fact, gained this money over many years or perhaps lifetimes, their riches accruing within the astral bank.

The reason that one would be tempted to use darker forces is clear. What is less clear is the temptation to use bliss. Bliss and ecstasy states are thought to be the province of saints, usually brought about by a sudden revelation of God. This bliss state, surprisingly, is remarkably easy to create. Positively, a bliss or ecstasy experience can serve the purpose of allowing a very closed mind to see the higher possibilities of life. However, the desire for bliss is often born out of glamour, as discussed earlier. Unfortunately it can also become an excuse for abandoning the material world and of relinquishing responsibility; this is not the spiritual way. We are not meant to abdicate our material responsibilities. Our very purpose is to evolve and grow in all aspects of our being. Growth does not come without fully embracing life as it is, and taking charge of one's own energy.

Some people achieve a bliss or ecstasy state through attending workshops, usually led by a charismatic leader. It is remarkably easy to manipulate this kind of energy and have people eating out of your hand, thinking you are some kind of divine being. Some leaders are unaware that they are manipulating the public in this way. They reason that everyone seems to be having a good time so it's OK, but it isn't. It becomes like a drug and after the initial burst of pleasure it will diminish and they then want more. It teaches them nothing, for bliss states, born from trance or astral connection, cannot be sustained. Usually after such an astrally contrived experience after 24 or 48 hours there is a huge anticlimax and the individual comes down from the drug of bliss. Unfortunately they will then crave another bliss fix and may fall prey to any unscrupulous charismatic individual who can provide it. These people are seeking a form of entertainment or happening and are unlikely to be ready to take on full commitment to the spiritual path. They believe, because of the strength of the bliss, that they are not only following the spiritual path but are quite a long way along it!! Rarely will anyone be the best judge of how far they have reached spiritually and indeed others are also rarely, if ever, equipped to give this information either.

Mass meetings where ecstasy states occur in some religious context also have the same effect. Hysteria with much fainting and wailing may occur and naive people believe this is somehow God speaking to them. These experiences, if they happen, must be directed positively or they can disastrously carry both the receivers and the implementers away from all reality. Spirituality is about balance, which, far from meaning that one must abandon the physical world, means we must embrace it and work within it to aid the evolution of spirit. If we were in a state of bliss all the time, we would progress very little.

Sometimes the enthusiasm for the spiritual journey will take you into areas that can deter you from your true path. Once the bliss experience dies, it will leave a vacuum which, as we have seen, can so easily be filled by a negative force. When one comes down from this state it will occasionally lead to depression as you look around and see the imperfections of life and think you do not want to be part of it anymore. Suicide, can in a few cases, seem like the only option.

It is the differences and imperfections in people that make them interesting and from which we can all learn the most. Life may not be easy, however, it can be a joy. Joy is the true essence of love and love is achieved through intelligent thought, compassion and balance. When you truly ask for the highest greatest good to work through you, this affirms that you are prepared to accept whatever that means. This may lead you away from glamour, but in its place you will find the permanent richness of balance and truth. There are many beings, both on the earth and the astral planes that would tempt us for their own ends or amusement. It's important to keep your eye on the goal of furthering your human state and not to abandon it.

CHAPTER FIVE

Channelling and Inspiration

Let no one persuade you to do evil or associate with evil in order that good may come of it and you may obtain knowledge. Never believe that any initiator of the right-hand path will require it of you.

Dion Fortune

Guides and Teachers

Where do we go for higher knowledge? Whom can we trust to assist us with the unseen forces with which we work as mediums and psychics? As in all areas of life we need advisors to help us along the way. For this reason, trainee mediums are often urged to find a teaching guide. This guide will be resident on the astral plane and will hopefully steer and work with you to further your spiritual knowledge and guard against adverse energies. The necessity, therefore, to attract the right energy with which to work is of paramount importance. Any energy the individual attracts is likely to be drawn by their own attraction of energy. Like attracts like. In those early days of astral connection this energy may only have a limited knowledge and it is common to hear from students that their guides have a very strong personality. Who or what are these beings? Are they really who they purport to be? Or are they an aspect of the individual's own personality?

We have seen in Chapter Three how thought-forms can be created and, given enough energy, will take on a life of their own. Are some of our guides just thought-forms? Through contact with this energy, whatever it is, we may be able to access a higher sense or knowledge. Mediums speak to their guides, but those with mental illnesses often talk to a secondary personality too! What is the difference? This question might seem anathema to those who adamantly believe in the spirit world, however these questions are important to ask. It is not relevant here to go into any depth as to the differences between mystical experiences and psychotic ones. However, it is worth relaying that the outward signs of 'spiritual emergence' and 'psychotic illness' are remarkably similar. Stanislav Grof, researcher of the scientific understanding of consciousness, author and teacher, says in *The Stormy Search for the Self*:

> Since modern psychiatry does not differentiate between mystical or spiritual states and psychotic episodes, people experiencing these states are often diagnosed as mentally ill, hospitalized and subjected to routine suppressive pharmacological treatment.

Far from being a mental problem, Grof and others suggest that many of these cases are actually psycho-spiritual crises. Equally, those who are either not intelligent enough, or have some unresolved psychological problems, may find that they are hearing voices which are not genuine guides, but a personality built from unconscious desires. Therefore the need for a sound teacher both on the earth plane and the astral plane is clear. I am always wary when I hear someone say my guide 'told' me this or that. It smacks to me of an abdication of personal responsibility and spiritual progress has no room for relinquishing responsibility. Releasing negative patterns and fear means we have a clearer energy and are therefore more likely to attract a clearer guide or energy to assist us. It is not uncommon for a trainee psychic to initially feel the presence of a loved and trusted soul in spirit. This aids reassurance for the medium, however, a question to ask is, does this trusted person have more spiritual knowledge than you?

Nonetheless, once you open up to spiritual forces you are likely to attract some kind of spiritual guide, and there is a feeling amongst mediums that there are specific spiritual beings that will assist us in this work. Whatever the energy is that assists us, we as humans need a form, so the medium will give the guide structure in order to see it in the conscious mind. This form often takes on an archetypal personality such as a wise Chinese man, a Native American, or Egyptian priest or priestess. You as a medium will grow, and just as a child starting in kindergarten needs one set of teachers, later on the needs change and a more advanced teacher is required. So it is with guides and teachers, and you will need a guide with knowledge that you can understand. As you grow so will your guides and teachers. It is preferable therefore, not to become too dependent on any specific guide energy.

Any guiding energy is likely to be only a little ahead of you in energy and knowledge. A loved one in spirit is probably a good place to start, and then one guide will, as it were, hand over to another and another as you evolve. One of the arguments put forward for having strong contact with a specific guide is that you can never be fooled if they are present. Unfortunately this is not the case, as it is very easy for a lower astral energy to masquerade as a higher being, as we discussed in the previous chapter. The content of communication will quickly tell you if this is happening, but even the most competent medium can sometimes be fooled.

This is one of the many areas of the work where people often seem to lose their intelligence. It does not matter what name a guide is giving or from where it originated. The question you must ask is, whether this information is ringing the bell of truth within my heart? If it is, then listen to it. If it is not, do not be swayed by the name of the guide. Listen to the song, not the singer, and if you feel it is not right for you then leave it alone. Think for yourself. It really is not good practice to relinquish your energy and control to anyone, no matter what name they give you or whether they purport to come from earth or from some wonderful-sounding place in the cosmos. There is no benevolent being in the cosmos that would make you do anything against your will; free will is sacrosanct in spiritual law.

Sometimes the presence of an angel-like being is felt. Angelic energies, if they are true, register on the note of the Heart, unconditional love, and, as such, they are generally good guiding and protecting energies to work with. As with other deities, saints and guides, we have given them names and qualities; here below are some of the archangels and healing energy associated with them:

Michael is heaven's defender. He battles against evil. He was thought to be the giver of the Ten Commandments and has often been called for at the time of death. He regenerates the body and is called the Prince of Light. It is foretold in the Book of Daniel that when the world is really in danger, Michael will once again appear. He was said to be the original slayer of the dragon, whose connections are with the earth. Many ancient sites are focal points of what has been called dragon power. There is thought to be an energy line running across England known as the Michael line. Michael seems to have a connection with England, and some believe that our patron saint St George's energy was transferred from the energy of the archangel Michael. (*See The Sun and the Serpent* by Paul Broadhurst and Hamish Miller). For healing purposes call on Michael for strength over adversary.

Gabriel The name means governor or power. Gabriel is the only angel who is sometimes referred to as being female. Mostly angels are seen as androgynous. Gabriel is the angel of truth and sits of the left side of God. He is the bringer of good news, particularly of births. It is said that Gabriel worked with the genes of early mankind and that Adam and Eve were his first experiments. For healing purposes call on Gabriel for conception and infertility.

Raphael is particularly associated with healing. Artists such as Botticelli, Titian and Rembrandt have depicted him. He is the protector of travellers and is the guardian of the tree of life in Eden. Raphael is the healer of the earth and an angel of the sun. He is seen to have a sunny disposition and apparently, if needs be, will guide you through hell. Call on Raphael for help with creative pursuits and any general healing.

Uriel is the angel of repentance, music and poetry. He interprets prophecies. His is a very fiery character and has been associated with absolute righteousness. He watches over thunder and terror. He is the perfectionist. He believes in order and it is said that on the Day of Judgement

---

O f all the mediums I have worked with, the most dedicated and, in my opinion, the one with most integrity was a lady called Ivy Northage, now deceased. In my earlier days as a working medium I had a few sittings with her during which her guide, called Chan, spoke to me with wisdom and strength. This lady had dedicated most of her life to true mediumship and allowed herself to be tested under strict scientific methods. There was no doubt of her honesty and integrity. At the end of the very last reading she gave me, I could distinctly see the presence of Chan and, as she finished, I watched Chan dissolve into her. I told her this. 'Yes,' she said, 'I still don't really know if Chan is actually a part of myself.' 'Whatever he is,' I replied 'the inspiration speaks for itself.'

Later this sentiment was echoed in her book, *Mediumship Made Simple*:

> I questioned Chan's reality. Was it part of myself hitherto untapped? I questioned him about this. He said, he was not in the least concerned whether people thought it was he or I as long as they listened to what we had to say.

---

he will destroy the bars of the gates of Hades, of which he is a doorkeeper. Milton, in *Paradise Lost*, describes him as the sharpest sighted spirit of all in heaven. Call on the healing energy of Uriel for clear inspiration and insight.

Raquel is the friend of God and watches over behaviours. He is the angel of earth and guardian of the second heaven. He is also associated with justice. Raquel will assist with healing and help for any legal or unfair situations.

Sariel (Saraqael) Sometimes depicted as one of the fallen angels, he redeemed himself in the war between the sons of light and darkness, as one of the fighting units of the sons of light. A good energy perhaps if you feel you have transgressed.

Remiel is the angel of hope and true visions.

Metatron is the angel of many eyes. A heavenly scribe, he is said to watch and record everything. His name could be derived from Mentor in Greek mythology, now a term for a 'guide' or 'measurer'. Another suggestion is the name consists of two Greek words for 'after' and 'throne' and therefore

---

When I knew Ivy, she was already an elderly lady and she would often say to people, 'when I die I am not coming back and nor is Chan, so if anyone says they are in contact with me they are either lying or mistaken'. As someone who had dedicated her life to mediumship I thought this rather strange and asked her why. She said, 'My time is to move on and I am not going to hang around.' At which level in the spirit world she is now resident I couldn't say, but I would hazard a guess it is one beyond the personality state, where we cannot make contact via personalities.

---

is described as, 'one who occupies the throne next to the throne of glory'. Metatron is mentioned in the Talmud and medieval mystical texts. He is seen as a guide and teacher.

In all of our work as psychics and mediums we must ask questions. Blind faith can make us blind and will not bring clear vision.

Channelling

In the past, mediums talked about 'inspirational speaking', a practice that has more recently come under the heading of 'channelling'. Channelling is a means of gaining access to higher knowledge. The medium will open their own channel of energy to allow information to flow through them. Healers also allow a flow of energy that aids health and wellbeing, and as such can also be classed as channellers.

The ancient Greeks were inspired by their muses, and information has also come inspirationally to many mystics down the ages. St John drew on his own experiences to reveal, 'important stages in the believer's developmental progression towards union with God'. This art, it seems, is not just given to the religious, but also many writers, poets, philosophers and musicians. William Blake spoke of his composing of the poem 'Jerusalem', whose words are used for England's patriotic hymn, as 'being dictated'. He said: 'I may praise it, as I dare not pretend to be any other than the secretary – the authors are in eternity.' Plato said:

> All good poets composed their beautiful poems not by art, but because they are inspired and possessed. There is no invention in him until he has been inspired and is out of his senses.

The poet Walt Whitman also said that his writings came from some supreme power, as did Francis Bacon, to name just a few.

Is it possible that all the many inspirations through the ages come from the same source? Whatever the beliefs of the individual are at the time, the source is ascribed to either an Eastern or Christian deity, angel or some other name. In this way, people who receive messages from an inspirational source feel they could be as easily interpreted to be from Allah or Yahweh or Christ or any other religious being. The sense the medium has whilst channelling is often felt to be beyond words; a sense of oneness with a higher energy. This is not dissimilar to any mystical experience where information is received, or there is simply a feeling of a profound connection with something beyond the mundane; powerful and intrinsically divine.

William James lists the characteristics of mystical experience as: 'indescribability, spiritual experience of ultimate truth, instability and passivity.' He describes his own experience by saying: 'I was in heaven, an inward state of peace and joy and assurance indescribably intense, accompanied with a sense of being bathed in a warm glow of light.' Under the description of a noetic quality, which generally is a form of mental perception, James indicates that these experiences are not related to the intellect in the usual sense:

> Although so similar to states of feeling, mystical states seem
> to those who experience them to be also states of knowledge.
> They are states of insight into depths of truth unplumbed by the
> discursive intellect. They are illuminations, revelations, full of
> significance and importance, all inarticulate though they remain,
> and as a rule, they carry with them a curious sense of authority.

In researching mystical teachings and models of spiritual development I have been struck by the similarity of content and meaning coming from completely different backgrounds across the globe, and in completely different times. These include: the Christian mystic St John of the Cross, who gave us three major stages of spiritual progress; the Qabalah; the mystical side of Judaism that has 22 levels or stages of growth; the chakras, St Teresa's Mansions, and Geraldine Cummins have seven levels or stages; and in Ken Wilber's work, *Integral Psychology* there are 11 charts with well over 100 models or maps of spiritual self-progress defined by various systems, including by philosophers, psychologists, mystical and religious writers.

It is particularly interesting that both St Teresa's 'Mansions', and the chakras both have seven levels or stages. These models were written 3,000 years apart. By St Teresa's own description she was inspired by God, and the mode in which she received the information might well be a description of what we now call channelling. We can't know exactly where and how the chakra information was first received, as it is part of the Upanishads, most of which were written down over 3,000 years ago. Indeed the Upanishads are one of the earliest writings known. What is certain is that both these models have inspired thousands of people since their inception. What is going on here? Is it that there are some truths which defy time? Is it part of some perennial knowledge? Or is it that spiritual truths are innately within us all? Channelled material does not always have a consensus on this, and although generally most mystics believe that some part of a god or higher state is present within us all, others refute this concept. For instance Cummins wrote, 'it is a preposterous presumption on the part of the mystic to call his own spirit God'.

As a matter of interest let us briefly, compare and contrast the chakra model of energies with the Mansions model of St Teresa of Avila.

The Chakra System

This system has a long legitimate legacy and is frequently used in psycho-spiritual experiential exercises. It is a dynamic system acting as an energetic spiral pathway of personal and spiritual growth. Its purpose includes describing and inspiring spiritual evolution. It can be perceived as initiation stages upon the mystical spiritual paths, which indicate shifts of consciousness and change of perceptions for personal spiritual growth.

Mansions

This is a mystical theology of the soul's journey by a 16th-century European Christian nun and mystic, St Teresa of Avila. St Teresa spent the majority of her life in a closed order and was educated in art, literature and basic reading and writing. She received the inspiration for the 'Mansions' whilst at prayer and contemplation. She saw a very clear crystal globe, made in the shape of a castle, which contained seven rooms she called, Mansions. Teresa interpreted this castle as the soul. The model was used to describe the course of the mystical life and the soul's progress beginning with the castle where there was no communication with God and where life was 'foul and dark', on into the Mansions, ultimately leading to the seventh where the soul transforms from an 'imperfect, sinful creature' coming in from the outside finally into the 'bride of the spiritual marriage'.

Bringing these concepts together, below is a diagram of four spiritual evolutionary models: Chakras, Mansions, and the models developed by Geraldine Cummins and myself. After which we compare and contrast St Teresa's Mansions and the Chakra model.

Chakras and Mansions
Stage One: Base/Humility
The Base chakra indicates an awareness of the self in the physical, mundane world. It is what connects us to our physical and material presence. In terms of development this is the instinctual energy that all living animals possess.

Models of Spiritual Development and Energy

CHAKRAS (Subtle Energy)	MANSIONS (St Teresa)	AFTERLIFE (Cummins)	INTUITION (Soskin)
1. **Base**	1. Humility	1. Matter	1. Instinctual
2. **Sacral**	2. Sin	2. Judgement	2. Tribal
3. **Solar Plexus**	3. Charity	3. Summerland	3. Personal Auric
4. **Heart**	4. Love	4. Colour and Light	4. Mediumship Empathy
5. **Throat**	5. Infused Contemplation	5. Flame	5. Inspirational Channelling
6. **Brow**	6. Visions	6. White Light	6. Vision
7. **Crown**	7. Union	7. Timelessness	7. Alignment

It is survival on the most basic of levels: how we feed ourselves, which in the modern world includes work; are we safe?; do we have warmth, clothing and our own space in which to live? Teresa's first stage, 'Humility' speaks of a resting time; a time needed for any temptation from the outer world to subside. This might suggest that Teresa does not think we are all automatically on a spiritual pathway, which differs from the chakra attitude that we are all journeying towards enlightenment, whether we are conscious of it or not.

For Teresa, there have already been major movements and change for an individual to reach the first Mansion. She speaks of the grace from God, which may have many different interpretations but could suggest some random unmerited favour from God. This concept may have been acceptable in the 16th century, however, is unlikely to be believed now, for there have been plenty of indications that people have had profound spiritual experiences who know little or nothing about the concept of God, and who, in Teresa's terms, lead 'sinful lives'. Is spiritual progress really that arbitrary? Intuitive experiences at this stage also have a physical aspect as they put us on alert to a 'sense' of physical danger like animals in the wild.

Stage Two: Sacral/Sin

The 'Sacral' second chakra is connected with creativity and emotions. This is the igniting energy. It is the rocket blast that gets us moving; the energy that gets us up in the morning, the energy that instigates action. It is also the sexual drive and passion, and it is interesting to note the title of Teresa's second stage 'Sin'. For a nun in her time, sexuality would not be seen in an open way and sex outside marriage was considered sinful. The chakras also correlate to physical areas of the body and the second centre is the reproductive area. Given that in Teresa's time most sexual encounters were deemed as 'sin of the flesh' could the title be connected? The second Mansion also infers an illusionary state when she talks about the problems of putting desire into practice and the horrors of the 'confusion the devil brings about'. For Teresa this is a time when temptation is still apparent and yet she encourages us not to lose heart, or cease striving to make progress for, 'even out of your fall God will bring good'.

The chakra model relays that personal ego and what are seen as lower desires are still very strong here, and any learning of self is likely to be achieved through relationships with others. Intuition here might develop through the sense of unity between the members of the family, tribe or society in which we live.

Stage Three: Solar Plexus/Charity

Teresa calls this stage 'Charity', and the Solar Plexus chakra relates to the 'little' or 'lower mind'. Teresa acknowledges the mind here also, with some degree of disparagement when she says: 'its love is still governed by reason and so its progress is slow'. In chakra terms the lower mental self, which could also be said to be governed by reason, is prominent.

Fear is also an element in the third chakra, which is connected in this stage by how we think about others and ourselves. The chakra model, and to a lesser extent the Mansions, also warns of the danger of identification with our roles in life. Intuition here could be developed through empathy and a deeper understanding of self and others. It is felt as 'a sense', having 'a hunch' and might induce discomfort because, paraphrasing John Rowan, 'it is as if we had no right to know things without proper evidence to back it up and we need to separate those intuitions we can trust from those that are fantasies'.

Stage Four: Heart/Love

Straight away we can see the correlation between Teresa and the chakra model in the titles. The fourth chakra is the 'Heart' and Teresa's fourth stage is 'Love'. The love of the Heart here is a love without judgement and is unconditional. It is love beyond emotions, which seems to echo in Teresa's fourth level. She says: 'It is where love is now free from servile fear, which has broken all the bonds which previously hindered its progress, it shrinks from no trials and attaches no importance to anything to do with the world.'

The Heart chakra is the first stage where the independent spirit is emerging. It is seen as the bridging point of departure between the lower mundane worlds and the higher spiritual realms. Similarly, Teresa says this is 'where the natural and supernatural unite'. In the chakras and Mansions the self is redefining itself, beginning to receive glimpses of the transcendent.

Many faiths in some way express that one can only reach God or enlightenment through embracing some form of divine love leading to the emergence of mature abilities. So for these authorities this stage appears to be guiding us towards a higher nature. Therefore intuition here senses inspiration through love and compassion.

Stage Five: Throat/Infused Contemplation
The fifth 'Throat' chakra takes us to a level of consciousness beyond the normal realms and it is associated with a higher form of spiritual communication. Equally, according to Teresa we have 'completely died to the world so that we may live more fully in God'. Her description seems similar to what the Theosophist spiritual teacher Krishnamurti calls a 'living meditation'. This means being in a constant state of spiritual awareness, where the spiritual connection is so ingrained it cannot be removed. Teresa concurs, talking of a union with God that is not the same as ultimate union, but one that has little chance of dissolving. She says the soul sleeps for a while giving the person 'a joy that is greater than all the joys of earth'. Intuition at Stage Five is a form of channelling of inspirational concepts. Teresa agrees but gives strong warning to discern whether the inspiration is truly godly and not 'from the devil who can make good use of imagination'.

It appears that as we go further up the ladder of consciousness we unpeel layer after layer, receiving longer and longer glimpses of the authentic self, bringing us further towards the divine. Both the chakras and Mansions give a sense of transmutation at this stage, whereby we can unite higher and lower states. It is at this stage that one receives profound contact with the unseen or psychic world. This concept is just as relevant in spiritual Self-awareness because until someone has had the experience themselves they are unable to understand or 'know' it in any deep sense. The danger here is not so much that higher inspiration can be found, but in the translation of the message. Nonetheless, intuition is thought to be more frequent and dependable here as the individual moves towards a greater trust of the authenticity of their message.

Stage Six: Brow/Visions

The 'Brow' centre is the energy of the priest or priestess, those who can see beyond the material planes. The very similarity of the titles here is interesting as the archetypal image of this centre is the third eye, an ancient Egyptian motif, which depicts visionaries. This stage includes psychic events and mystical experiences and is a stage that brings illumination, intuition and profound insights.

The sixth chakra state is the evolved person, the saint, seer or sage. The third eye motif illustrates the possibility of seeing beyond the clouds of the material world, to greater spiritual heights, and therefore having access to greater visions and insights. This is a state which is beyond any influence of society or family and suggests that here we are now moving beyond even the transpersonal, towards greater and greater alignment with our spiritual natures.

At first Teresa's title of the fifth stage, 'Vision' is perfectly in line with the chakra third eye visionary state. However, the sixth Mansion is very much more difficult to either compare or contrast as Teresa presents us with a long narrative on the perils of this stage, with several meandering pages which seem somewhat self-indulgent in nature. Nonetheless, she also talks about visions and again advises that they may not always be what they seem and that the ability to see beyond the material is not always a happy state as the 'true reality of our world overwhelms'.

That we can experience difficulties at any and every stage of development is clear, but Teresa labours the point, to the extent that it has the effect of distracting our thoughts away from the spiritual back to the personal. Teresa's description here is full of conflict, pain and anguish, and so personal is the writing, it occurs to me that Teresa believed herself to be at this stage. Intuition here is of a visionary nature and the individual embraces their intuition as a greater form of truth. Teresa alerts us to the difficulty in making sense of visions when they can be so different for different people. It could equally be argued that true visionaries are profoundly transforming to themselves, their communities and the world.

Stage Seven: Crown/Union

In chakra terms everything is known here, there is no doubt, no fear, and intuition leads us into the higher realms beyond the material view of the world, where visions and reality are aligned.

Teresa suggests a similar notion with the 'spiritual marriage being the deepest centre of the soul'. She places God firmly within this stage, as the soul for Teresa, 'must be where God himself dwells'. It is the divine mystical union of oneness with God, which many other mystics describe. In whatever way these models describe this last stage, it is clear they agree that it takes us to a state so different from the average consciousness it can bear no resemblance to the mundane world. In the Mansions it is the total dissolution of the personal through the absolute 'union' or 'marriage' with pure consciousness. In the chakras it is the total integration of spirit within our lives. It is where the higher will and the individual will unite.

These models portray spiritual development as some form of journey. Teresa says she puts the action completely in the hands of God with constant reference to 'God's grace' and 'if God is willing', and so on. She even says that no matter how strong you think you are, you cannot enter all the Mansions by your own efforts. Yet this statement is somewhat contradicted throughout as she also constantly implores us to make our own effort in resisting temptations and becoming discerning. This then implies that the individual, as well as God, has some effect on the spiritual journey and she describes a very contemporary stance in self-awareness: 'It is absurd to think that we can enter heaven without first entering our own souls, and without getting to know ourselves and reflecting upon our nature.'

It seems, therefore, that she also acknowledges the individual as taking an active part and not a submissive role in the process. Teresa clearly equates the final union as being so complete there is 'no difference between self and God', so for Teresa the soul has, in effect, been acting as a magnetic force throughout, drawing the individual towards the divine union. Teresa writes of the spiritual union: 'I used unexpectedly to experience a consciousness of the presence of God of such a kind that I could not possibly doubt that he was within me or that I was wholly engulfed in him.' This 'unexpected' experience is frequently noted by spiritual aspirants, however, few people are in permanent contact with it. As Teresa perceives the soul in its true state as God, we must assume that God for Teresa has been there all along.

As I delved deeper into the meaning of these spiritual models I was particularly struck by the similarities between the seven Mansions and the seven chakras, so much so that I was forced to ask the unlikely question of whether Teresa could have come across the Eastern concepts in her lifetime? It is believed for instance that Christian missionaries carried Yoga through India into China in the 5th century. Indeed, communication between East and West was much more prevalent through the ages than we imagine, through trading and missionaries. Whether Teresa had some Eastern knowledge we may never know, but if she didn't, why are these models so similar? Teresa states they are from God, which some modern channellers also claim. It is either an amazing coincidence, or alternatively it might give credit to the notion that there is some immortal universal collective consciousness. Does this then give credence to the notion of a perennial philosophy and evidence of a possible transcendent unity of religions?

Channelling is currently used to describe an array of communications with a higher source. In some cases the word 'channelling' is used to describe a form of trance mediumship, whereby the medium allows an entity to speak though them. There are some differences, however, the principal one being that trance mediumship usually occurs by the connection with a discarnate spirit, that is, someone who is deceased. Channelling can be obtained from a connection to entities or energies not necessarily having had a life on earth. More recently we have seen channellings from energies without any identity, but which originate from a universal consciousness. Being pedantic we could say that channelling is a form of trance, with the difference being that no separate entity is controlling the channeller's energy. From the medium's point of view the feeling of channelling is remarkably similar to that of a strong trance state; with most forms of highly connected mediumship the mediums do not remember the content of the material.

There are many accounts of mediums bringing through information of which they had no prior knowledge and displaying talents that they themselves did not possess. There was, for instance, the case of the well-known medium Pearl Curran, who channelled Patience Worth. Having little education, Pearl was virtually illiterate, and yet her mediumship produced poetry, novels and other literary compositions, works which were way beyond the skills of such a simple woman, as was her use of obscure Anglo-Saxon words whilst in trance. Where did these skills come from?

Whether even a full trance state completely eradicates the personality of the individual medium is a subject worthy of discussion. A simple, uncomplicated person with neither aspirations nor cares, can, in certain circumstances, make a better natural medium than a more sophisticated individual. An uncomplicated person is often free from the intellectual reasoning that will bring doubt to bear and therefore disable a link, which requires some form of surrender. Simpler people are often able to open freely without inhibitions, hence the flow of information is less impaired. However, it seems that to connect with energies beyond the astral requires intelligence, integrity and a permanent commitment to spiritual energies, especially within the real lived world of the medium. With the difficulties involved in trance work, increasingly the medium is asked to raise their consciousness to be able to connect to a higher source. Like attracts like. And if we raise our energies beyond the astral planes we may be able to bring through even higher inspirational messages.

Most modern religions have started and been perpetuated by some inspirational message from discarnate beings who have profoundly affected our societies and faiths. For example, in the Old Testament Moses received the Ten Commandments. Around 1000BC came Solomon, followed over a period of time by other prophets. Later in the New Testament we see John the Baptist receiving messages. Their channellings were often preceded by words such as, 'the word of the Lord came unto me'.

The Bible, mainly from St John 8, gives us various descriptive accounts of a form of channelling:

The words that I speak unto you they are spirit, ye are from beneath, I am from above, ye are of this world and I am not of this world. I do nothing of myself but as my Father hath taught me I speak these things and he that sent me is with me. He that is of God heareth God's words. The Father is in me and I in him … in my Father's house are many mansions … the words that I speak unto you I speak not of myself but the Father that dwelleth in me, he doeth the works for I have given unto them the word which the Father gavest me.

Note the phrase, 'my Father's house has many Mansions'. Is this likely to be the inspiration for St Teresa's model? The list of some form of channelled material is endless: Richard Rolle became known as the father of English mysticism through his channelling, which included transcendental music; Joseph Karo a Jewish mystic; Mohamed channelled the Koran; and more recently Edgar Cayce, Madame Blavatsky, Alice Bailey and many more.

Madame Blavatsky (1831–91) who telepathically channelled the Master Koot Hoomi gave us the concept of a hierarchy of adepts, initiates and masters, the energies of creation, forces of evolution and the workings of universal consciousness. In her seminal work *The Secret Doctrine*, Madame Blavatsky shows how every level of attainment allows us knowledge and greater experience of the cosmic mind as we move upwards from ordinary person to initiate, to master and onwards, up to the planes of planetary and cosmic realities. She said that 'this progression necessitates the corresponding development of power and responsibility'. It was upon these doctrines that Madame Blavatsky and her friends founded what became the metaphysically orientated, and highly influential, Theosophical Society. F W Myers devoted a large part of his life to intelligently exploring channelling. Through his diligent research he was, in the end, left in no doubt as to communication between the spiritual and material worlds.

Another most inspiring channel was Alice Bailey who died in 1949. She channelled the entity know as 'The Tibetan'. Her channelling set down the fundamentals of modern spiritual and psychic development. One of her best-known works is *The Rays and the Initiations*, in which, alongside Blavatsky, she added several important concepts to Western metaphysics. The most significant of these concerned the body's energy system, the chakras. These were previously little known in the West, but which nowadays are taken for granted when considering such matters as healing and psychic unfoldment. Alice Bailey brought us knowledge of kundalini energy, the astral, etheric and causal planes. Although there had been some earlier contact with the concept of Eastern metaphysics through translation of oriental literature and individual visits to the East, there is no doubt that these ideas were popularized through Alice Bailey's efforts. Her writings have great influence, as within them we may glimpse some of the deep spirituality common to all great mystics and their works.

The seven rays to which Bailey referred are embodiments of seven types of energy, which demonstrate to us the seven qualities of the universal light force. They do not, however, seem to comfortably equate to the seven chakras. According to Bailey these seven qualities have a seven-fold effect upon matter and form, and are to be found in all parts of the universe. They also have a seven-fold interrelationship between themselves. We can perhaps grasp this concept if we remember that light pours down through the many layers of matter. Just as light shining through water, or a prism, can then be seen as the seven rainbow colours, so the seven rays equate to the many builders, lords rulers and deities. The whole area of what was described as occult was greatly served by Bailey and other mediums in the past, and we owe them much.

Recently we have seen a form of channelling that shifts away from communication with single entities into a broader vista. Furthermore, some mediums have become aware of communications, not just from one entity, but also from a group. These groups have been variously labelled as the 'White Brotherhood', 'the Teachers', 'the Planetary Logos', 'the Spiritual Hierarchy' and 'The Professors'. These are purported to be a combination of entities including wise discarnate souls who have come to the end of their karmic connection with the earthly existence. Also we have seen publications of channelling purported to be from light-beings residing beyond our solar system. We are told that this group of beings is active at this time because of the enormous shift of consciousness occurring within humanity. When this Gestalt type of energy is contacted it can give an overview for the individual and for the planet.

For those who have worked with an individual guide, the difference of linking with a group energy is marked, for these energies are not as soft, sweet and nurturing as our own individual communicators. They are compassionate, but their compassion is beyond emotion and they can seem quite stern in quality, answering our questions without frills or fuss. These beings are often contacted through the astral, although they need not be astral entities themselves. They use the astral in the same way as we use radio frequencies. Many spiritual and psychic teachers have felt their presence. They generally do not stay long in their link and always come straight to the point.

Astral contacts, as we have seen, have inspired and assisted us. However, the next stage of development for humanity demands that mediums attune their whole being to a level beyond the astral, and consequently beyond personal information. So, instead of the melding of energies between the medium and the discarnate spirit during the psychic connection, the whole vibration of the medium must now be raised, not just during the link but also within the lived world of the individual. There are of course many different vibrational layers and attunement beyond the astral; indeed the possibilities for any medium are endless. The higher the vibration the less personal information comes through. For this higher communication to take place the medium must have expunged most of the negative aspects of self. Being a pure instrument does not mean you are perfect; mediums and channellers are human beings like anyone else, with some form of advanced self-awareness having taken place.

To channel this energy one has to set aside the little self and the little mind, and the instrument or channeller of this information has to have integrated themselves to the highest universal forces they can reach. In my opinion, anyone who has worked on themself in a deep way, who has searched within for their connectedness to the core and Source of everything of which we are all a part, can obtain channelled information.

In one of my many channellings I was given the message that the greatest

I n 1989 a huge shift of consciousness occurred for me. I had been happily working as a medium for many years. At this time, my astral guides seemed to step back. However, this was not in any way alarming for me, rather it felt like a natural progression. At the same time I had information bombarding me from all directions so I reached up and asked for guidance from the highest possible Source. When the information started to come through it felt like I was held in a beam of energy, a melting of consciousness between the light force and myself. Having experienced many forms of mediumship throughout my career I immediately knew that this was a very different frequency to any I had hitherto been linked. I instinctively knew it was beyond the astral planes. As is often the case, after the sessions I had no memory of what had been said, so the sessions were recorded.

What was this new energy? I was curious and asked to what or with whom was I communicating. The answer came back, 'a unison of light forces: original thought'. I had never heard this term and did not really understand what it meant, other than it was very different from any other connection I had encountered. Whatever it was, it was not personal and was not an individual entity. I set up a session each week with a recorder and after six sessions the message came, 'We will now dictate a book'. Publishing a book was something I had not even

desire of everything in the cosmos is to expand. It seems to me that the need to channel at this time is part of the ever-present thirst for greater possibilities. This may not be the highest type of psychic attunement, nor is it indicative of one who has reached the end of their journey. It reaches to a different frequency from the astral levels, giving us the opportunity to rise beyond aspects of illusion and glamour. Individuals who channel from this considered. The amazing speed with which the book came out was certainly not a normal occurrence; I finished channelling ten sessions in the April of 1990 and by July of the same year the book *The Wind of Change* was in print. I still was unsure as to its purpose and did not have any emotional connections to it. Some months later I picked up a book called *Channelling* by Jon Klimo. I was shocked and amazed to read: 'When an individual is aware of life in its infinite sense, he is also aware of the benefits of matching this vibration with the vibration of original thought!'.

It was explained to me that this connection requires the energy of the channeller to have expanded in order to accommodate the link with higher consciousness. I certainly had experienced quite a different state and energy in myself at this time. I felt free from fear and able to speak and live my truth even though it was difficult for the people with whom I lived and worked. However, in no way am I saying I had suddenly become some advanced being.

During the period when four of my channelled books were published I was often asked what or whom are you channelling. In pondering on how best to answer this question and endeavouring to be completely honest, in the end I felt the most truthful reply was that it was I – the highest aspect of myself in alignment to the highest energy I was capable of reaching.

energy may not be divine beings, nonetheless, they have allowed the divine in them to speak. For the purpose of giving individual consultation it has little use, as it is too far removed from the personal state. The higher the frequency, the less personal the content. Most people who come for a sitting are not looking for global consciousness information, they are seeking information about their own personal lives.

All the way through our psychic development, we have seen how new opportunities present themselves at every turn. The view is different with every step and with each step our frequency and energy changes. The individual's desire must be to seek truth and find the deep core spirit of themselves, for without their true intention there can be no real expansion. As we relinquish the veils that cloak the true self, our energies become lighter, with the result that their frequency changes. Like, as always, is attracting like. During the process of channelling we have to let go of the little self, therefore our psychic abilities expand and we can contact finer and finer vibrations.

So, what then is the highest Self? Some people equate it with the inner guiding teacher, or even with one's conscience, and both views are equally valid. As in life it is always preferable to go to the top, so let us aspire to the highest part of self. It has been called the god within. God, however, is an emotive word for many. There seems to me to be a spark of some universal higher energy within us all. In unfastening the outer protective garments of our personality we have allowed ourselves a glimpse of that spark, and of the greater Self and higher consciousness.

The further we go on our spiritual journey the more aligned our state, and the potential for higher teachings. For so very long we have depended only on structures, and the higher the channelling the less the structure. We may receive a name, but the name does not validate the message. Perhaps from the apostle, John, we get our best advice: 'Beloved, believe not every spirit but try the spirits whether they are of God, because many false prophets have gone out into the world.'

More recently the art of channelling has taken off, with many books and tapes being produced. They are of varying quality, and many seem to talk at length about the necessity for humanity to lose its fear. My own channelling books, published over 20 years ago, speak mainly of the many changes in store for the planet and for us.

In my opinion one of the best examples of channelling are the works of Alice Bailey. Written in the middle part of the 20th century much of her teachings were written for the blossoming number of psychics, mediums and channellers. They are as relevant now as they were when they were written. I would urge any student to ponder on her works; you may not always agree with what she says, and some of her, now, rather old-fashioned, ways of describing things may be hard. The use of 'man' for instance is now considered to be politically incorrect. However, her words are thought-provoking and stretch the mind. I do not agree with 100 per cent of what she writes and found it particularly hard to digest the use of the word 'master'. However 'master' was used in her day more as a description of a teacher and not of someone who had absolute power. Since her death the Lucis Trust has brought out very helpful compilations of her works including *Serving Humanity*. This work has a section on 'The Transmission of Teachings' (originally taken from *A Treatise on White Magic*) from which a selection is quoted here:

> Some transmitters [channellers] work entirely on astral levels, and their work is necessarily part of the great illusion. They are unconscious mediums and are unable to check the source from whence the teachings come; if they claim to know that source, they are frequently in error. Some receive teachings from discarnate entities of no higher evolution, and frequently of lower than themselves. Some are simply abstracting the content of their own sub-consciousnesses and hence we have beautiful platitudes, couched in Christian phraseology and tinctured by the mystical writings of the past, which litter the desks of disciples, working consciously on the physical plane.
>
> It is necessary for those who want to act as true transmitters and intermediaries to keep their eyes on the horizon and seek thus to extend their vision... They must seek to increase its scope that they hold on to the truth that all things are headed towards the revelation and that the form matters not. They must seek pre-eminently to be dependable instruments, unswayed by passing storms. They must endeavour to remain free from depression, no matter what occurs; liberated from discouragement; with a keen sense of proportion; a right judgement in all things; a regulated life; a disciplined physical body and a whole-hearted devotion to humanity.

'Unswayed by passing storms', 'dependable instrument', 'free from depression' etc. are words of encouragement in finding within ourselves an equilibrium, a balance on all levels. Without this, Bailey makes it clear that no advanced knowledge can be channelled.

She continues:

> ... many methods are tried, suited to the nature of the aspirant. Some have brains that act telepathically as transmitters. I deal with the safer and rarer methods, which utilize the mental vehicle as the intermediary between the soul and the brain, or between the teacher and the disciple... the higher mental methods are more advanced and surer even if rarer.

In her works she often talks of the need to rise up to the mental levels. I take this to mean the higher mental attributes of humanity, as in the sixth chakra energy of the higher mind or visionary state, beyond the emotions and the craving for the 'little me'. Being beyond emotions, however, is not the same as denial of the emotions. First we need to understand our emotions, to see them for what they are, to use them positively and not be drained or swayed by any that are fear-based. Then, and only then, can we hope to rise to the higher mind, to the true visionary state. Not the state of the idealist, whose notions are largely based on fear and the need for control, but visions beyond the demands of society and beyond the thousands of years of influence from astral energies.

Of her own channelling she says:

> The training of the aspirant, the indication to him of possible trends and lines of evolution and the definition of the underlying purpose is all that it is wise to impart at the present stage. This has been attempted in these instructions and there has been given also some new teaching anent [regarding] the emotional vehicle. In the next century when man's equipment is better developed and when a truer meaning of group activity

is available, it will be possible to convey more information, but the time is not yet. All that is possible of me is to grope for those feeble words, which will somewhat, clothe the thought. As they clothe it, they limit it and I am guilty of creating new prisoners who must ultimately be released. I talk in symbols I manipulate words in order to create a certain impression; I construct a thought-form which when dynamic enough can impress the brain of a transmitting agent such as yourself. But as I do so, I know well how much must be left unrelated, and how seldom it is possible to do more than point out a cosmology, macrocosmic or microcosmic, which will suffice to convey a temporary picture of divine reality.

As most of her works were written in the middle of the 20th century, when she speaks of the next century it is actually now. She breaks down forms of 'transmitting', as she calls it, into three categories. Firstly 'Higher Clairvoyance', which speaks directly from mind to mind, whereby a conversation is carried out entirely on the mental levels. Secondly, we have what Bailey calls 'Telepathic Communication'. This is channelling direct from teacher to pupil. Thirdly is 'Inspiration', which utilizes the mind of the medium by transmission to the brain. In this section she makes a bold statement and one which flows through much of her work. 'Mediumship is dangerous.' Asking the question why, the answer comes back:

because the mental body is not involved and so the soul is not in control. The medium is the unconscious instrument, he is not himself the controlling factor, and he is controlled. Frequently also the discarnate entities who employ this method of communication, utilizing the voice apparatus of the medium are not highly evolved and are quite incapable of employing mental plane methods. Inspiration is always safe whereas mediumship is also to be avoided.

These are harsh words to hear, especially for a trainee psychic and medium. She does say that some forms of mediumship have their value but constantly emphasizes that the astral levels, if not to be avoided, must be used only as transient stepping stones to clearer connections on the higher mental planes.

I have worked for many years as a medium, and I do have some sympathy for this stance. The vast amount of illusion and delusion that may be present in this area can be a minefield for any neophyte in the psychic fields. The forms of channelling that are beginning to arrive, and to which she may well be referring, are not so connected to the astral levels and do not take control of the medium. Bailey says, students:

> ... would do well to remember that it is the teaching that is of moment, not the supposed source. By their intrinsic value alone these writings and communications must be judged.

This seems to be another way of telling us to judge the channelling by its content and not the supposed entity that brings it through.

The medium is likely to be doing their best to achieve the highest level they can, however, they may not always be the best judges of the validity of their own connection. Mediumship can range from the banal to higher inspirations that aid spiritual evolution. But how does the medium know? We cannot judge ourselves no matter what the link might be giving us. As mediums we can only train ourselves in expansive knowledge, imbue intelligence and will to the highest greatest good.

In the 1990s there was a spate of channelled books. Prior to this period few publishers would touch them. Some did eventually, and then more, and consequently channelled works gained a lot of publicity. They purport to come from many different sources. My own first three channelled works from 'original source', and the last one, had definite influences from what I called the 'professors' – a group of energies I had been working with particularly for my students in higher consciousness classes. We are told by Bailey not to consider who or what these energies are, but to listen to the truth of their voices. I agree with this statement, however, curiosity and rigour mean I want

It may seem surprising but I was completely unattached to the channelling I received. I spoke the words but never remembered them. I transcribed my channellings from the tapes and gave them to the publishers. Consequently, I was asked what this or that meant from the words of my books. I must have often looked an idiot because firstly I never remembered them, and secondly they seemed to penetrate a part of my mind that was unable to articulate anything about them afterwards!

to know what is going on here. To call a link just an energy means very little to our inadequate brain, we have to call it something. Aware that my new link was like nothing I had experienced before I struggled to find a description. 'Original thought' is equally vague but it was the title given to me.

For the writing of *this* chapter I have, after 20 years, revisited them. There are some projections for the future, for instance, in *The Wind of Change* it speaks of a massive movement of peoples. We have to remember that this was channelled before the Berlin Wall came down and when the Internet had barely started and most people did not even possess a computer. We can see that there have indeed been vast movements of peoples, for different reasons including wars, cheaper transport costs, the opening up of boundaries, economic reasons and so forth. Some predictions, as far as one can be aware, have not yet come to pass, such as genetic changes. Although, with the fast moving knowledge that is continually emerging on genetics and how we can use it to eradicate diseases and possibly extend life, this might yet be true. Maybe one day we will all be genetically modified!

In another of my channelled books, *Transformation* it says:

> Each soul always finds its true home, in its true place in its true time. The land mass is moving much faster than you can see. Underneath the earth there is a shaking away.

Of course our planet is always moving, and from time to time throughout history we have had massive changes to our environment. So these words, in the context of the volcanoes, earthquakes and tsunamis we have encountered lately, do seem to have some validity. However, it is not something we can absolutely pin down to being unusual.

Asking the question about the changes, I was given that it was not so much about what we were doing to our planet but rather it was 'wheels within wheels', meaning that there was coming a synchronicity of change within the whole of the cosmos and three major cycles were coming together to radically change both the physical and spiritual aspect of our planet Earth. It was reassuring us that it was a natural change, and although it would obviously affect the peoples and all living things on the planet, not only would we survive but the energies coming in were enabling us to take on a greater consciousness which would bring in more balance and peace.

> They [the energies helping our planet] are working very strongly
> on the higher planes to help lift and help expand consciousness
> but this expansion has to come by the will of the individual.

In other words it's not just up to the leaders of the world, it is up to each one of us to eradicate fear and raise consciousness:

> Again we remind you of the unison of light workers and that
> includes you. It needs to happen through individual choice or it
> cannot happen at all.

In my last channelled book it seems to suggest that channelling will not be so prevalent in the future because we will have the knowledge to hand, within ourselves:

> When channelling comes into actuality through the spoken word
> it permeates through the mind of humanity. It creates energy of
> realization, not on a logical or factual level, but it becomes part of

your dream world and as it does it begins to manifest in matter. Everything mirrors everything else, and everything is part of everything else, but to bring actuality – materialization of the cosmos down into matter, it needs to seep though different layers of consciousness landing within the human mind. As it lands within the human mind it then takes place within the human state.

So what was the purpose of these books? In my case I started channelling to find my own answers and I did it with good faith. One of the messages I received about channelling said it was not about the words but more about the opening up to higher inspirations. The purpose therefore was about accessing a higher energy level. The words I received were a symptom and not the cause. What does seem to be a constant theme in channelled works is the very real necessity to lose our fear. Here is a quote from my channelling:

> Now is the time for your impregnated cellular fear, which is different from the emotional fear, to be cleansed. As you already know, this is not done through meditation, however powerful, but by the sheer willingness to simply let go. It is achieved by the will, and through the connection of honesty, integrity and absolute commitment to truth within you. This will allow you to open up to clean the Solar Plexus centre, to enable the light force to impregnate. Listen to the word impregnate; conceive within the Sacral centre the conception of light. In this conception of light, the cells that are made within that area enlighten and can help the birthing process of the new humanity; the impregnation of light within the cells dissolves, burns up, clears and purifies all that is remnant of the old stuff. This is why your dreams, your expectations your acknowledgement of light and the possibilities that the light creates, are paramount to the birth of the new child.

'A new child', could infer a birth of a new species, a different kind of man. The message in all my channelled works is about the necessity to raise our con-

round the time my second book *Cosmic Dance* was published,
I was leading a weekend workshop in London. There were 29
participants. Out of these, 23 of them had come specifically for me
to tell them where and when the spaceships were coming to collect
them! I had put no such information in any of my books. It turned
out that, because I had used the word 'ascension' as a description of
a shift of consciousness, and, at the time, there was what I would call
an 'ascension fever' among some New Agers, they thought I had some
extraterrestrial insights into the arrival of ETs to save the chosen ones!
Ascension fever is the belief that extraterrestrial beings are watching
and waiting to take people away to other planets. These participants
also believed the chosen ones were being picked up by extraterrestrials!
There were 23 very disappointed people that weekend, particularly one
lady who, on the strength of her beliefs, had sold her house and arrived
at the workshop with her suitcase!

sciousness, allowing this new and greater possibility to occur. Unfortunately
some people interpreted the words with their own and incorrect meanings.

This reveals that however careful one is as a medium, the words can
sometimes be manipulated to mean what the seeker wants to believe. Beliefs
can be dangerous, but beliefs are neither absolute, nor set in stone. At best we
can use them as a scaffolding to take us forward. Shortly after this, and other
bizarre instances, I decided I would never put my name to a channelled piece
of work again. Many people believe that if you channel you must be some
kind of higher being or god, and that the information is therefore infallible. I
do not believe this. A medium can, and must, do their best; only hoping that
the words and energies produced by these works help to inspire and allow
people to question and think for themselves, and open up to greater possibilities. My books were not about extraterrestrials and definitely not about
Armageddon! This idea of ETs coming to save the chosen ones still persists.

I n December 2006 I moved to the south of France primarily to look after my ageing father-in-law. I find myself living close to a mountain I had never heard of before, called Bugarach. According to a growing number of people this is where the space ships will take us away in 2012! The year 2012 has become just one of the many predictions down the ages of the end of the world. I am planning a good New Year's Eve party for 2013!

To want to be rescued by some god, deity or extraterrestrial is, in my opinion, a way of avoiding real life here and now. Only by taking responsibility for our fears, thoughts, our physical world and ourselves will we progress forwards in our spiritual journey.

Aspects of spiritual development can give some people the notion that someone or something will take over their responsibility. This, in my opinion, is an illusion, a giant fantasy, and an excuse to abdicate responsibility for our world and ourselves. Channelling can be helpful and does inspire. Hopefully the words of the channeller can stretch our minds to greater possibilities and give us the impetus to find the truth within ourselves, to transform nega-tivities and to bring these into all aspects of our lives; for, as each person eradicates some fear, it helps dissolve the negative energy in the astral and consequently brings a brighter energy field to our world.

I finish this chapter then with an excerpt from a passage in *The Wind of Change*:

> We would like to paint you a picture: Imagine an ordinary light in an ordinary room. Over the light is a dark cloud. Individuals have had to grope and feel their way around the dark room, stumbling without light to guide them as they searched for the way out and failed to find it. They have looked everywhere but to themselves. They have stumbled, strutted and groped around. They have

collapsed in a heap, despondent and despairing. But finally through acceptance of themselves through an inner realization dawning, as they sat there in the dark room they have discovered how simple the answer is: they have merely to reach out, lift the edge of the cloak, which is your own darkness, and immediately the light is there. Dear Children, the light has always been there for you but you just didn't see it.

CHAPTER SIX

Higher Consciousness

The secret of truth is not unravelled by questioning or giving away your wealth and position. You cannot exalt the heart with mere words. Pain is the price that the heart has to pay.

Rumi

The need to develop one's higher consciousness is not always recognized in psychic and healing development, as most people only want to know about their emotional, mental and physical lives; or, they want contact with a loved one in spirit. For authentic and transformational psychic work one's own development is of paramount importance and just as you have onward personal development (OPD) in many positions in life, so it is advisable in the psychic and spiritual world. Linking to higher consciousness energies may not give as many specific facts about the sitter's personal life, however, it will give a more spiritual outlook. Having the ability to see beyond the clouds, gives a greater worldview and brings richness to the sitting. This will enable the psychic to obtain further information that may not be obvious to the sitter at the time. In this way we can see potentials, pitfalls and possibilities for that person and therefore be able to give them their own unique guidance.

Higher consciousness energy, as described here, is of a different frequency to the astral energies described in the previous chapter. Because this energy is more refined and as always, like attracts like, psychics will be unable to connect to the higher consciousness energies without having undergone some personal higher consciousness development themselves, enabling them to bring their own energy in line with this frequency. Analogously, it would be like trying to receive a radio programme on medium wave when it is being transmitted from FM (there is a feeble pun here!).

The writer and mystic Peter Ouspensky (1878–1947) devoted most of his life to the development of consciousness. Originally a student of Gurdjieff, he branched out on his own to explore, teach and write about what he called 'self-consciousness'. He states that we cannot obtain the higher states of consciousness by 'desire or decision alone'. The only way to obtain what he called 'objective consciousness' is through 'the development of self-consciousness'. He states, 'it is a result of inner growth and of long difficult work on oneself'. He also acknowledges that flashes of insight do occur to people and they can be made more or less permanent only by the use of special and dedicated training. The difficulty, as he sees it, is that people believe they already possess it, so why should they involve themselves in a long-drawn-out search for self when they are already there! This identifies a constant problem in spiritual and psychic development as we can only see what we can see in the present, from the perspective of where we stand. It is almost impossible to describe what a shift of consciousness means for any individual until they receive it.

Higher consciousness can be perceived as connected to the higher chakra centres. These centres do function naturally, however, their higher function rarely reaches the ordinary everyday consciousness in most people, and when it does, it is often sporadic. Ouspensky and many others tell us that only by waking up from the illusion and sleep of our normal consciousness can we reach a greater perspective and 'remember ourselves'. This concept is similar to that of many other spiritual and mystic teachers, when they suggest that the

S ome years ago I was upset and hurt by someone's harsh words. I relayed this to an innately and naturally spiritual person. His reply was, 'Ah yes Julie but it's only the little I that is hurting.' I laughed, how right. It's only the little I that responds negatively. The greater and deeper Self has no pain.

deeper, higher aspects of self, removed from the 'little I', are already present within us, waiting to be acknowledged and used.

Throughout our psycho-spiritual development progress there are copious shifts of perceptions. Some of these are subtle and hardly noticed, however, some are profound and affect us to the very core. Many people will not want to reach a higher state of consciousness as it takes them beyond the clouds of everyday living and mundane concerns. Getting an overview on ourselves, other people and the world is not all love and light, for it often reveals very uncomfortable truths. On the other hand, in terms of psychic work, it must be true that we would wish for the highest levels we can attain.

The greater the shift the more likely it is to cause disturbance in one's life. Whilst spending months immersing myself in interviews for my master of philosophy research, with students who were attending psycho-spiritual courses, the word that kept reoccurring from these interviews was 'hard'. They described aspects of themselves that, in the process of letting go of the negative mind-sets and working with an array of psychic energies, pushed and challenged them. Changing one's perspectives alters the way we deal with life and how we respond to the people around us. After listening to weeks and months of interviews there was a point when I sat down and cried out: Is this work ethical? Is it really assisting them? Spiritual development with any depth comes at a price and it is hard to push beyond the little self, to see ourselves as we truly are. What did emerge was that the students undergoing spiritual development who really made the big leaps, the real shifts of consciousness, were those who had undergone some profound life-changing events. This can be a difficult time in someone's life. It has a name: 'Dark Night of the Soul'.

The Dark Night of the Soul experience is prominent in mystical and spiritual literature including that of the Christian mystics. It is often relayed as a form of deep spiritual transformation which may come with trauma, and the sacrifice of one's previous life. When it occurs it could be defined as a profound sense of loss of self. It brings into sharp focus the way we have looked at our world in the past and the way we look at it now. The ideas, notions and beliefs by which we have previously lived, can alter dramatically. This can bring some form of crisis in one's life. Nonetheless, it can also mark the beginning of a new and more fruitful existence. This deep spiritual transformation often begins when old systems, mind-sets and beliefs, break down, and we are then forced to confront ourselves and ask the ultimate question: Who am I? Why am I here? Where am I going? And how am I going to live my life?

Of all the interviews I obtained for my research there is one in particular that succinctly illustrates this journey. This student had begun to question everything and he wondered, *what was the point of coming to the development classes? What was the point of doing the job I was doing?* He also started to wonder, *what was the point of the life I was living?* These questions led directly to his *unease.*

This professional man in his late 20s had been an enthusiastic student, and had progressed well in his intuitive development, but suddenly his attendance waned dramatically and when he did come to class he seemed agitated and angry:

> I couldn't concentrate. I felt like I was drifting and falling asleep
> and I think now, when I look back, it was part of the process.
> It was a process going on in my own energy. I wasn't happy about
> this and I seemed to be seeing things in terms of getting it right
> or wrong.

Around this time it begun to *dawn* on him that he was actually uncovering himself. His dilemmas lasted a long time and he was becoming increasingly uncomfortable with himself.

It wasn't very pleasant because it was all about me wasn't it? I
did every possible thing I could to mask it, avoid it, whatever,
but I now recognize it as a valuable part of my personal process.
I can say this now, but I learnt it the hard way. I also noticed a
lot of changes going on with me physically. It was a stage that
I was unprepared for. Physically my body started to come out
in different kinds of rashes and things. I became really angry,
very irritable and emotionally slapped a lot of people around at
the time, and I kept blocking it and I realized that something
strange was happening. It all built up and finally culminated on
a particular day when everything in my life turned upside down
in one morning. It was a catalyst point when everything that had
built up just came out. There wasn't any more blocking-off to
do. I was not in control. I had an inability to hold onto money,
which was my biggest problem, and it had come to the point of
no return on the same day. Also, my relationship just collapsed
overnight which was probably the right thing to happen but that
wasn't the way I saw it at the time, and I realized the reason that
I was holding on to the relationship was the wrong reason. My
world fell apart mentally because that was where I was holding
most of these things and things could not have got any lower. All
the constructs around me were just wiped. I couldn't physically or
mentally cope with that moment so I just had to surrender to it.

'Masking' it and avoiding it, and then finally reaching a breaking point when
his world fell apart is a graphic description suggesting some form of death
of self. He continues:

Finally, I just sat down and thought I'll ask for some help. I felt
that the only way to understand it was to let go. And when I did
I had this overwhelming experience of peace, and by the evening
I felt so balanced and so peaceful. When you let go, all fear
evaporates. I just had to surrender to it and that for me was quite

a turning point. The most difficult bit was learning to be more of who I am and actually taking away all of those things that I thought were right and weren't. This was a crisis point in my mind, in my fears and they evaporated almost as fast, but at the same time it didn't mean that some of the situations disappeared. And I think that's quite an important point because many people come looking for solutions to things but the solutions aren't necessarily the way they expect them to be, and it doesn't mean that you look at the world really differently, but it is different if you feel different, or see it differently but actually the same things are happening. It affected me to the very core, but I had a sense that I would have to go through it.

'All the constructs around me were just wiped', and 'it affected me to the very core' are very pertinent descriptions of a Dark Night of the Soul experience. It is when one's previous structures of living disappear and there is nothing to hold on to. Finally, as this student experienced, we come to a state of 'surrender' or 'acceptance' of the situation, and equilibrium, healing and peace arrive. This form of experience could be seen as a form of death; the death of the past and the self that belonged to it, with no turning back. This death of self has some correlation to the known phrases of bereavement: denial, anger, bargaining, depression and acceptance, as described by Elizabeth Kubler-Ross in *On Death and Dying*. Another pertinent aspect of this student's story is that the external aspects of his life did not change, but his response to them did. When our energy and responses alter, it changes what happens as we start emanating a different energy and acceptance of what is. This then can have a profound and ultimately beneficial effect on all aspects of our lives.

Dark Night experiences happen when everything we have previously lived by falls away; the rug is pulled from under our feet and even our faith may leave us. We are utterly alone. Psychologist and pastor David Elkins, writes of this with heart-felt words in *Beyond Religion*. For him his Dark Night corresponded to the death of his son. He says that after his Dark Night experience he became 'a more sensitive person, a more effective pastor, a more sympathetic counselor'. He also goes on to say: 'Our souls grow strong and we develop an authentic capacity to console others but, we cannot celebrate this growth like an egoistic victory because the price we paid was far too high.'

Losing everything that makes sense of our world is 'hard', however, out of these experiences we come to a transformed self. Buddhist monk Sogyal Rinpoche states that change and death are part of the human condition and:

> ... to believe otherwise is folly. We so desperately want everything to continue as it is, that we have to believe that things will always stay the same.

Rinpoche, suggests that we meditate on the impermanence of things and 'arrange our lives accordingly'; we must learn 'detachment or letting go'. This concept of 'letting go' has similarities with what Christians describe as 'dying of the self'. Letting go of any aspect of self is not an easy process, as another student explained:

> I think the depth of knowledge gets deeper with the process, almost like an onion, where you keep taking the layers off, and as another layer comes off it's a thicker layer, that's how it feels and so therefore in a way sometimes you think, well hold on a minute, what is it giving to me in my life?

As described here the 'peeling of the onion' of the outer layers or lower aspect of self is an unfoldment and can be a painful process, which the data suggests requires confrontation of difficult personal issues. Another student recalls this period:

> I do remember feeling a tremendous amount of fear, I had to confront things and that it was right. I hadn't felt such depth before.

When constructs change, it can bring out fear and may sometimes give the feeling that you might be going mad. Extreme aspects of this spiritual shift, as in the Dark Night of the Soul, may be transformative but they can be terrible to live through. Even if it were possible for a teacher to instigate this upheaval, which is debatable, one would have to question the rationale and the minefield of ethical considerations of sending someone down the road of the Dark Night, which has historically taken mystics close to the edge of sanity. Nonetheless, evidence suggests that no deep authentic spiritual transformation occurs without change, and some dying of self on various levels taking place. Another student describes this:

> It seemed to me that I was slowly working through my worst
> fears in my life, and every fear that I think I have ever had started
> coming up over a period of years. It was so horrible, but actually
> facing them wasn't as bad as I thought, in the end, and after I got
> over them I realized it wasn't as though I was being rewarded,
> but what I gained from it was tremendous. After every set of
> circumstances something wonderful happened, even in my own
> transformation or events or you know, something great happened
> and it felt like for me anyway I needed to pursue things as they
> came up and I couldn't not look at them. So when it was a horrible
> fear, although it was so horrible and I wanted to run away, yes I
> gritted my teeth.

Phrases like, 'I gritted my teeth' and 'I knew I had to push through my fear', explain that the will of the individual must be engaged in the process of working through, letting go and finally accepting oneself and one's life for deep transformation to occur. Spiritual and mystical literature also imply that any deep spiritual process may necessitate a clearance process. Change is rarely comfortable and can induce anxiety and fear. However, this crisis point is the very thing that makes the big difference and which leads to greater transformation. Another student describes the feeling of becoming aware of self.

Things come up, and that hurts. Looking at oneself so honestly, can hurt, but I found once I worked through the hurt, bit by bit, and again looked at myself unconditionally and said OK fine that's in the past, not if only but let's say next time let's do it differently, now having the tools to see things differently and to react differently.

Your energy is a magnetic force, and any change in it will alter your life. By allowing a shift of focus you have let in the radiance of a different light, which will uncover your true self, and higher consciousness will ultimately manifest itself through you. Conscious awareness of deep spiritual truths may be a long way down the path for most, but even in the early days when you are experiencing the sparks of illumination and the feeling of being pushed, you are already on the road to transformation.

It was once said to me that of all the people incarnate at any given time, only 1 in 60,000 were awake in consciousness. This is echoed in the words of Plato who spoke of all mankind being like prisoners in a cave who face away from light. They are unable to see themselves or anyone else because they are in darkness, shackled, observing life only through the shadows on the wall. When one of these people leaves the cave and finds that reality bears no resemblance to the shadows, returning to awaken and inform the others, he is met with derision, ridicule and aggression. He is trying to share his new-found knowledge with those too blind or too frightened to accept it. Does this sound familiar?

In taking our awareness beyond the usual levels, we enter an unknown territory; one with very different scenery and no perimeters. This experience can be daunting, very often throwing the individual into shock. Yet right from those early days in your development, when you had the sense of being pushed, you are likely to have undergone some sparks of light or moments of illumination. These moments are often transitory but enable you to receive glimpses of a transcendental way and serve to reveal that there are much greater possibilities ahead.

These glimpses often first occur where groups of spiritual seekers congregate. It is important not to confuse these moments of awareness with the bliss states spoken about in previous chapters. Bliss experiences are usually astral-based and will do little to further your spiritual growth. The best ways of identifying the difference is to ask yourself if you have a desire, or even a need, to go back. Do these moments last? If they do not last more than a few days, almost certainly they are not true enlightenment. At best these types of experience serve to let us know there are more and greater states of awareness. True glimpses *can* occur in seminars and workshops; just as often they arrive in silent times or even when one is doing mundane things. They have a sense of truth, a sense of knowing beyond the rational. Alternatively, transitory bliss states may lead you down blind alleys. They can lead to frustration and lure you towards the endless circle of illusionland. This is not the stuff of spiritual growth, it is the stuff of the dependent devotee, the workshop groupie and all those who long for another 'happening'. It feels glamorous, but as the glamour fades, and in extreme cases, it can leave the individual with deep and utter despair, causing the bereft student to wonder why their god has deserted them.

Allow any transcendental glimpses to fill you with the wonder of living. Let the door be open to detached observation of self and realize that our true essence and being are nothing to do with labels. We are not our jobs, our hobbies, our bank balance or our looks. In finding the ability for detached examination we begin to realize the real self, wherein our divine origin lies dormant. When we become aware of this we are no longer prisoners in the darkness of the senses which have, in the past, ruled our lives. With the dawning awareness of higher consciousness we begin to acknowledge our lives, not with the 'little I' but the real I, the hub of our wheel, the core of our being, the soul force, the truth. At this point there is recognition of the possibilities of greater being.

Students frequently believe that if they find the right teacher, this individual will know all the answers and will navigate their lives for them. Whilst it is certainly true that a good teacher, or teachers, often form an essential part of your progress, only charlatans or ignorant untrained teachers will offer to sort out all your difficulties. Truly advanced souls will not solve your personal conditions. Higher consciousness involves spiritual maturity and that means taking absolute personal responsibility for your life. A genuine teacher will be concerned with drawing out the true essence of their students, helping them to know and understand themselves; awakening their mind to their greater possibilities, encouraging them to be self-reliant and think for themselves.

Higher awareness on one level leads to higher awareness on others. From the moment we reach out tentatively from the fog of illusion, and the instant we consciously say 'I want to expand and help myself and humanity', we send an unmistakable vibrational message out to the higher planes. On these planes there are energies that exist for the express purpose of serving humanity. Immediately one transmits this message, with the will completely in place, these energies are drawn towards the sender. Communication then takes place.

Very often at first this occurs through sleep or through some astral frequency, as this is the only level the young seeker can reach. Information is most often conceptual and not intellectual. The student may then feel they have been in a place of learning in their sleep, but are unable yet to grasp what they have learnt. They will then increasingly receive inklings of something; something they cannot as yet completely understand. The outer layers of self have to be removed and this can take years or even lifetimes to complete. Once that call has gone out, you can be certain that your progress will be assured. Trust all that happens, then, happens right. Be aware, look, listen and see everything as a learning process, both the good things and the bad. As you draw your energy into higher and higher states, your own vibratory frequency will expand. You will at some point connect with, and align to, the increasing number of energies that are registering on the higher planes. You begin to act as an important connection between the dense physical existence and the higher spiritual realms. This bond of energy is seen as important for the coming times and for the expansion of consciousness of the entire planet.

'The Source', 'all that is', 'divine energy' or whatever words you wish to describe the living energy that runs through us all, is omnipresent. It is thought to be as present in the souls in Plato's cave as much as saints, gurus and divine beings. It is only by acknowledging the divine in everyone and everything, including ourselves, that we can begin to fulfill our true potential. Every step of the way looks different; the man at the top of the mountain describes a very different picture from the one at the bottom. They are both right. They, as we all do, see their own life from the perspective and position in which they stand.

You eventually grow to become your own guide and teacher. In this adult stage of spiritual growth you become part of the ever increasing group energy that, step by step, bit by bit, is taking us to the point where the coalesced energy will bring the world into a new state. We will then move over as one into the greatest evolutionary leap humankind has seen.

Many musicians, poets, playwrights dancers and singers have inspired us along the way. J B Priestley's, dream vision in *Man and Time* is worth quoting here:

> I dreamt I was standing at the top of a very high tower alone, looking down upon myriads of birds, all flying in one direction; every kind of bird was there, all birds of the world. It was a noble sight, this vast aerial river of birds. But now in some mysterious fashion, the gear was changed and time speeded up so that I saw generations of birds. I watched them break their shells flutter into life, weaken, falter and die. Wings grew only to crumble, bodies were sleek and then, in a flash they bled and shriveled and death struck everywhere and at every second.
>
> What was the use of all this blind struggle towards life, this eager trying of wings, all this gigantic meaningless biological effort? As I stared down, seeming to see every creature's ignoble little history almost at a glance, I felt sick at heart. It would be better if not one of them, not one of us all had been born if the struggle ceased forever.
>
> I stood on my tower still alone, desperately unhappy, but now the gear changed again and time went faster still and it was rushing by at such a rate that the birds could not show any

movement but, were like an enormous plain, sown with feathers. But along this plain, flickering through the bodies themselves, there now passed a sort of white flame, trembling, dancing then hurrying on; and as soon as I saw it I knew this flame was life itself, the very quintessence of being; and then it came to me, in a rocket burst of ecstasy, that nothing mattered, nothing could ever matter, because nothing else was real, but this quivering, hurrying lambency of being. Birds, men or creatures not yet shaped and coloured, all were of no account except so far as this flame of life travelled through them. It left nothing to mourn over behind it; what I thought of as tragedy was mere emptiness of a shadow show, for now all real feeling was caught and purified and danced on ecstatically with the white flame of life. I had never before felt such deep happiness as I knew at the end of my dream of the tower and the birds.

This inspirational piece reveals to us the despair that is a common reaction to the realization gained from seeing further than the mundane and beyond the astral planes. This is the Dark Night of the Soul. It is the darkest hour before the dawn. It is lonely, however, if we are able to catch the essence of the 'flame', described by Priestley, we then come to a better understanding of ourselves and our fellow humans. Through this greater understanding and compassion we are able to take the healing energy, ignited by our connection, out into the world; not just as healers and psychics or those who do good works, but by the energy of our very being.

When you, as psychic or healer, have gone through this resurrection of being, the type of readings you give will change. You will probably find that fewer of the sitter's personality and human situations will be revealed, and when they are they will be in reference to their spiritual progress. Contact with discarnate beings in the astral will only arrive if it is for the higher good. Communication through the astral may accommodate a connection to beings beyond the astral, which still need to communicate through this familiar energy. Proof of survival or other psychic evidence will come by touching the very core and heart of your sitter.

In future times it is going to be increasingly important that any proficient psychic practice necessitates knowing the difference from the personal auric, astral and higher forms of intuition. It is extremely unlikely that anyone can imagine a state beyond their present view. Therefore we always think our present stand is the only true one. Analogously, for those who have not experienced it, reaching beyond the astral is like trying to communicate with a little child on subjects that only an adult mind can understand. Only the constant dedication to seek the truth, beyond ego, illusions or excuses, will guide you through the foggy areas of the astral to the true energy of the third eye, the true visionary state. These are the senses beyond the clouds, beyond illusion and the little desires of humanity. Intent is all; intent to what is good. Transpersonal psychologist, with over 50 years of scientific research, Charles Tart describes some good examples in his excellent book, *The End of Materialism*.

Reincarnation

I have heard many psychics putting the cause of a person's difficulties onto a past life that often seems to be glamorous and dramatic. Belief in past lives is not essential for heightened consciousness. A psychologist could have a field day with interpreting what seems, to some, to be a previous life. The most likely interpretation they would give is that the person is connecting to an alter ego or other personality to account for some difficulty in facing reality. Another interpretation could arrive from the Eastern theory that we are all one, and energetically therefore we can connect with everyone that is and has been. A scientific explanation might be that the release and recycling of the particles that form our make-up could mean we link with the particles of someone in history. As good psycho-spiritual practitioners we want to help the client move forward to receive a more beneficial life. Sometimes linking to a possible past life does the opposite. The reason why most people do not remember their past lives is because they can start again in this one, unencumbered by any mistakes and distresses from the past.

This was made clear to me many years ago when I had a student who had only just started walking again after being paralysed for seven years. Doctors were unable to explain why this healthy girl, who was a dancer, suddenly lost the use of her legs. It was on the second evening when something set off a thought in my mind. I asked her if she had been regressed. 'Yes,' she replied. 'Was this before you lost the use of your legs?' I asked. 'It was a week before,' she replied. 'What were you told?' I asked. Her reply was shocking; 'The regressionist told me I was Egyptian and I had my legs cut off.'

Was this suggestion enough to bring about her paralysis? Did she will it upon herself? Was it that she once again connected to the Egyptian life? In the regression she had been hypnotized. Although hypnotism has some very positive uses, false memory can occur. That is, the hypnotist creating an altered state has inadvertently taken their client into the astral and hence could have picked up someone else's life. Whatever happened in this case we cannot know, but the effect was traumatic and had affected this young woman negatively for many years.

One day, one of my colleagues came into the staff room and said, 'Well that was my third Mary Magdalene this week!' We laughed as we had all experienced clients who believed they were such people. Famous biblical names cropped up time and time again. I have met many Mary Magdalenes also, and Jesus, and I once gave a sitting to a man convinced he had been Judas Iscariot. When explored, this man had a tremendous amount of guilt that originated from a childhood experience, and nothing to do with being Judas Iscariot except that he identified with the imagined conflict of the biblical figure.

What is going on here? Is it a psychological disorder? Can it be truly another life? In many of my own experiences with sitters who believe themselves to be a reincarnation from another life, the reality is that they are personifying a trait or situation hidden within their unconscious from something in this life. People will often convince themselves of obstacles in the form of past lives, or many other things that are born out of a fear of the future and give them excuses from taking responsibility for their own present existence. Whatever we may have been in this life or others, for heightened levels of consciousness we need to release the past fears, negativities and excuses. If a past life *does* emerge during a sitting, my advice is to quickly establish how it is affecting the sitter and intuitively provide good positive advice, so they can let it go, move forward, and be healed from the past and its influences.

Pitfalls in Spiritual Practices

Along your spiritual path there may be upsets, some of which will be caused by having expectations of others. Working unconditionally will spare you from disappointment. Of course as sensitives we are concerned with the very many troubles of our world, but our miserable feelings will only serve to energetically play the record of disharmony over and over again and this will fuel the negative thought-forms of the world. If you personally feel you can do something to help, do it. This, however, is not always possible, so visualize the negativity in a bubble of light and let it go in peace.

You may find that those with whom you are learning like to compare their progress with each other and this can lead to what could be called 'spiritual snobbery'. It is the playground level of, 'I know something you don't' and comes from the mistaken idea that one is further down the road than others. This is dangerous and absurd. We are all on the same road. The fact that some are slightly further down the path means nothing. We will all arrive there in the end, whatever mode of transport we take. We can learn from everything and anyone around us, and often from the person closest to hand. You can learn from the daisy under your feet, from the wonder of a child, and often we learn much from the fool. Other people's journeys are not our concern, unless we have been specifically asked and then we can try to reach them on their level, whatever that is, finding the correct guidance for them. After which we leave them to stand on their own two feet.

We like to think that any establishment that is set up to be spiritual is filled with spiritually aligned people, but one often finds a distressing amount of pettiness and gossip in these places. This presents one with a wonderful opportunity to rise beyond these lower vibrations. Keeping that higher energy present at all times will positively affect others, or alternatively jettison you away from that place, and if it does, it is right that it does. Disturbance in these places can bizarrely come from people trying to be all 'love and light', and trying to be too nice. If by being nice you are not being truthful, it will be sending out a discordant energy, which will be picked up subconsciously and set about troublesome and confused communications. There is no good energy in falsehood. In the polishing of stones, grit is necessary. It is the irritant of the grain of sand that stimulates the oyster to produce the pearl. Spiritual polishing works in a similar fashion.

One of the most misinterpreted aspects of spiritual development is materialism. The inclusion of this subject in a chapter entitled Higher Consciousness may seem incongruous; nonetheless, as we have seen, everything is a mirror, an echo of everything else. In our quest for higher consciousness, a balanced perspective on money with an ability to integrate that perspective fully and comfortably with our spiritual endeavours is essential if we are to break free from the illusion that surrounds this aspect of life. In each lifetime everyone receives what they need for their progress. For some people that may mean they become very wealthy and learn lessons from having riches, whilst others can learn from being poor and having to struggle. The need for money often takes people where they would not have worked or gone, and wherever that is, it will be right. We cannot be in the wrong place since we can just as easily be spiritual in any place.

The foregone conclusion by some that you can't possibly be spiritual if you have money is untrue, however, the old adage 'money can't buy happiness' is equally true. Happiness is a by-product of right living; seek it for itself and you will never find it. Happiness and contentment are within. Money is only a form of energy and exchange; it is subject to the same laws as everything else in the cosmos. In modern times money is seen to be the devil, which is a distorted view and one that quite possibly has its roots in the envy of those who do not have it. Like any other energy it is potentially dangerous or wonderful. If one is greedy, or uses money to exert power over others, this obviously goes against the spiritual flow. It is the obsession with, and the worshipping of, money that is evil, not the money itself. As energy, money is best served when it is allowed to flow freely.

A troublesome aspect of psychic work is the question of just how much should be charged, if anything at all. People must, of course, judge for themselves. Living as we do in a material world we need money in order to live. If you are a person of means, and in all honesty would not resent doing the work for nothing, then do so. In these days this is an unrealistic scenario for most people. The guides and helpers on the spiritual planes have indicated that they are totally disinterested in what we charge. They only care about the positive attunement, energy and alignment that we make. They know very little of materiality. All they care about is the opportunity to help and heal. If you set a fair price, one with which you are comfortable, to able-bodied adults that is fine. If people are genuinely unable to pay then accept a donation; an exchange of energy, no matter how small, will bring a more positive outcome.

One of the hardest things to understand is what constitutes unconditional love. No true student of spirituality would want to act in an injurious way and we all realize the need for harmony and peace.

Deception and lies, even so-called white ones, emanate an unharmonious

---

I once gave a sitting to a woman who was married but secretly had a couple of lovers and a few 'friends'. When I suggested that this might not be very fair to any of these men she replied, 'Oh I thought that was what unconditional love was about!'

---

vibration. Truth has a clear resonance because it has a healing force. Truth, when spoken, always has a powerful quality even if you don't agree with what is being said. It is sometimes hard to speak and live your truth, however, on this there can be no compromise.

Within each field of development, there are the creations of structures and boundaries and therefore the potential for imprisonment within them. In each case they must, at some point, be forged through, for if we are not careful we can find ourselves trapped at each and every stage by the limitations of structures. We belong to a limitless universe where boundaries are superfluous to our needs. The idea of limitlessness is impossible to grasp for the little mind. However, if we can see structures not as something unmoveable but rather as scaffolding that helps us climb, and at some point the scaffolding must come down, we can move more effectively. Stepping stones and not cages are required for growth. The object of any spiritual work is to liberate and release the consciousness and to expand its field of contact. The greatest and truest desire in humanity is the desire to expand, evolve and grow.

It is a good thing to remind ourselves that there are no limits or absolutes, other than the ones you set yourself. If we take time to look and listen we shall instinctively know the right path for us. Although, particularly at the early stages, we only get glimpses of it, the beacon of light is ever within. We know deep in our being that one day it will be revealed and when it does we will no longer be attached to the outcome. At that point we will have ceased to care, not through selfishness but rather through the knowledge that all is well; knowing that we are part of the 'all-that-is', is the greatest security and the only truth.

After this stage there will be the giant leap of consciousness, which is the total melding of the self into the pure timeless light of Source. This, perhaps, is the real resurrection spoken about in different ways by various faiths. Here, from the unity of the larger group soul, the energy of the individual expands and rarefies. The energy of light at this point is so intense that the individual energy dissolves into it. This is the total transcendental state; the closest stage of the highest consciousness. It is beyond human powers of description, although from time to time it is possible to receive conceptual glimpses of it. In the crucible of white light all facets of the body dissolve. This is not the end, but only another stage of the eternal journey.

There is a growing sense that humanity is on the verge of some kind of leap of consciousness. More people are increasingly working with the Heart, unconditional energies. Many faiths speak of having to come to unconditional love before they can move beyond the densest energies. I cannot measure this, and I doubt if many can. From research and from the sense I have had when working with unconditional energy, I know that this emancipates us in so many ways, and has the ability to take us into a very different peaceful and healing state.

In one set of channellings I received the message that, in our energies, humanity was at the equivalent stage to late adolescence. Those who have had children of this age well know the pitfalls and the dangers. In our late teens, the world is all ahead of us. We have not reached the stage of cynicism nor yet been dragged down by the trials of life. Adolescence can be a potentially dangerous age where there is a desire to break down the existing boundaries and explore. Is humanity straining to come of age and, just like any young person, are we pushing against the authority of society and religions? If so, at some point we might need to begin to take charge of our own actions, thoughts and feelings to enable us to direct our own destiny. Let us hope, therefore, that humanity takes the best of this energy and uses it in abundance to steer us away from fear and begin to create a new and better world.

Each shift of consciousness is preceded by what, to some, seems like a test, with some situation occurring that intimately affects aspects of the person's life. It is completely understandable that this feels like a test, and we need to ask the question, who or what is doing the testing? Some would believe it is the hand of God or another deity. But is it? The unpalatable fact is that we do not *consciously* put ourselves in a position that may be uncomfortable and might radically change our lives. Whatever the situation is that pushes us, it probably needs to push us. We are rarely willingly to do it ourselves, however the magnetic energy of our individual consciousness draws to it the situation and occurrences that we need to make the necessary changes. Like attracts like, and the level of one's consciousness draws its own energy. In this way you could say that it is the individuals who are testing themselves.

If you accept the whole premise of energy work you will know that whatever happens to us, wherever we go, whoever we live or work with, is all part of the process. With greater consciousness we obtain more choice and it is good that we implement this choice. Everything that happens is giving us something very rich in experience which, if we allow it, will assist our growth. All situations, and people we engage with, produce discovery and unfoldment, and a further opening to the real and the true. This in turn constitutes a responsibility and opens up that which hitherto has not been recognized or employed.

So, as they say, be careful what you wish for! The moment you send out that call to spirit, life will continuously present you with all you need to further your progress. This might mean, and often does, a radical change in all that you have known, believed and loved. The major shifts in our spiritual growth are not achieved by psychic phenomena, however amazing, but through the expansion of intuition; in(ner) tuition and the subsequent energy that creates. This magnetic force, bit by bit, brings recognition and an increase in the occasional sparks of truth relayed by the deep soul self.

The number of psychics in our world today is growing. The reason for this might be that society is no longer particularly worried about its existence and it has been many years now since psychics were put to their death, in the West at least. The energetic reason suggests that there is a growing sensitivity of the peoples of the world. All over the planet, those who are sensitive are registering energies beyond the mundane and their eyes are being opened to a new world that hitherto has been hidden to us. This in turn is helping us to reach out further and expand our consciousness. Unfortunately, too many psychics are so pleased with their abilities, they are getting stuck in the glamour of the work rather than seeing it for what it is – a stepping stone to far greater possibilities, not just for themselves or their clients but for all humanity.

Through the many ages of our civilizations we have evolved from the cave man to incarnating such geniuses as Einstein, Shakespeare and the Dalai Lama. The capacity of humanity is unlimited. Just take the last 100 years, which is nothing in the millions of years of our evolution; at the turn of the last century modes of transport like cars and airplanes, that we now take for granted, were not around. Electricity was in its infancy and it would be another 50 years before any kind of real computer, and only in the last 25 years have these been readily available to us in our homes. The Internet, which has made a huge difference to our lives in the last few years, was not even in most people's dreams 100 years ago. What might we see in the next 100 and, more to the point, what sort of consciousness will we need to accommodate this?

CHAPTER SEVEN

Where Do We Go To From Here?

All that is necessary for the triumph of evil is that good men do nothing.

Edmund Burke

Development and growth are integral to our world; from child to adult, from bulb to plant, from chrysalis to butterfly. Development and change is ever present, and human development has accelerated considerably in the last 50–100 years. What does that mean for society, religions and our psycho-spiritual practices?

If we look again at the chakras, this time as a parallel model of humanity's evolutionary stages, we can equate the Base level to the physical, where survival was paramount, as in early man's cave-dwelling past. This is the instinctual energy. The second level is the Sacral, which is when man evolved and discovered that he could cultivate his own food, leading to the development of communities and tribes. This tribal energy was our saviour, as groups and societies began to work together, but also has been our downfall, as with the hundreds and thousands of years during which our communities grew in size, splitting into competing groups. Consequently most of humanity is now hard-wired to a tribal consciousness, which means we continue to fight each other.

As we moved into the third Solar Plexus stage we gradually began to acknowledge our emotions and find compassion; we also saw the growth of the mind. Now we could communicate with our fellow humans all over the world in real time. The world is becoming our tribe, and there are early signs of humanitarian feelings, to help and work together with our global neighbours. Jeremy Rifkin suggests in *The Empathic Civilization* that empathy gives us the best hope for survival propounding that we become 'homo empathicus'!

Does this mean we are analogously reaching towards the Heart-loving unconditional levels in evolutionary energy terms? A look at any news programme might seem to suggest otherwise, yet we also see the shoots of empathy, compassion and even some love for our fellow humankind. Acclaimed biologist Alister Hardy, drawing from the fields of psychology, animal behaviour, psychic research and anthropology, suggests that spirituality is natural to the human species and has evolved because of its biological survival value. If this is true it also suggests that we have an even greater need to be spiritual for the continuation and survival of humanity.

For thousands and millions of years we have evolved, developed and grown, step by step. During this time, nature has advanced pretty well at its own speed, allowing us to gradually incorporate the changes into our physical, mental and emotional state. Now, with the ability to actively manipulate our genes, will we force changes at seemingly unnatural speeds? How will we cope? Most people resist change, yet we live in a constantly changing world, every minute of every day. The passing of the sun, the planets and even as you read these words, the earth is hurtling across the sky at thousands of miles per hour. Stasis creates stagnation, and stagnation creates disease, or to put it another way dis-ease. Often people kick and buck against what they feel is change to their status quo. This is pointless, as life will, if necessary, force natural changes.

Continuously we are hearing that scientists have discovered the gene for various illnesses and congenital diseases. Recent knowledge has altered the very food that we eat, and through these enormous discoveries it is now perfectly feasible to feed the world. It might not be too long before we can order the child we want. This is playing with nature on a grand scale, and the implications are enormous. I suppose one could argue that as we are part of nature, and it is we who are implementing these changes, it is in one sense natural, although many would disagree.

As I write this I am seeing an increasing number of articles telling us that 'the code of life' has already been discovered by scientists, leading to major breakthroughs for cures of hundreds of illnesses. We stand, therefore, at perhaps the most exciting, and some would say alarming, brink of massive changes; none more so than those from new revelations in genetics. These discoveries will quickly change us and our world to the very core; already work is underway to complete tests on a pill that, if taken every day from middle age, will not only enable us to live much longer, but many diseases that now take our lives will be eradicated. Scientists believe this pill can be on the market within the next 10 years. When such drugs become available, they will be gobbled up by most of the West, so what does this mean for the rest of the world? Due to modern medicines we already live longer and there are now thousands of people reaching 100 years of age! No more will we live to just the biblical three score years and ten. What will we do to accommodate people living, not just to 100, but maybe 200 to 300? How will society cope with this?

Modern birth control methods have, in my lifetime, already changed whole societies and the way they live. If we are analogously only 18 years old in our evolution and energy, had we not better grow up fast? For these reasons alone, it is vital that we shift our consciousness very quickly indeed. We will need higher mental faculties, stronger emotions and a heart-felt intuition to do what is right, what is good and what will bring us into perhaps the greatest step in evolution that man has ever trod.

'... wrong, comes up to face us everywhere', from Christopher Fry's *A Sleep of Prisoners* (*see* Chapter One) is a very pertinent description of events in terms of what we are discovering from the television, internet and phones that have become our personal computers. There are fewer and fewer places for evil to hide, and for atrocities to go unnoticed. Will we, as Fry's verse asks us, 'wake up'? We can now, in real time, communicate with the whole world. We can register our feelings, our hopes and fears on the social networks. We can see how people in other parts of the globe live, and things that would never be made public in the past are there for all to see. We therefore cannot ignore the difficulties of peoples in other parts of our world. In so many ways the world has already become a global village and we now understand more and more that what is done in one place affects others, particularly in the case of the environment. Let us hope that with all the information we have to hand, that information acquired is not, in itself, confused with wisdom.

Before he became Buddha, Prince Siddhartha Gautama was kept in wealth and privilege away from any pain or evil. One day whilst on a ride outside the palace he encountered, for the first time, beggars and disease. His previous vision of the world was shattered and, such was the shock, he renounced all the joys, pleasure and privileges of his birth, and drifted around for years as a poor monk. So great was his dramatic experience, it altered his perception of the world forever. After many years, he became spiritually enlightened. Will our greater knowledge of the world bring about our enlightenment? And what about our growing psychic faculties, how will this affect, if at all, such a monumental time in humanity's history?

Over my life I have watched the whole Mind Body Spirit movement evolve from being near impossible to get any information, to now when so many books, films, DVDs and the internet are full of information on these areas. All roads eventually lead home. Large amounts of products can be superficial and misleading at best, and extremely misleading or even dangerous at worst. The astral energies built up over thousands of years are powerful, full of humanity's fears, desires and woes. These are still present, and our task now is to clear them. Fear, in all its guises, must be addressed for us to move into a better world. When the Arab Spring started in 2010, and I watched when those people rebelling against their repressive regimes were interviewed, time and time again I heard the words, 'our fear has gone'. This elimination of fear has enabled them to try to make a better life, even sometimes at the most awful costs.

Fear can be perpetuated throughout societies and is still being used to imprison whole populations of peoples. Commonly used by leaders of all kinds is the fear of hell, the fear of abandonment, the fear of financial collapse and the fear of death. Fear stops us, it distorts our thoughts and it makes us ill. Our fears resonate out into the atmosphere and are held in the astral planes. Just as through dubious hypnosis people can be drawn into 'false memories', which have nothing to do with them but feel so real, so we can be drawn into negative states which may or may not be anything to do with us personally. Energetically, if we have little or no fear, this negative magnetic force cannot attach itself to us. The challenge for us all, each and every one of us, is to consciously engage our will in intentionally dissolving fears. Through our dreams, hopes, positive desires and, most importantly, the things we do, think and say, we can create a more productive and better world.

A symbol associated with Christianity is the fishes, epitomized by Jesus calling his disciples 'fishers of men'. The last 2,000 years have been recognized as the age of Pisces, the fishes. We have now entered the Aquarian age, and the emblem for this new stage is the lone water carrier. Water in Greek symbolism denotes the source or spirit of life, and in this image the individual holds it in their own hands. Could this illustrate the ascendancy of the individual and the flow of spirit, which is now in *our* own hands?

Knowing and working with unconditional loving energies is right and good, however, this does not mean guides, deities, gods or space men will rescue you! The age in which we now find ourselves is a grown-up one. It is the age of responsibility and growth, the like of which we have never seen before. The opportunities this could bring for humanity are endless and wonderful, if, and it's a big IF, we can stop apportioning blame on our leaders, politicians, priests or parents, and instead embrace and take responsibility for our own energies.

The following quote from *A Treatise on White Magic*, by Alice Bailey, touches the essence of what we must do, and encourages us to move forward. This is spoken to all those people who, in one way or another, have sensed there is more to life, and that they have consciously started on their spiritual journey. (For modern parlance I have altered the gender words):

No glamour, no illusion, can long hold the person who has set themselves the task of treading the razor-edged path which leads through the wilderness, through the thick-set forest, through the deep waters of sorrow and distress, through the valley of sacrifice and over the mountains of vision to the gate of deliverance. They may travel in the dark (and the illusion of darkness is very real), they may travel sometimes in a light so dazzling and bewildering that they can scarcely see the way ahead. They may know what it is to falter on the path and to drop under the fatigue of service and of strife, they may be temporarily sidetracked and wander down the bypaths of ambition of self-interest and of material enchantment. But the lapse will be brief. For nothing in heaven or hell on earth or elsewhere can prevent the progress of the person who has awakened to the illusion, who has glimpsed the reality beyond the glamour of the astral plane and, who has heard, even if only once, the clarion call of their own soul.

Once we have heard that clarion call, no matter how softly it calls, sooner or later our progress is assured. We have come to a time when this progress must accelerate very quickly indeed if we are to meet the extraordinary events, discoveries and knowledge bombarding us from all areas. How can we do this? No real spiritual progress occurs until the energy of the individual is cleared and resonates a truly loving state. Energy is not something to which you can pay lip service. It is not something through which we can earn 'brownie points'. The intent has to be completely genuine to engage the energy. Only by embracing the knowing that we must do this, for and by ourselves, can we reach inside the depths of our being. Also, when acknowledging the difficulties that our mind-sets, prejudices and fears manifest, wherever they emanate from, can we ensure that they are completely eradicated. This unfoldment of self, bit by bit will clear away the 'veils of illusion' that all mystics down the ages have known, and consequently this will bring a clearer resonance of energy to ourselves. One light in the darkness can assist others to see their way forward.

One of my favourite classic books is George Eliot's *Middlemarch*. This is the story of a woman called Dorothea, who wanted to make a difference. The haunting words of the last page I have paraphrased here:

> She had no desire for great acclaim or being praised above other women, feeling that there was always something else that she might have done if only she had been better and known better. Her full nature spent itself in deeds, which left no great name upon the world. However, the effect of her being on those around her was incalculable. For the growing good of the world is often dependant on un-historic acts and all those Dorotheas, who live their unknown lives authentically and rest in unvisited tombs.

This story is energetically sound as it tells us that we can, and will, make a difference; not by being famous or standing on some podium making speeches; not even by becoming a healer or psychic; but in all our daily thoughts, words and actions, which in turn affect those around us and then those around them, moving outwards into the world. The heroine of this story is conscious of her actions, and her mindfulness allows for positive changes in herself and those around her.

Mindfulness of our thoughts, emotions and actions is a very productive way to move forward, and it is essential to being consciously aware. Most people's minds are unfocused, and their thoughts flit from one thing to another. Their intent is therefore constantly dissipated, and their mental energy shifts around in random ways. By focusing on our thoughts we begin to see this dissipation at work, and we become aware of just how much energy we lose. Bit by bit, through disciplined meditation, we can bring our thoughts into focus and work more productively. Before we begin our meditation it is crucial that we engage our will and intent on the task at hand. We can start by making an affirmation that during the meditation our minds will not be seduced by past or future things, keeping our thoughts on the moment, and in the present.

Mindfulness hopefully leads us towards an instinctive desire to bring this mindfulness into all that we think, feel and do, not just our meditations.

Ask what and where is your true intent? And the answer must not be an airy-fairy explanation of what we would like it to be, but what it really is. Knowing oneself and how one's mind-sets and patterns have dictated our thoughts is essential. Intentions are a powerful energy and result in an outward force around us and into the world.

To really reach into the depth of our being, at some point there must be some deconstruction of self. By looking deeper, the student begins to see through their own thoughts and habits, becoming conscious, very often for the first time, that there are profound splits and paradoxes inherent in their thoughts. In doing this they can become aware of the ego's skilful ability in self-preservation and with that knowledge they are likely to be shocked by their own, sometimes devious and artful, defensive excuses. At some stage the ego must be revealed and they must consciously uncover and face their negative mind-sets and habits that may have originated from past experiences and possibly a whole lifetime of reinforcements. There is a saying 'face the devil and he will disappear'. If the devil is the personification of our fears then by shining the light of truth onto our fears, the devil lives no more.

It is the deconstruction of beliefs, thoughts and social patterns by psycho-spiritual students that is considered to be an important part of the process of unfoldment, leading the way to a clearer and more accurate intuition for oneself and for others. When this deconstruction occurs, a great deal is happening with the individual, and they are often experiencing profound splits in their psyche, which in turn can create uncertainty and fear. This stage of development is hard, but necessary for progress.

Buddhist thought says that the primary cause of human suffering is the persistent belief in permanence. When self-awareness deepens, we will have greater access to intuition. As time progresses, people welcome and become more confident in these intuitions and insights, acknowledging that change is not only possible, but also essential for their growth. Their intuitions then become active tools and they can then direct them for their own development. In effect their own intuition becomes their own personal teacher.

If a period of uncertainty is almost inevitable for spiritual transforma-tion, and intuition is of help, then using intuition throughout the spiritual development process might seem preferable and desirable. Gradually, through the unpeeling of self, the individual becomes conscious of a 'knowing state'; a state of being, in the present, when our intuitions will serve us most. Intuition, by its very nature, is immediate. It is true that sometimes we will receive intuitions about the future, however, it is most successful when we use it to tell us what to do in the moment, in present time. We cannot change the past, we can however make the future better and we do that by knowing what to do now, here, today, in the present time.

Modern psychology has assisted us greatly, as we can now realize why people do bad things, and why they are held in the prison of their previous experiences. We can, sometimes just by knowing we can, alter the negatives that do not serve us and keep us from seeing clearly the way ahead. Every thought has energy, every emotion has energy, and every part of us emanates energy. Fear is an energy that brings dis-ease. It is just as much a disease as any physical one. We acknowledge our physical ailments; let us now put every bit as much emphasis on our other ailments.

More recently we have seen a new form of inquiry going under the name of evolutionary psychology, which is the study of the way the higher mental functions have evolved through time. These include parental influences, love, language, helpful and destructive tendencies, emotions and morality, including the ability to find and punish those who appear to deceive us. Evolutionary psychology works alongside neurophysiology, concerning itself with the circuitry in the brain. It is uncovering some fascinating theories in the advancement of humankind. Evolutionary psychology is scientifically based and has little or no time for spiritual matters, nonetheless, it does give us some important information on the whys and wherefores of how we work. It is important to remember that we are physical beings as well as spiritual beings, and that much of what we are can be identified as originating in animal behaviour.

Another new science is epigenetics, which tell us that our biology and genetic activity are influenced by their connection and interaction with the environment; 'instead of being victims of our genes, by controlling our environment we have the power to control our biology and become masters of our own fate'. (*See Spontaneous Evolution* by Bruce Lipton and Steve Bhaerman.)

In these changing times we increasingly need to acknowledge and build bridges between science and spirituality. Research into quantum theories is revealing some connections between the two areas. Dean Radin who has carried out many years of Psi research, including for the US Government, says in his book *Entangled Minds: Extrasensory Experiences in a Quantum Reality*:

> ... the fabric of reality suggested by quantum theory and the observations associated with psychic phenomena bear striking resemblances. They are eerily weird in precisely the right way to suggest a meaningful relationship.

Advancement in the science of the brain reveals that most of our patterns are set during the period from birth to seven years. This gives new meaning to the saying 'give me a child until he is seven; he's mine for life'! In the brain there are neural pathways, which are a programming chain for neurons and synapses. The brain plots a course with these neural pathways. With an intense emotional experience the brain invests a lot more energy in the recording of that experience. In response it will release neurotransmitters to deal with the experience, including endorphins, which reduce perceptions of pain and stress, and dopamines, which give us pleasure and improved nerve conditions. Intense experiences in our lives mean we are more likely to revert to the saved response mechanisms created at an early age in the brain. Primal hard-wired responses are much stronger than learnt ones.

Imagine for a moment all those pathways in your brain and all those experiences that could have cemented themselves within you from an early age. When we are in heightened states of fear, these pathways and experiences are automatically revisited. We can then begin to understand how difficult it might be to un-learn and create new responses. Scientifically we know that is possible, for instance, in a stroke victim where a large area of the brain is damaged, the brain learns to create new neural pathways around the non-functioning damaged area. This is achieved chemically and electrically. Through implementing our minds and physical being we strengthen these new pathways by constantly reinforcing the actions and intent. This is how affirmations can assist us, by putting different and more positive notions into our brains. It is only in the action of *doing* that the brain makes new and better pathways.

When I ponder this, I think of the small roads in Devon. The roads are winding and roll over hills and valleys, often in a spurious and roundabout fashion. They are there because once, a long time ago, one donkey forged a path. Then the next donkey found it was easier to follow this path, then another then another. When concrete and tarmac were put down it was on the path of the original donkey track. And so it is with the pathways in our brains. One action, one emotion, one thought was reinforced, causing the hardening of that path until all the energy naturally follows it. Now, with conscious knowledge, we can choose new ways of being and create for ourselves more proficient pathways, void of fear that in time will become the norm. We can only succeed by doing it. A master potter knows he can make a pot; he may design the pattern in his mind, he may think on it and he knows it is possible, but the pot is not brought to actuality until he puts his hands in the clay and makes it.

In the words of a student:

> I think the mind sets in patterns very quickly and I like when people come up with ideas that make me see things from a different direction. I find that refreshing, and sometimes just a simple thought can shift your whole attitude to the day or the week or some aspect. The smallest shift can turn a problem into an interesting phenomenon and I like that. I like the capacity of the mind to just suddenly take one step to the side and the whole world changes and sometimes people come up with an idea or thought or whatever and that just clicks something and perhaps we see things differently and that I find beneficial.

'Mind-sets' changing very quickly is a revealing observation, which was stimulating for this particular student. However, changing ingrained mind-sets for most is hard and requires the engaged intent and will of the individual. This change is only possible by the individuals themselves. We can choose to keep helpful beliefs, and we can choose what we feel and think, despite the apparent fixed notions from the past. Psychic work is one aspect of this enormous change, and working with energies undoubtedly alters our perspective in all sorts of ways. Discovering our psychic potentials is part of the path, but it is not an end in itself. It will assist us if used correctly. Our psychic and intuitive selves know, really know, the truth.

Being a medium or psychic, sensing and feeling the thoughts and emotions, aspirations, mind-sets, hope and fears of others, is a privilege. It takes you to a place of understanding of people with very different thoughts, feelings and mind-sets to yourself. Our job as psychics and mediums is not to persuade people to act and live like us, but to find their own truths and answers, and to help them think for themselves, emancipating them from their suffering and pain. Consequently the more breadth of vision you achieve, the greater the ability you have to give others this breadth. People are in great need of this for their own world, and the world needs it to embrace the changes that confront it.

Theories and Philosophies

Spiritual experiences are seen across different cultures and backgrounds, advancing the theory that there might be not just a perennial philosophy but a perennial experience that is present with peoples of all religions and cultures. This is the theory that our true nature is intimately linked, and at one with the sacred. Words from various faiths may be different, but many follow the same themes:

- The kingdom of heaven is within you – Christianity
- Those who know themselves know their Lord – Islam
- Those who know completely their own nature know heaven
  – Confucianism
- Look within, you are the Buddha – Buddhism

Is there perhaps a 'built-in' human state that mystics and spiritual teachers down the ages have discovered? There is another possibility that many mystical writers hint at but rarely make explicit, and that is, instead of the notion that we can have a direct relationship with God, we go one step further and suggest that our true authentic self, our life force, highest Self or soul energy is God already? Could this then be described as not so much perennial philosophy, but a perennial Self, present within us all? And if this is the case could we, by uncovering, acknowledging and attuning to it, obtain some form of spiritual Self-awareness, with some possibility of gaining complete 'union' with God, or whatever description you wish to use for the ultimate energy in the universe?

Our awareness of the world has been radically altered in the last hundred or so years; for example, when we first saw our planet Earth from space in the 1960s, or when the big bang theory opened up different possibilities for the creation of the world. Stephen Hawking propounds in *A Brief History of Time*:

> So long as the universe had a beginning, we could suppose it had
> a creator. But if the universe is really self-contained, having no
> boundary, nor edge, it would have neither beginning nor end, it
> would simply be. What place then for a creator?

In a chapter from *A New Renaissance* entitled 'Reinventing the Human Species', Frank Parkinson writes:

> If everything that exists in our universe today was once contained
> in a primeval dot of energy then the timeline of our self leads
> back to the moment of creation. We not only have God within but
> are still in some significant sense within God.

To some this concept may be sacrilegious, but why are we so afraid of our possible power?

This concept was echoed in the now famous speech by Nelson Mandela, quoting from Marianne Williamson: 'Our deepest fear is that we are powerful beyond measure. It is our light, not our darkness, that most frightens us.' Revealing our power might be seen as arrogance and be threatening for some; however, as Williamson continues: 'as we're liberated from our own fear, our presence automatically liberates others'. Our presence is our energy. It is our response and our being. Are individuals, and that means you, ready to take on that responsibility?

Some form of unconditional love is to be found through all faiths around the globe. Does this concept hold the key to the perennial energy? If so, contemporary spiritual development that actively uses this concept as part of its development process could have many advantages, cutting across the dogma of religions into the experience of spirit, for and by the individual. Unconditional love is a very particular energy. In this state of Heart we are in perfect balance, unaffected by negative emotions and we lose our fears. It energetically allows us to cross over the bridge to higher energies, higher perceptions and love beyond measure. In the Heart, or unconditional loving state, we are free from the chains of the past, the energy dissolves away all those things that stop us becoming the best we can be. We are in a state of acceptance or, as mystics call it, surrender. This is not a passive or negative acceptance but one born through love.

For thousands of years we have been searching for truth, visions of utopia through different ideals and philosophies. Could it be that the resolution of humanity's problems lies not in the hands of any philosopher or particular political persuasion, religious leader, or ideal, no matter how good. Each regime, each philosophy, each faith has been called into question or disappeared, coming and going, age after age. A *new* leader, a *new* idea comes along and we are told it will be our salvation, but very soon the *new* ideas fade, and then another prophet in the guise of the next *new* man or woman at the top arrives and the whole process begins again. Equally, it could be reasoned that the *new* age and contemporary spiritual Self-awareness is another idealistic concept. Giving power to the individual, for instance, may just be another spiritual concept. So are the new spiritual concepts any better than the religious models of the past?

Science loves structure, models and paradigms but some scientists also acknowledge that uncertainty and anxiety are necessary consequences of a creative universe. Many people are mistrustful of uncertainty as it can open a Pandora's box that seriously calls into question a model of reality, which may have taken hundreds of years to establish. There are strands of science that still completely ignore or even scorn any investigation into intuitive psycho-spiritual areas. Equally, those on the spiritual path often ignore or scorn science. In both cases this is a myopic view. Perhaps one of the most enlightened people living today is the Dalai Lama. In his book, *The Universe in a Single Atom*, he relays his exploration into science. If this enlightened and highly spiritual man takes the time to investigate scientific areas, who are we not to do the same? Perhaps it is understandable that science on the whole ignores any psychic work, intuition, and spirituality, when part of the process of this development often brings up fears and uncertainties with no definitive models. Nonetheless, recent discoveries in science are also drawing us away from former beliefs. It might be argued that any movement, group or organization, after a time, often creates its own bias and structures. So is the modern spiritual movement in as much danger as any other movement from creating structures and building up doctrines?

If we look at the new movements, some have already shown signs of locking onto dogmatic ideals that, in their extreme, give little room for an intuitive response. Some people, thankfully not all, in these new movements are just as dogmatic and fixed in creating a myopic view and missing out some greater possibilities. For instance, in the green movement those who do not take on board science in its bid for the natural world, could miss out on life-giving discoveries; peace movements that state we must not draw arms at any cost may play into the hands of a dictator; animal rights campaigners killing in the name of their cause; feminists fighting for their legitimate rights as women turning against all of the male gender; and emancipatory movements that believe so much in civil liberty that they allow the worst kind of abusers free to hurt and kill again. Of course this is not true for all people connected to the above organizations, and all of these movements have an important role to play. The new Mind Body Spirit movement can equally create models and structures and many of their ideas seem just as biased; many support alternative medicine to such an extent that they avoid conventional medical treatment at any cost. I have personally encountered people who refused orthodox treatments and, due to lack of the appropriate medicines, unnecessarily died.

The difficulty with intuition is that it is right in the moment, for and by the person. However, and this is a crucial point, it may not be the right approach for any other person. We can only judge in the moment for ourselves and being in the balance of the Heart will bring courage to do what is necessary, particularly if it goes against people who think you are wrong. The philosopher Immanuel Kant in his Critique of Practical Reason suggested that 'there is an absolute truth if only we could find it'. Yet if one lives and works intuitively, there may never be an absolute truth, as each moment has its own unique meaning for the individual. Psycho-spiritual work celebrates people's differences, and endeavours to work with them. In one interview a student states:

> I'm more open. I'm sure I can accept that there is more than
> one way of living life. I didn't know what that one way was, but
> I had a feeling that there was one way and I just had to find it.
> I don't think that is the case any more. It has made me look at
> things. This work helps you become autonomous and helps you
> to stand on your own two feet. When you tune in, you receive the
> information. The strongest feeling was being connected to my
> own greater guidance.

Is this 'greater guidance' an authoritative voice? It is easy to find authority in academia by the papers that are published. Nonetheless, if you wrote 100 papers on spirituality, or for that matter intuition, it might not necessarily mean you were a more spiritual or intuitive person, or indeed have had a spiritual or intuitive experience yourself. You might have much diverse information about spirituality but, if you have not realized it yourself, can you legitimately be called an authority? And even if you have had such experiences can you be an authority for anyone else's spirituality?

Kierkegaard gave us the notion that each of us requires individual self-awareness and each of us is unique. So would this not mean that uniqueness demands different solutions to different problems for different people? If each moment in time is unique, and each person brings their individual perspective, experience, needs and desires, there is unlikely to be an effective spiritual model, map or guide that suits each and every individual. This suggests the necessity to be open to applying different ways of learning for different phases of psycho-spiritual growth with different people. A programme without any form would be hard to practise, so rather than using any programme as a set model, it might be used as a kind of scaffolding which is movable and flexible to the needs of the individual. This mutable approach does not necessarily mean a complete lack of structure as some focus at various times can assist.

Self-development infers some form of better state or person. Kant says that the aspiration to become a better person is 'our duty', and 'the achievement of the highest good in the world is the necessary object of will determinable by the moral law'. He sees this as only being possible through 'the observance of the soul' and argues that 'the moral law commands us to make the highest possible good in the world the final object of all our conduct'. These are commendable sentiments, but with so many interpretations of what might constitute a 'better person', where does that lead us? Could it be, for instance, that a better person may not be just one who does good deeds but one who lives by their truth?

Change often involves difficulties and real transformation is often simultaneous with crisis. Crisis can, and does, bring in new ways of living and thinking that might not otherwise have been discovered. How many people would consciously put themselves into a position of crisis? Life itself tends to implement change if our world has become stagnant and we need to grow. Growing pains occur as a necessary part of our transformation. Recent scientific paradigms are embracing and even assuming unpredictability, as chaos, to be an inherent cosmic expression that is deeply embedded within the core of reality. The philosopher Martin Heidegger believed that anxiety is coincident with freedom and proposed that the 'authentic self' is very aware of this.

At the start of every spiritual awareness class, I always ask the students to start practising Detached Loving Observation of Self: detached to remove the little self, so one can begin to see oneself devoid of the cloaks and clouds surrounding us; loving because this exercise is not one of being critical; and observation to acknowledge ourselves as we truly are. On the second week of one of my courses, I asked the group how they had got on in their observation of self. 'Well!!' said one student, 'in my observations this week, I have realized that everything that comes out of my mouth is a lie.' The whole class was shocked. This sounds rather extreme, however, if you consider how we are all conditioned to speak and live by other people's constructs, one can see how this statement could be more prevalent than it might sound. This particular student was brought up in a family who told her from an early age to be 'nice' at all times. She only came to class a couple more times, and then told me how sorry she was to leave but at this time of her life she just could not bring herself to change her life and her lifestyle. I completely understood. Many years later she emailed me to say she had given up her job in England and was now living abroad. She had trained as a healer and was now working in the psycho-spiritual field. Once some light is brought to bear on ourselves we may put it aside for a while, but when something is revealed it cannot hide away indefinitely.

Self-deceptions and making excuses create conflict in the energy field of the individual, and bring obstacles to inner peace. Wellbeing, both spiritual and physical, seems to depend on a commitment to the truth and, as they say, the truth will set you free. Telling the truth about an experience is an essential part of any psychotherapeutic process, and is equally relevant to spiritual wellbeing.

If confronting one's truth is essential to the spiritual process, it may necessitate asking awkward questions. This might have the effect of making the person feel vulnerable and uncertain. So what can be done to assist the process? In obvious cases of life changes, such as physical disabilities or abuse, change will be enforced. Equally, changes that are encountered in spiritual development can be every bit as difficult and often need huge adjustments for the individual. For some people this may necessitate psychotherapy or other assistance. Some years ago I came across a well-meaning university lecturer who was beginning to lead her students in personal growth and self-awareness. She relayed to me that after each class she felt absolutely drained, as so much 'stuff' was emerging from her students. If the leader of any such group is not equipped with the knowledge of holding the group energetically in the Heart, this often occurs. I have also observed this in untrained psychics who might not give the necessary attention to balancing their own energies.

A student recalls how making spiritual connections through 'attunements' helped:

> Certainly over those first two or three years my evening
> attunement changed and deepened. Some nights I didn't feel I
> was very still or very clear and other times I was. Sometimes, I
> was very confident and clear about what I was doing and it was
> effective, other times I wasn't quite so sure. It felt a little bit, you
> know, the quality of it varied quite radically. But over a period I
> was able to develop with a system of attunement so that I knew
> when I was in tune. Although sometimes it was hard after a day's
> work to do, after a period I made myself achieve that attunement
> however long it took, so that I knew when I had reached it and
> when I hadn't. There was a more consistent level of attunement
> that I was gaining after and during that period and since.

This student felt able to create his own system of regular attunements to assist growth. When asked if that attunement infiltrated their day-to-day living the student replied:

I have observed that people often have trigger words. These bring strong images, memories and feelings to mind. They may be pleasant associations or very negative ones. It often isn't possible to know what are the trigger words for every individual. For instance, strawberries and cream may conjure up delightful images for one person, but if perhaps someone is allergic to strawberries they will instantly feel negative. Trigger words are different for different people and it takes some unpicking to find what they are and why the person has them. We emotionally respond to trigger words and they are closely associated with highly valued concepts and beliefs.

> Yes because those nights when I felt that connection it generally made me feel more at ease with myself and more focused and purposeful when I started the next day. I felt like I was connected to where I should be whereas without the attunement I felt I was drifting slightly, and passing time a little bit, rather than getting to grips with something. So yeah, it certainly did indirectly. As that system of attunement became stronger, then my ability to stay in my own energy increased.

Attunement in this context is firstly connecting to the innermost core of your being and then connecting to the highest greatest Source and bringing together the two, creating a oneness with oneself and the universe, as already described earlier in this work.

Over many years of running psycho-spiritual groups I have found some fascinating trigger words in students. Two of the most common trigger words are 'will' and 'God'. Sometimes the word 'will' creates a negative response because, for some, it is associated with someone having will over them in a negative way. Someone who has lived in a repressive country or had a repressive parent, for instance, would respond in that way. If you say these trigger words, the person will almost certainly stop listening and their energy will be directed towards the negative pathway associated with it in the brain. Identifying them can be a useful tool in the uncovering of self.

When what I call the 'G word' (God) comes up, many responses are often negative as it often conjures up memories of being told about hell and damnation. The concept of God, to some, is a way of religion controlling us. What or who is God? Is God a man (it usually is for most people) with a long white beard, as often seen in artist's pictures? Is God some person who dictates our lives? Just as the devil is a personification of our fear, maybe God is a personification of peace and love? Therefore, in our exploration of self, perhaps we need to find the god or good within. The description of a god or gods have divided humanity throughout history; each tribe insisting their own vision of God is right, and often killing those who do not think the same way. So it is quite understandable that the very mention of the word often brings negative connotations to many people.

Latterly, I have found that more and more people like to talk about God (if they do at all) as an energy, the source of the universe or a force in the cosmos, usually a force for good. This then begs the question, what is good? For most people something good is something that makes them happy, peaceful and contented. Arguably something good may come out of an experience that is uncomfortable, traumatic and one that subsequently allows greater knowledge and awareness to emerge. Ascribed to St Augustine is a thought worth pondering on: 'There is a place in people's hearts that does not exist, into which pain enters so that it might.'

What is certain is that most of us are searching for something greater than the little self and many students of spirit have a sense of a higher power. If, as the scientists tell us, we are all made from particles that are recycled, meaning that you or I could have bits of Napoleon, Jesus or Hitler in us, it gives meaning to the notion that we are all one, all inextricably linked. This concept is not new, as ancient faiths also believed this. And it is now being mooted in some scientific explorations. Whatever you may believe, it is surely true that we all want the best, and all hopefully want to be the best we can be. That best of us is likely to be within us, waiting to be discovered. And as

Shakespeare said: 'what's in a name? A rose by any other would still smell as sweet.' It is the energy in the intent for good that is important, regardless of any name we choose to ascribe to it.

Spiritual Authority and Education

Increasingly it is propounded that truth, not surprisingly for those who see themselves as spiritual beings, first and foremost comes from one's own experience. This is seen to provide direct and uncontaminated access to the spiritual realm. 'Truths' provided by the dogmas of religious traditions, or by other people, parents, scientists or even putatively spiritual masters, might well be erroneous. Scientists do sometimes get things wrong, and a spiritual master can lapse into a contaminated-ego mode of functioning. So-called truths coming from others, whatever their pedigree in spiritual matters, may not be relied upon. However, testing them with one's own truth, experience and intuition will enable the individual to know whether it is right for them.

Over the last 30 years the use of a different kind of learning has emerged in social sciences and self-awareness programmes called 'experiential learning'. This is not just experiencing and acknowledging aspects of self within the classroom, it is also making use of the knowledge in real life situations. *Experiential Learning* by David Kolb describes an educational cycle where learning is seen to be achieved by having an experience, reflecting upon it, formulating concepts and generalizations and testing the implications of concepts on new situations.

Group input is thought to assist experiential learning, whereby the student brings real issues to the class in which the whole group can contribute. It enables the student to reflect upon an issue. This is then integrated with the individual's system of constructs, through which he views, perceives and evaluates the experience to give it added meaning. In this way the students effectively provide their own textbook, with information and examples illustrated through their own lives. It creates a real learning situation as, week by week, their progress helps them get closer and closer to their inner Self. First this involves a series of releases of unwanted aspects of self, which is seen to open the door to deep awareness and greater possibilities. This takes courage on the part of the individuals, and requires a sense of adventure for their own journey. As Abraham Maslow says in *The Farther Reaches of Human Nature*: 'One cannot choose wisely for a life unless he *dares* to listen to himself, his own self at each moment in life.' The decision to 'dare' to look at oneself, no matter what that will reveal, is seen as one of the most important elements towards advancement, and one that cannot be stage-managed.

Although there are many arguments against this approach, gaining spiritual truths by way of experience stands at the heart of contemporary spiritual development. So where does this leave the spiritual teacher? Indeed, is there any need for one if knowledge is within us all? Where should we go for our learning? Could we just stay at home and meditate?

Psycho-spiritual learning requires openness and transparency but how can we expect students to find their own authenticity if the facilitators have not implemented theirs? Transference and counter-transference are often just as present with the teacher as the student. To counterbalance this in spiritual Self-awareness it might be appropriate if the facilitator were required to develop their own spiritual self-awareness. For instance, it is commonly accepted that to become a psychotherapist the practitioners must go through the same process of psychotherapy themselves. Yet, despite the growing interest in implementing spiritual programmes into higher education there seems to be very little work in the spiritual education of the teachers involved. Psychic, healing and spiritual development groups, as well as institutions of education, need leaders who have themselves undergone a deep inward spiritual journey. Working for and by the individual has its many critics, seeing it as self-indulgent. Having models, formulas and structures is the way most educators have worked for a very long time. Perhaps now is the time for change.

There is a saying, 'we teach what we need to learn'. I have often said I have probably learnt more from my students than they have learnt from me. One important thing I have acknowledged is that 99 per cent of people, at the core of their being, are good souls. People do bad things sometimes. Most often it is because they feel threatened, they are fearful and hurting, or that they have issues from the past which have wounded them and, like any other animal when wounded, they fight back. Any therapist knows that if you say to anyone 'you made me do this' or 'you made me like that', the response will always be a defensive one, and the person will just not hear it. As adults, no one makes us do anything. We do things that are born from our mind-sets or beliefs, and because we are hard-wired to do them. Let us then begin to unravel the fixed wiring of our being and start today to be the best we can be.

Every day, thousands of people all over the world see some form of psychic practitioner. This puts them in the position of guide and teacher. So, as psychics and healers we are in a wonderful position to assist this transformation. Working from the open balance of our own energies we can inspire, we can reveal, and we can positively assist the journey of humankind towards its next and important evolutionary shift.

The 19th-century educationalist Johann Heinrich Pestalozzi, said that:

> ... to elevate human nature to its highest, its noblest, requires developing whatever of the divine and eternal lies within its nature... Man is someone who is developed in his innermost powers and man will only become Man through his inner and spiritual life and a spiritual life is not to be found by a person in any outward expression of religiosity but only in the innermost sanctuary of his being.

When, in the course of my research, I came across similar quotes to this one, from mystics and educationists, some of which were written years or even hundreds of years ago, at first I was delighted to find similar concepts for the betterment of humanity. However, it also brought some sadness, as I realized that the knowledge of these great people of the past is largely still not accommodated in most forms of education.

The elevation to the divine, which Pestalozzi suggests lies within us, is echoed in contemporary spirituality. Although these principles have been present throughout history, very few examples of finding the spirit within us have been identified, let alone actively used within education. Research has shown that the 'soul' or 'inner' essence is not so much developed from reason or logical faculties, as propounded by Plato; it is found by contacting our inner core spiritual Self and authenticating this knowledge by actualizing it in our real lived world. In this sense it might be seen as a 'living education'.

Since World War II the individual has received more attention, and it is increasingly considered that the world has many voices, all of which are valid. This might be fundamentally grounded in multicultural political ethics, and it could be argued that political ethics and multicultural sensitivities are certainly important. However, can they form the basis of spiritual practice or commitment? We could take the perennial view that spiritual forces are within us all, regardless of culture, nationality, society or clan. By this token, contemporary spirituality generally could be seen to resonate with the notion of the freedom of working 'outside the box' or a set structure of beliefs. In the past, for many, it was felt that there was only one true way to God. In the present climate, to believe that one way to God is the only way, seems myopic, limiting, and possibly simply wrong. For all its faults, our modern world does at least allow the possibility of autonomy, which in spiritual terms means individuals can find their own way to God, giving them their own authentic experiences of spiritual truths.

Within many countries that have a multiracial population, moral ethics may be conflicting. It makes sense to include different faiths and beliefs in education, but can any of their ideas give us an authentic spiritual experience that we can use within our individual lives? Religions, some of which are hundreds or even thousands of years old, would probably argue that their faiths hold all the keys. If this is the case then why is there such a growing desire for spiritual experiences outside a religious structure? It could be argued that there are many roads to God, or even that all roads eventually lead to God or spiritual enlightenment. One of the aspects of contemporary spiritual development is that one can select different values and techniques to achieve this, however, to obtain any kind of deep spirituality, it would seem likely that at some point a student must choose a road and continue with it, at least for a time. The framework of an established religion might give people safety by following a well-trodden path, yet some of these well-trodden paths have incorporated hatred and fear. Safety is important, but it could be argued that any movement or change is likely to disrupt the individual's life, so any change of self may never feel safe.

Many leaders of spiritual groups hold their students too long, which creates a dependency that will never allow the people to be comfortable enough to think for themselves. Just as when a child is learning to walk, if the parent hangs onto them it will dramatically slow their progress. Facilitators and leaders must allow the growth of their students, allowing them to sometimes make mistakes, and be glad, really glad, when the student comes to the point where they say, 'I don't need you anymore'. Like a good parent the leader must at some point let go. If the student has already established connection with the innermost part of their being, they will feel safe whatever life throws at them.

The argument against any work on self is that it promotes selfishness. Ironically it is by knowing oneself that we can better understand and have compassion for others. We then can achieve an empathy that is real and consequently will want to aid our friends and families, our society and the world. Psycho-spiritual students generally do acknowledge the greater picture in life, which can lead to a more altruistic way of living. One student said they now have:

> ... a broader mission, not just earning bread-and-butter money, because my profession is researching things, so instead of trying to publish another paper I think of things in a bigger frame now and I feel I have a mission to somehow combine the psychic and spiritual work with other professional work.

Future Possibilities

The whole area of contemporary spiritual education is still forming, and evidence suggests several possibilities including education in different faiths, examining the bigger questions of life, moral and ethical issues, and more experiential spiritual learning. What if every teacher, as part of their teacher training, underwent some psycho-spiritual work on themselves? This would then help and support them to feel their individual strength and commitment to truth. Even some basic psychology and simple meditation, implemented in schools, would at least put the children in the mode to look within. If children and their parents understood themselves better, it would be likely to lead to a more rounded and less violent world. Bringing experiential learning into education would be beneficial. One simple way is to encourage students to keep a journal with their own experiences, and then bring these into group discussion. This helps them to realize how their thoughts and actions are manifesting in their lived world. To hold a group together requires a developed mind, empathy and heart, which is a form of empathetic mediumship, enabling learning for, and by, the individual. In short, we need vocational teachers and true visionaries to emerge. For this to happen, our society must realize the enormous benefit of having clear leaders, strong in themselves and open to all possibilities.

It has been said that vocational teachers are born and not made. This is likely to be true, however, if we provide a good environment and endeavour to cut away the poisons of the past, both individually and globally, there is every possibility that one's true vocation will appear. Visionaries are not just people with good intention but those who see beyond the clouds, who have an instinctive clarity that is not imprisoned in a box or structure, who are free from fear and have courage to do the right things. These are the people whom society has all too frequently labelled as mad or bad or both, and many throughout history have been put to death, only for their ideas to then be implemented after their death. Throughout our journey of energies and extra-sensory perceptions we see how necessary it is for us to have open-hearted and open-minded people. Through the lifting of the veils of illusion we can all become visionaries of our own world, which will energetically affect the people around us and, ultimately the world.

Teachers and facilitators cannot measure spirituality, for who can judge such a non-definable aspect as the spiritual Self? What exam board, or examining process has the qualification? Maybe only a god can do this, and if that god or some part of divine energy is within us, it is possible that only the individual can be the final judge. What teachers can do is to both help identify and dissolve the negative aspects of self that cloud the true being and at the same time, help them make a connection with their innermost spirit to illuminate and therefore reveal the way forward.

Most people who have included some psycho-spiritual learning in their life will say it has helped them, particularly in actualizing their new-found knowledge. Being a psychic, medium or healer, or implementing spirituality, may not always provide us with a life without difficulties, illness or sorrows. Life is likely to continue to present us with challenges, problems to be solved, bereavements to be grieved, and all the myriad experiences an individual may encounter. It may not make the bumps in our road disappear. What it can do is provide us with a stronger vehicle with which to ride more easily over them.

Bibliography

Avila, T, 1989, *Interior Castle*, Image Books, London, 1989,

Bailey, A, *Serving Humanity*, Lucis Press, London, 1987

— *Discipleship In The New Age Volume 1*, Lucis Press, London, 1944

— *Discipleship In The New Age Volume 2*, Lucis Press, London, 1955

— *A Treatise On White Magic*, Lucis Press, London, 1967

Blavasky, HP, *The Secret Doctrine*, Theosophical University Press, California, 1988

Borges, J L, *The Book of Imaginary Beings*, Avon Books, New York, 1969

Bouma, G, *Religion and Spirituality*, Cambridge University Press, 2003

Broadhurst, P & Miller, H, *The Sun and The Serpent*, Pendragon Press, Cornwall, 1989

Cummins, G, *The Road To Immortality*, Psychic Press Ltd, London, 1967

Daniels, M, 'The Myth Of Self-Actualization', *Journal of Humanistic Psychology No. 28*, 2002

Dawkins, R, *The God Delusion*, Transworld Publishers, London, 2007

D'Adamo, Dr. P, with Catherine Whitney, *The Eat Right Diet*, Random House, London, 1988

De Quincey, C, 'Consciousness: Truth Or Wisdom?' *Institute of Noetic Sciences Review, Volume 51*, 2000

Elkins, D, *Beyond Religion,* Quest Books, Wheaton, 1998

Eliot, G, *Middlemarch*, Penguin Books, London, 1994

Farrer, F, *Sir George Trevelyan and the New Spiritual Awakening*, Floris Books, Edinburgh, 2002

Fortune, D, *Sane Occultism*, The Aquarian Press, Wellingborough, 1967

Freud, S, *Standard Edition of The Complete Works Of Sigmund Freud*, Hogarth Press, London, 1953

Grof, S, *The Stormy Search For Self*, Thorsons Press, London, 1995

— *Psychology of the Future: Lessons From Modern Consciousness Research*, University Of New York Press, 2000

Happold, FC, *Mysticism*, Penguin Books, London, 1970

Hardy, A, *The Spiritual Nature of Man*, Clarendon Press, Oxford, 1979

Hawking, S, *A Brief History of Time*, Bantam Press, London, 1980

Heron, J, *The Facilitator's Handbook*, Kogan Page, London, 1989

Heron, J, *Sacred Science*, PCCS Books, London, 1999

Humann, H, *The Many Faces of Angels*, DeVorss and Co, Los Angeles, 2000

James, W, *The Varieties of Religious Experience*, Penguin Classics, New York, 1982

Judith, A, *The Wheels of Life*, Llewellyn Publications, Woodbury, 1990

Jung, C, *Collected Works*, Routledge & Kogan Paul, London, 1960

Kant, I, *Critique of Practical Reason*, Liberal Arts Press, Arlington, 1956

Kilmo, J, *Channelling*, The Aquarian Press, Wellingborough, 1988

Knowles, M, *The Modern Practice of Adult Education*, Cambridge Adult Education, Cambridge, 1990

Kolb, D, *Experiential Learning*, Prentice-Hall, London, 1984

Krystal, P, *Cutting the Ties That Bind*, Element Books, Shaftesbury, 1990

Kubler-Ross, E, *On Death and Dying*, Routledge, London, 1997

Larimore, W; Parker, M; Crowther, M, 'Should Clinicians Incorporate Positive Spirituality Into Their Practices? What Does The Evidence Say?' Society Of Behavioural Medicine, 2002

Le Shan, L, *How to Meditate*, Back Bay, Boston, 1999

Leadbeater, CW, *The Chakras*, Theosophical Publishing, Wheaton, 1996

Lipton, BH & Bhaerman, S, *Spontaneous Evolution*, Hay House, California, 2009

Maslow, A, *The Farther Reaches of Human Nature*, Viking Press, New York, 1971

— *Towards a Psychology of Being*, John Wiley and Sons, Chichester, 1999

Myers, FWH, *Human Personality and its Survival of Bodily Death*, New York University Books, 1961

Myss, C, *Anatomy of the Spirit*, Bantam Books, London, 1997

Nelson, J, *Healing the Split*, State University of New York Press, 1994

Northage, I, *Mediumship Made Simple*, Buckland Press Ltd, Kent, 1986

Olivelle, P, (trans.) Upanishads, Oxford University Press, 1996

Ouspensky, PD, *In Search of the Miraculous*, Arkana, Routledge and Kegan Paul Ltd, London, 1987

— *A New Model of the Universe*, Arkana, Routledge and Kegan Paul Ltd, London, 1984

Peters, R (ed,) *The Concept of Education*, Routledge and Kegan Paul, London, 1973

Parkinson, F, 'Reinventing The Human Species: An Evolutionary Crossroads', article from *A New Renaissance: Transforming Science, Spirit, and Society*, Lorimer, D & Robinson, O (eds.) Floris Books, Edinburgh, 2010

Radin, D, *Entangled Minds*, Paraview Pocket Books, New York, 2006

Rinpoche, A, *The Tibetan Book of The Living and Dying*, Random House, London, 1992

Rifkin, J, *The Empathic Civilization*, Tarcher, Cambridge, 2009

Rogers, C, *Freedom To Learn*, Macmillan College Publishing Company, New York, 1994

Rowan, J, *The Transpersonal*, Routledge, London, 1993

Rumi, *Gardens of The Beloved*, Maryam Mafi and Azima Melita Kolon (trans.) Element: an Imprint of Harper Collins Publications, London, 2003

Samuels, A; Shorter, B; Plaut, F, *A Critical Dictionary of Jungian Analysis*, Routledge, London, 1986

Schlemmer, PV, *The Only Planet of Choice*, Gateway Books, Bath, 1997

Scott, C, *The Initiate*, Routledge & Sons, Ltd, London, 1920

Soskin, J, *The Wind of Change*, Ashgrove Press, Bath, 1994

Soskin, J, *Transformation*, The College of Psychic Studies, London, 1995

Tart, CT, *Open Mind, Discriminating Mind*, Harper Row Publishers, London, 1989

Tart, CT, *Transpersonal Psychologies*, HarperCollins Publishers, New York, 1992

Tart, CT, *The End Of Materialism: How Evidence of the Paranormal is Bringing Science and Spirit Together*, New Harbinger Publications, Inc., Oakland, 2009

Trevelyan, GO, *Magic Casements*, Coventure, London, 1980

Vaughan, F, *The Inward Arc*, Authors Guild Backprint.Com, 2000

Welwood, J, *Towards a Psychology of Awakening*, Shambhala, London, 2000

Whitmore, D, *Psychosynthesis In Education*, Destiny Books, Rochester, 1986

Wilber, K, *The Atman Project*, Quest, Wheaton, 1980

Wilber, K, *Eye To Eye*, Shambhala, Boston, 1996

Wilber, K, *Integral Psychology: Consciousness, Spirit, Psychology, Therapy*, Shambhala, London, 2000

Willard, D, 'Spiritual Formation In Christ: A Perspective On What It Is and How It Might Be Done', *Journal Of Psychology and Theology*, Volume 28, No. 4, 1998a

Index